# Faith, Love, and Hope

# Faith, Love, and Hope

## A Spiritual History of The Firs
## (Centennial Edition)

KATHERINE B. JEFFREY

*Foreword by Bruce G. Whipple*

WIPF & STOCK • Eugene, Oregon

FAITH, LOVE, AND HOPE
A Spiritual History of The Firs (Centennial Edition)



Wipf & Stock
An Imprint of Wipf and Stock Publishers
199 W. 8th Ave., Suite 3
Eugene, OR 97401

www.wipfandstock.com

PAPERBACK ISBN: 979-8-3852-7583-0
HARDCOVER ISBN: 979-8-3852-7584-7
EBOOK ISBN: 979-8-3852-7585-4

VERSION NUMBER 03/20/26

# Contents

# Foreword

The question "What is that in your hand?" that God posed to Moses at the burning bush (Exod 4:2) came to Otis and Julia Whipple during a prayer meeting when a young missionary recruit described how the Lord led him, in response to that same divine question, to serve as a missionary in China. This verse represented a particular challenge to the Whipples, who were at the time facing an uncertain future. Otis's construction business was failing because of the effects of World War I, he has just recovered from a near-death encounter with the 1918 Spanish Flu, and the family was in deep poverty. The question, however, remained: "What is that in your hand?" Though "virtually nothing" was the only apparent answer, the Whipples realized in it a deeper calling: would they be willing to give up everything to follow Christ? This question and its implications became the soil in which the spiritual legacy of The Firs would be planted and nourished. In her first book, *Work of Faith, Labor of Love*, and now in this updated retelling, *Faith, Love, and Hope: A Spiritual History of The Firs (Centennial Edition)*, Katherine Jeffrey (née Brown) eloquently describes this story in detail, from the beginning to the present.

Katherine's story also needs mentioning in this context. Among the dearest friends of my parents, Grant and Bernice Whipple, were Ron and Dorothy Brown. Ron and Dorothy were from Vancouver, British Columbia and were frequent guests at The Firs, attending many conferences and gatherings and serving actively on The Firs Council. Ron had a deep interest in the Firwood summer camp and it was because of him that The Firs was able to purchase Reveille Island, a ten-acre property approximately one hundred yards offshore from the Firwood swimming beach. The value of this property for The Firs has been immeasurable. Perhaps Ron and Dorothy's most important contribution, however, was encouraging their daughter Katherine's connection to Firwood and the entire Firs ministry. The result, eventually, was the gift Katherine herself has been to The Firs: the preservation and telling of this history through her own work of faith and labor of love has been and will continue to be a gift for generations to come.

As a grandson of Otis and Julia, having come of age at The Firs, and now in retirement being close at hand and able to participate voluntarily, the significance of The Firs to me is summarized well in Heb 10:23: "He who promised is faithful." The only endowment of The Firs has been this promise. Yet a century from its founding it is possible to look back and see what God has accomplished through this ministry. There are multitudes of Christian believers and leaders worldwide who met Christ at The Firs. This has occurred despite the challenges associated with the aftermath of WWI, the Great Depression of the 1930s, WWII, and the subsequent social upheavals and revolutions that continue today. God has guided and protected The Firs through these times and against the theological winds that have threatened to uproot it from its firm biblical soil.

My hope is that your reading of *Faith, Love, and Hope: A Spiritual History of The Firs* will challenge you also with the question "What is that in your hand?" May God bless you as you ponder its implications for your own life.

Bruce G. Whipple, M.D.

# Preface to the Centennial Edition

"We give thanks to God always for all of you, remembering you in our prayers, unceasingly calling to mind your work of faith and labor of love and endurance in hope."[1]

THE 1980 EDITION OF *Work of Faith, Labor of Love* traced six decades of ministry at The Firs Bible and Missionary Conference in Bellingham, Washington from its founding in 1921—what we might now think of as "the Whipple years." It made an effort to identify something of the unique soil out of which The Firs sprang: the compelling witness of nineteenth-century faith missions (especially those pioneered in England by Hudson Taylor and George Muller), trust in the Scriptures as the infallible Word of God, and an intentionally interdenominational character. These influences, in a weave of God's ordaining, shaped the spiritual convictions of Otis and Julia Whipple and, through them, the early generations of The Firs family and fellowship. To use an arboreal metaphor, this was the Old Growth or Primary Forest of The Firs: it was a *Work of Faith*, committed, through radical dependence on God's promises in Scripture and his provision in response to prayer, to "helping people believe,"[2] and a *Labor of Love*, characterized by unanimity in decision-making and generous interdenominational hospitality, recognizing believers as "all one in Christ Jesus." That remarkable early history, which may be largely unknown to

1. 1 Thess 1:2–3, NAB (Revised).

2. From this distance, one reflects with a kind of wonder at the simple, audacious faith that sent the Whipples regularly to their "Promise Box" when they needed specific guidance from the Lord. It is also striking how thoroughly they leaned on "the whole counsel of God," receiving clear direction often in Old Testament narrative, prophecy, and Psalms.

current friends of The Firs, is preserved here, with modest corrections of detail and some additional content and documentation.[3]

This updated volume continues the story of The Firs up to and beyond its centennial year (2021), focusing on its Second Growth, following Grant Whipple's retirement as long-term executive director, entrusting the ministry to new and younger leaders. What began as a family story has since the late 1970s grown into a story encompassing an expansive and diverse network of believers. And here, the third quality of the famous Pauline triad of faith, love, and hope is especially relevant.[4] In the new chapters that make up the second half of this book, *Endurance in Hope* may be thought of as the overarching theme.

The author who, as a twenty-something graduate student at Regent College, Vancouver, researched and wrote *Work of Faith, Labor of Love*, has been entrusted with creating this new, expanded, and updated history. For many reasons, the surprising opportunity to revisit this project after four and a half decades presented an immense challenge, not least because of my geographic distance from the Pacific Northwest since the early 1980s and thus my considerable detachment from the day-to-day and year-to-year details of The Firs' ongoing ministry. Moreover, as a seventy-something grandmother, I am now older than many of the "old-timers" who kindly welcomed me into their homes and archives in the late 1970s. Nonetheless, I have taken to heart the Wendell Kimbrough hymn, based on a favorite Firs theme-text (1 Cor 15:58), "Your Labor is Not in Vain."

Current and former members of The Firs community have not only supported this project with their prayers; they have been unfailingly generous in providing documents, memories, and perspective that have allowed me to shape this narrative. I am deeply grateful to those who shared their thoughts with me, both in person and via phone and email conversations, and as deeply regret the opportunities lost to talk to members of The Firs constituency I was unable to consult or who have passed into the Lord's presence over the last several decades. Though I have

3. Biblical references in this revised edition have been modified from the King James Version, which was used exclusively in the early years, to the New King James Version, which preserves the cadence and poetry of the KJV but replaces archaic pronouns and idioms. In the new chapters (14 and following) and in chapter epigraphs, other translations, where noted, are sometimes preferred.

4. Faith, hope, and love (which we know as the "three theological virtues") are featured also in 1 Thess 5:8 and, most memorably, in Paul's famous "love chapter" in his first epistle to the Corinthian church (1 Cor 13:13).

made every effort to recount and verify details faithfully, responsibility for any errors of fact or interpretation in what follows remains with me.

The world has changed in incalculable ways since 1980. The culture we took for granted in the last decades of the twentieth century is now the stuff of humorous anecdote or nostalgia: big hair, power suits, and clunky personal desktop computers—the first generation of now ubiquitous "devices" that would eventually upend our lives with worldwide connectivity, social media, and a 24-hour news cycle, collapsing time and space and tempting us into myriad (often addictive) "virtual" worlds. Things were overall simpler on the other side of the turn of the millennium: we were all, on average, trimmer, healthier, and less sedentary; most children still lived in two-parent households and shared family dinners around the table. Social connections came through churches, neighborhood associations, service clubs, community sports leagues, summer camping, and, for many, conferences at places like The Firs. The border between the United States and Canada was not only famously "undefended" but also laid-back; crossing at the Peace Arch in Blaine, Washington required no passport and typically only the most neighborly of official interactions. We had yet to confront the realities of international terrorism on our own soil or of mass immigration, much less a series of global health epidemics, including a viral pandemic called Covid-19 that brought everything everywhere to a virtual standstill in 2020 and 2021.

The pace and breadth and depth of cultural transformation have been, for those who lived through it, deeply disorienting, even in the church. The Christian community, broadly speaking, has itself changed profoundly in the last half-century—either by tracking the shifting culture or attempting to withstand the cultural tide. The revivalist ethos initiated by the Jesus Movement, with its youth-focused, relational evangelism and contemporary Christian music, became somewhat institutionalized in evangelical churches in the 1980s and 1990s. These changes breathed fresh life into many congregations, but a diminished emphasis on discipleship and personal holiness and a tendency to package worship as entertainment were sometimes accompanied by trendy, shallow preaching. Meanwhile, the pro-life and pro-family initiatives of the Moral Majority movement, reacting against the secular societal drift, enjoyed a decade of considerable cultural and political prestige, but alienated many.[5] High-

5. The perception of self-righteousness and hypocrisy in the Moral Majority was a considerable liability, and one to which virtually all conservative Christian churches and organizations are (fairly or unfairly) vulnerable.

profile ministries, megachurches, and parachurch organizations grew in number and influence, as did an often-problematic cult of personality surrounding eminent pastors and Christian celebrities. Heightened exposure brought heightened scrutiny: sexual and financial scandals in many corners of the Christian world generated headlines and cynicism, diminishing the institutional credibility of the church writ large and making "religion" an especially negative concept.[6] Self-inflicted wounds and the unedifying spectacle of public infighting within the church community also harmed the gospel witness. And whereas public affirmation of faith-based communities and ministries like The Firs, once common in the "human interest" or "lifestyle" pages of newspapers and on the public airwaves, became vanishingly rare, a single public attack, even a baseless accusation, could go viral in an instant and cause immeasurable harm.

Even within the ostensibly evangelical ranks, many churches have recently adopted a nuanced or revisionist (sometimes completely naturalistic) view of Scripture and de-emphasized traditional biblical doctrines or ethical norms, overlaying secular creeds (e.g., "Love is love") with gospel language and treating Jesus as a champion of contemporary causes and a model of non-judgmental tolerance and affirmation.[7] More conservative churches, meanwhile, which hold firmly to a high view of the authority and reliability of the Old and New Testament scriptures as the Word of God, are increasingly countercultural; in linking the Great Commandment with the Great Commission, evangelism with discipleship and service, obedience to Christ with love for "the lost," they can seem more anachronistic in twenty-first-century America than ever before. In many ways, these divergent tendencies within the evangelical camp are replaying aspects of the so-called "modernist" controversies of the early twentieth century, but with new fervency, greater stakes, and bigger megaphones—particularly as the passions and allegiances of a

6. Whereas in 1990, 90 percent of the American population identified as Christian, that number has plummeted by nearly 30 percent in recent years; conversely, the number of religiously unaffiliated individuals (sometimes called "nones") has dramatically risen, especially among the young. The religious vacuum has for many been filled by alternate dogmas and causes associated with progressive or populist movements.

7. This may perhaps be regarded as the second generation of "Moralistic Therapeutic Deism," which was identified by sociologist Christian Smith as the preferred faith of the young, replacing a robust, theologically-grounded Christianity, in his groundbreaking 2005 book *Soul Searching: The Religious and Spiritual Lives of American Teenagers.* For a trenchant analysis of the recent drift of some prominent evangelical pastors and institutions, see Basham, *Shepherds For Sale.*

highly polarized American political discourse have intruded into pews and pulpits.

Like all Christian ministries, The Firs has been affected by these currents and forced to navigate an ever more complex social and spiritual milieu. Members of the Firs constituency have not always found change to be easy; nor has the line between appropriate change and potential mission drift always seemed obvious. Personnel issues have occasionally challenged the ethos of "all one in Christ Jesus," and several tragedies and controversies have unsettled the peace. The Firs has reluctantly relinquished some of its founding missionary tenets. It no longer has a fulltime resident staff living on site. Dreams of expansion were tested in the late 1990s and ultimately relinquished. The current challenge would seem to be "strengthen the things that remain" (Rev 3:2), consolidating The Firs' properties and holdings in light of a reconfigured ministry profile, primarily focused on evangelism and discipleship of the rising generation.

Through ten decades, The Firs has sought prayerfully to adapt to changing cultural needs, but always in the light of its unchanging scriptural mandate. To explain itself in forthright but winsome ways to an often-skeptical community, to embrace neighbors who don't necessarily embrace it. To render unto local "Caesars" appropriate deference, while remaining uncompromising in its fidelity to Christ and his kingdom. And above all, to live accountably before God, modeling behavior and a demeanor consistent with his character, thus "helping people believe."

By God's grace, The Firs endures in hope, renewing and reinvesting the moral and spiritual capital of radical faith and self-sacrificing love that has sustained it since the 1920s and that will, pray God, continue to carry it well into and through its second century of Christian ministry.

To that end, and in thanksgiving for the hundreds of individuals, often hidden and unsung, who have poured their lives into the work of The Firs, this volume is prayerfully dedicated.

Katherine B. Jeffrey

# *Work of Faith, Labor of Love*
1921–1977

# Prologue (1977)

In the opening hours of a Firs couples' conference in the early 1970s, two men introduced themselves to each other and struck up a warm and animated conversation. Before they had exchanged many words, however, their lives' strange cross-purposes came into sharp relief: one was German-born, the other Czech; one an eminent computer scientist, the other a diplomat; one active in Christian leadership, the other a religious seeker. The scientist learned, moreover, that during World War II this new acquaintance had endured bitter suffering at German hands. The next morning as he met with conference leaders, his heart was heavy with sorrow for his country's—and by implication, his own—part in the collective horror of those years. Please pray with me, he asked, that this man will find it possible to forgive me and that I, in turn, can minister to him the healing love of Christ.

Pray they did. And somehow through long hours spent together, the healing came for both, their new-found friendship a living commentary on Ephesians 2: "For he himself is our peace, who has made us both one, and has broken down the dividing wall of hostility . . . So then [we] are no longer strangers and aliens, but fellow citizens with the saints and members of the household of God" (vv. 14, 19, ESV).

As the retreat drew to a close on Sunday noon around crowded tables in the conference dining room, the diplomat turned to Grant and Bernice Whipple, seated next to him, and remarked quietly, "I want you to know that The Firs for me is holy ground." Asked to explain, he continued, "In this place, this weekend, someone whom history made my enemy over thirty years ago has asked my forgiveness for his part in my wartime suffering." Then after a thoughtful pause, he added, "In being here and in knowing him, I have begun to believe in the reality of the Christian gospel."

This first-time conference guest could not have known how many others have used similar language to describe The Firs. The unique atmosphere which defines The Firs for many people, its special sense of sanctuary, regularly prompts people to speak of it as "a place apart," "a holy place." But why is this so? After all, what immediately strikes the eyes when one is introduced to The Firs is the size, diversity, and apparent prosperity of its operation. It owns some of the finest recreational property in the Pacific Northwest. The thirty-two-acre main conference center situated in the quiet Geneva suburb of Bellingham, Washington has attractive accommodations for more than two hundred guests, and is the site of some fifty camps and retreats each year. Six miles away on scenic Lake Whatcom there is an additional, heavily timbered waterfront property called Firwood, which houses upwards of 150 campers for each week of its summer camping season. And atop Mount Baker, in the nearby Cascades, stands the beautiful alpine Firs Chalet where students, churches, and guest groups enjoy winter ski retreats.

Programming at all three locations is versatile, adapted to the changing needs of an ever-growing Firs constituency. Parenting and singles' conferences, pastors' and lay leaders' retreats, and family camps have significant current priority. Trip camping is becoming a staple of the annual conference schedule, with sailing, canoeing, backpacking, and bicycle trips being offered for junior high and high school campers, and boating excursions and "conference on wheels" bus tours on the agenda for adults. All this, added to the regular round of Bible studies, luncheons, fellowship groups, leadership training programs, missionary projects, and youth programs sponsored and hosted by The Firs' personnel.

The resident staff members who make The Firs their home and its ministry their life's vocation are, as a group, forward-looking. But they are also deeply committed to the sources of their vision and to the traditions that have nurtured it for six decades of conference ministry. All hold to The Firs' doctrinal position, its uncompromising adherence to the inspiration and authority of Scripture and consequent emphasis on biblical teaching, its thorough grounding in what may fairly be described as conservative American evangelicalism. But all subscribe, additionally, to its missionary emphasis and to financial and operational principles bearing the clear imprint of late nineteenth-century interdenominational faith missions—particularly those pioneered by George Muller of Bristol, England and his compatriot and friend, James Hudson Taylor.

It is in these allegiances to the past, to the distinctive twofold inheritance of a theology rooted in America and a spirituality sprung essentially from English sources, that the sense of "holy ground" is faithfully preserved, even in the midst of change and growth. There is probably no better metaphor for The Firs as a whole in this sense than the original 20' x 20' honeymoon cottage in which, in 1921, the work began. "May The Firs cabin never be torn down," said Isobel Kuhn in 1940, "no matter how badly 'enlarging' is demanded! It is sacred with the footsteps and the smiles of many a saint of God."[1]

Forty years later, the cabin still stands at the heart of the Geneva conference property, though its walls have been pushed out and partitions removed. The present Firs lounge, by retaining rather than replacing that historic inner sanctuary, bears witness not only to God's repeated injunctions to "enlarge the place of your tent, and stretch out the curtains of your dwellings" (Isa 54:2) but also to the special character of the original dwelling; it stands as a concrete memorial of God's dealings with those who have gone before.

The Firs' debt to the past extends past 1921, though, and must in part be gleaned from the annals of church history. Well beyond the reach of present memory, in the remote middle years of the nineteenth century, God was at work shaping lives and ministries that would in turn shape the character of The Firs as it emerged from inconspicuous origins to become an influential center of Christian activity and witness in the Pacific Northwest.

## ENGLAND: THE "LIFE OF FAITH" IN AN AGE OF UNBELIEF

England in the middle decades of the 1800s would have seemed to most an unlikely seedbed for the modern resurgence of faith ministries and missions. Although popularly remembered as an "age of progress" marked by the secure and stable reign of Queen Victoria, freedom from international conflict, and an impressive array of domestic reforms for which outspoken critics like Charles Dickens had long been clamoring, the 1850s and 1860s were riddled with anxiety and restlessness. Churches and chapels were crowded with worshippers (for most Victorians, church attendance was an important component of respectability), but beneath

1 Kuhn, "My Spiritual Mother," in Brown, *Work of Faith, Labor of Love*, 211.

the rather shallow and complacent profession encouraged by "natural religion," skepticism was rampant. As one church historian has observed, "never has any age in history produced such a detailed literature of lost faith, or so many great men and women of religious temperament standing outside organized religion."[2] Even among regular parishioners, many were devoting their most serious meditation to the revolutionary new philosophies of Hegel, Marx, and Darwin.

Darwin's *Origin of the Species*, published in 1859, confirmed for many the apparently irreconcilable antagonism of science and faith that had been growing for more than a hundred years. Now, every new discovery in biology, astronomy, or geology seemed to call Scripture—or at least traditionally held views of Scripture—into question. John Ruskin echoed the sentiments of many when he exclaimed over the insufficiency of his own inherited faith to withstand the "evidences" of science: "If only the Geologists would let me alone, I could do very well, but those dreadful Hammers! I hear the clink of them at the end of every cadence of the Bible verses."[3] On the continent, "higher critics" were busy with their own hammers, chipping away at one-secure beliefs as they re-edited and, in effect, rewrote much of the biblical text.

The sense of spiritual abandonment underlying the optimistic mystique of the age was perhaps nowhere more memorably penned than in Matthew Arnold's poem "Dover Beach" (1851): "The Sea of Faith / Was once, too, at the full, and round earth's shore / Lay like the folds of a bright girdle furled. / But now I only hear / Its melancholy, long withdrawing roar, / Retreating to the breath / Of the night wind, down the vast edges drear / And naked shingles of the world."

Yet it is in the midst of this doubt-ridden era that we find a humble saint in the port city of Bristol bearing quiet but extraordinary testimony to the presence of a living God. "I have joyfully dedicated my whole life," wrote George Muller, "to the object of exemplifying how much may be accomplished by prayer and faith."[4]

In 1833, Muller left a full-time pastorate to establish an orphanage in Bristol as part of The Scripture Knowledge Institution for Home and Abroad, without financial backing, endowment, or funded property—indeed, without any form of visible support.[5] Determined to take Scripture

2. Vidler, *Age of Revolution*, 112–13.

3. Ruskin, in a letter to Henry Ackland (1851), *Works* 36.115.

4. Cited in Pierson, "Proof of the Living God," 1.70–86.

5. See Pierson, "Proof of the Living God" for a brief recapitulation of the faith

seriously, straightforwardly, and to rely upon it, Muller appealed to God alone rather than human benefactors for the means to gather, feed, house, clothe, and teach Christian truths to hundreds of destitute and orphaned children. And as year after year came and went, the work prospered, and ever-increasing needs were consistently met, often with astonishing specificity. Muller's work at Ashley Downs may not have eradicated the skepticism of his era but it provided both a challenge and encouragement to a church struggling with unbelief: God could be trusted.

Some of the distinctive features of the Bristol orphanage, moreover, were to provide models for later faith ministries such as The Firs, with which Muller himself was to have no direct contact. It was Muller's habit never to solicit funds or to take up public offerings; even in his pastoral ministry he had chosen rather to place small "freewill offering" boxes so that those who were truly led to give would give in secret, without compulsion. He decided, additionally, that the work would "owe no man anything"—that debt should not be incurred for any purpose. In essence, Muller's example was one of simple dependence and steadfast, childlike trust. "It is a most wholesome lesson," he was prone to say to his colleagues, "for Christian workers to learn that all true work is primarily the Lord's and only secondarily ours."[6] That versions of this statement are frequently heard at The Firs and that its spirit is so deeply understood is no accident. The spiritual affinities are strong.

Among Muller's more immediate descendants in the life of faith was the pioneer missionary to inland China, James Hudson Taylor. Taylor was born within months of the establishment of the Bristol orphanage work. As a young man, when he pledged to take the gospel to the Orient, he was greatly influenced by Muller's quiet, consistent testimony to the faithfulness of God.[7] It was not until he was actually in China, however, laboring with the Chinese Evangelization Society, that he came to the attention of this man he so much admired. In 1856, having been in China only a matter of months, Taylor wrote to friends and family in England of a humiliating incident in which all his personal belongings had been stolen. There was no appeal for assistance, only an expression of gratitude that he was being schooled so rigorously in the life of faith. Somehow the letter came to the attention of George Muller who, feeling a bond of sympathy and compassion with the young missionary, sent sufficient

principles of the Bristol ministry.

6. Pierson, *Muller of Bristol*, 271.

7. Taylor and Taylor, *Growth of a Work of God*, 61.

funds to cover the loss and pledged his spiritual and material support to young Hudson Taylor's endeavors.

There was a profound spiritual kinship between the two men. Like Muller, Hudson Taylor was convinced that a faithful God would supply every need, and that both solicitation of human support and indebtedness were contrary to his intention for his children. The issue of debt was in fact determinative of Taylor's decision to withdraw in 1857 from the mission with which he was associated:

> To me it seemed that the teaching of God's Word was unmistakably clear. To borrow money implied, to my mind, a contradiction of Scripture—a confession that God had withheld some good thing and a determination to get for ourselves what He had not given . . . If the Word taught me anything, it taught me to have *no connection with debt*. I could not think that God was poor, that He was short of resources, or unwilling to supply any want of whatever work was really His.[8]

When Taylor returned to England in 1860, he and Muller met for the first time, and it was largely because of the older man's support and encouragement, as well as his example, that Taylor was able to venture wholly on faith in founding the China Inland Mission.[9] In June 1865, with a prayer for twenty-four willing, skilled laborers, he opened an account for the C.I.M. and waited for a miracle. The principles on which the new work was to operate were as radical as those Muller had adopted: "We can afford to have as little as the Lord chooses to give, but we cannot afford to have unconsecrated money, or to have money placed in the wrong positions. Far better to have no money at all, even to buy food with, for there are plenty of ravens in China."[10]

The organization of the mission was simple: biblical precedents informed every area of concern. In the early 1870s a council of Christian friends was formed, which shared responsibilities at the home office in England. From the beginning, this council group, like the staff of overseas workers, was an interdenominational fellowship, comprised

8. Taylor and Taylor, *Growth of a Soul*, 430.

9. Muller's support was a mainstay for the missionary. In late February1869 Taylor received a letter from England saying, in part, "We are just back from Bristol. The sympathy expressed for you and those with you . . . was very sweet; and none spoke more warmly of you than dear Mr. Muller." *Growth of a Work of God*, 161.

10. Taylor and Taylor, *Growth of a Work of God*, 42. The reference to ravens comes from 1 Kgs 17; in the midst of a drought, God sends ravens with food to the prophet Elijah.

of Methodists, Baptists, Presbyterians, Plymouth Brethren, Anglicans, Quakers, and Pentecostals, among others. As one of Taylor's letters records: "We decided to invite the cooperation of fellow believers irrespective of denominational views, who fully held the inspiration of God's Word, and were willing to prove their faith by going to inland China with only the guarantee they carry within the covers of their pocket Bibles."[11]

The China Inland Mission was thus established, as the burden of a man of faith in a skeptical generation. Its impact on China, on foreign missions generally, and on the whole Christian world, was to be immense; notably, its legacy would extend to a Bible and Missionary Conference half a world and half a century away on the shores of Lake Whatcom in western Washington.

## AMERICA: REVIVAL AND RECONSTRUCTION

To understand aright the fruitfulness of the early years of the C.I.M., Taylor's biographers remind us, "it should be borne in mind that Mr. Taylor, among others, was reaping the aftermath of the great Revival of 1859" in which "Christian hearts were kindled in a new sense of oneness, and awakened to the fact that God by his Holy Spirit was using a class of workers hitherto largely excluded from the spiritual ministries of the Church."[12]

Although it spanned two continents, this midcentury awakening seems to have had its origins in America. In 1857, amidst financial panic and agitation over issues that would later shatter the Union, a group of New York businessmen, at the invitation of lay evangelist Jeremiah Lamphier, began to meet for one-hour noonday prayers meetings. These Fulton Street gatherings, named for the address at which they were initially held, were almost immediately attended with a marked demonstration of the presence and power of the Holy Spirit. As the movement outgrew its first venue and spread throughout the city, it gained widespread public attention. A *New York Times* editorial on March 20, 1858, pronounced "the great wave of religious excitement" to be "one of the most remarkable movements since the Reformation":

11. Taylor and Taylor, *Growth of a Work of God*, 42. Hudson Taylor himself had been raised among Wesleyan Methodists but left the church over doctrinal issues as a teenager. Though he was later rebaptized by the Plymouth Brethren, he never formally became a member of that or any other denomination.

12. Taylor and Taylor, *Growth of a Work of God*, 48–49.

> In this City, we have beheld a sight which not the most enthusiastic fanatic for church-observances could ever have hoped to look upon: we have seen in a business quarter of the City, in the busiest hours, assemblies of merchants, clerks, and workingmen, to the number of some 5,000, gathered day after day for simple and solemn worship. Similar assemblies we find in other portions of the City: a theatre is turned into a chapel; churches of all sects are open and crowded by day and night.

Despite their simplicity—their sole object and program was prayer—similar gatherings were soon being held all over the country, "from the forests of Maine, the crowded City-ports, the manufacturing towns, the new cities of the West, the villages of the southwest, and even the mines and mountains of California," according to the *Times* editorialists. Unlike other previous "awakenings," they observed, this revival was especially distinctive in its "deep, earnest, and moral" tone and its interdenominational character.

A Welsh immigrant named Humphrey Jones carried the message and the impact of what he had seen back across the Atlantic in the summer of 1858. Within weeks, the awakening became local news as well, and new converts began to fill the pews of established congregations in Wales. Ireland, Scotland, and England were to be touched in the same dramatic way. In 1859, shortly before Hudson Taylor was to return home on furlough, he received word that "the Revival has reached London and hundreds are being converted."[13]

In America, possibly the greatest single product of the awakening was Dwight L. Moody, destined for a ministry of immense proportions. For several years, however, his influence—like that of a book by American Presbyterian William E. Boardman, entitled *The Higher Christian Life*—was to remain somewhat hidden, as the States were plunged into Civil War.

The war years had a generally debilitating effect on American Christianity. Although there were instances of revival in both Northern and Southern camps, the very nature of the struggle, with antagonistic forces both claiming allegiance to sacred principles, tore at the heart of the church. Those who were drawn into the conflict soon saw that while simple black and white discriminations were seemingly at the center of the confrontation, the issues, like the uniforms, were more often a muddy

13. Orr, *Second Evangelical Awakening*, 87.

blue-grey. And once the "holy war" was over, there were many disillusioned crusaders in the ranks.

The era of Reconstruction, not surprisingly, produced disparate responses and interpretations. Some carried an almost militaristic zeal with them into successive decades.[14] But for the most part, Americans were weary of the scandal of intolerance, weary of conflict, and content to replace the "new world" theology of their pilgrim-spirited forebears with a more secular (though still tacitly Christian) American dream. Fanaticism, even evangelical enthusiasm, was out of favor; religion was expected to be, above all, reasonable.

New social conditions in the post-war era had a dramatic effect on the church. Much of the country was transformed, almost overnight, into an urban, industrialized nation. Because of the rapidly rising demand for labor, the late nineteenth century saw wave after wave of immigration from Europe. But ideas also migrated: empiricism, humanism, skepticism, and a host of other "isms" that were prevalent in England and on the continent made themselves felt on a popular level in America.

To the already deafening clamor of European free-thinkers were added the American voices of Ralph Waldo Emerson and John Dewey, and the church had few apologists equal to the task of refuting them. The secularization of education, championed by Dewey and effected by the trend of increasing state jurisdiction, was compounded by the liberal drift in leading seminaries. From the late 1860s through the next several decades, many American pastors and theologians travelled to German to seek out the enlightenment of higher critics first-hand. Returning, they promoted their new teachings to generations of seminary students.

Evangelicalism's second wind in the United States was to come essentially as a reaction against all such modernizing tendencies and as an attempt to recover the fundamentals of historic, biblical Christianity. Dwight Moody, after a season of spiritual drought and uncertainty, emerged in 1872 as a potent spokesman for the conservative forces. With singer Ira Sankey, he embarked on a preaching tour of the British Isles, where evidences of awakening attended his ministry, so that by the time he returned to his own country in 1875 his reputation as a revivalist was firmly established. Subsequent meetings in New York, Philadelphia, Chicago, and Boston saw powerful outpourings of the Holy Spirit.

14. This was the era in which the Ku Klux Klan and the (anti-Catholic) American Protective Association were established.

William E. Boardman, who had joined Moody and Sankey in London during their English campaign, stayed on and conducted a series of conventions related to the principles of personal holiness espoused in his *Higher Christian Life*. Through the interest and cooperation of Church of England evangelicals, a ten-day gathering at Oxford was organized in 1874 and attended by more than a thousand people; a similar convention at Brighton nine months later drew three thousand, including Hudson Taylor, who was temporarily home from China.[15] In 1875, the convention was moved to Keswick; from that time, annual summer conferences "for the promotion of practical holiness" retained the Keswick site and adopted its name.

A Christian conference movement was also taking hold simultaneously in the United States. Under increasing pressure from liberal churches and seminaries, and following a precedent set at Lake Chautauqua, New York in 1874, various strands of resurgent theological conservativism united in a series of non-denominational Bible conferences:

> The Believers' Meeting for Bible Study met in Chicago in 1875; its later annual gatherings were often at Niagara-on-the-Lake, Ontario, and became popularly known as the Niagara Bible Conference. The Niagara Conference was in part based on English models, as was the Bible and Prophetic Conference called in New York in 1878 at Holy Trinity Episcopal Church . . . In 1886 and 1895, similar conferences were held at Chicago and Philadelphia while on a smaller scale many other such meetings were held in various cities.[16]

The prophetic, dominantly premillennial, strain which characterized the early American conference movement was in part reflective of

15. While on the mission field, Hudson Taylor had been exposed to and deeply affected by "holiness" teaching, as recounted in the chapter entitled "The Exchanged Life" in Taylor and Taylor, *Growth of a Work of God.*

16. Handy, *History of Churches*, 291. The 1878 Niagara Bible Conference published an influential fourteen-point doctrinal statement that spelled out what all faithful Christians should believe: the verbal, plenary inspiration of the Scriptures in the original manuscripts; the Trinity; the creation of man, the fall into sin, and total depravity; the universal transmission of spiritual death from Adam; the necessity of the new birth; redemption by the blood of Christ; salvation by faith alone in Christ; the assurance of salvation; the centrality of Jesus Christ in the Scriptures; the constitution of the true church by genuine believers; the personality of the Holy Spirit; the believer's call to a holy life; the immediate passing of the souls of believers to be with Christ at death; the premillennial Second Coming of Christ. A shorter and better-known list of "essentials" or "fundamentals" that prevailed into subsequent generations was fivefold; see below.

the influence of John Nelson Darby, founder of the Plymouth Brethren. Darby discovered in North America a receptive audience for his dispensationalist teaching, which was subsequently popularized in Cyrus I. Scofield's influential Scofield Reference Bible (1909, revised 1917). With its Bible charts and graphics, including "end times" prognostication, it added new urgency to missionary endeavor. Moody repeatedly delivered missionary challenges and was influential in sending hundreds of Christians abroad. At a Mount Hermon conference in 1886, dozens of college men responded to his call and to the example of the "Cambridge Seven" who had gone to China three years earlier.[17] From this beginning, a Student Volunteer Movement for Foreign Missions was organized, adopting as its slogan "The evangelization of the world in this generation."

In 1888 Hudson Taylor himself visited North America on his way back to China. "I wanted to see Mr. Moody," he later wrote, "and had heard of over two thousand students wishful to consecrate their lives to God's service abroad." Taylor met with members of the Student Volunteer Movement at a Northfield summer conference and attended numerous other meetings. His most important engagement, however, proved to be the Niagara Bible Conference of 1888, one of the results of which was the birth of the North American branch of the C.I.M.[18] When Taylor continued on to China he was accompanied by a band of volunteers from Canada and the United States.

Missionary zeal contributed the strongest positive motivation for the American Bible Institute movement, which was also taking hold in this era—providing an alternative theological formation to that offered in increasingly liberal seminaries and colleges. In 1882 the Missionary Training Institute of Nyack-on-the-Hudson, known by most simply as "Nyack," was established. Four years later, Moody founded the Chicago Evangelistic Society, which was to become Moody Bible Institute. Before long, similar institutions sprang up in Denver, Los Angeles, Minneapolis, Philadelphia, and New York—bastions of orthodoxy in which a "back to the Bible" emphasis dominated the classroom experience. Scripture was understood to be the primary textbook in every course and the five fundamental doctrines set forth in the declaration of the 1895 Niagara Bible Conference (the inerrancy of Scripture, the virgin birth, the deity

17. C.K. Ober, cited in Taylor and Taylor, *Growth of a Work of God*, 442, note 1. See also the biography of C.T. Studd by his son-in-law, Norman Grubb.

18. For the story of the origins of the C.I.M. in North America, see Taylor and Taylor, *Growth of a Work of God*, chapter 30.

of Christ, the substitutionary atonement, and the physical resurrection and bodily return of Christ), each of which was a specific refutation of current liberal tenets, found a central place in Bible School teaching.

The "fundamentalist" movement was already well underway when, in 1910, two prominent California laymen associated with the fledgling Bible Institute of Los Angeles (Biola) published a twelve-volume series of articles reflecting conservative evangelical doctrine entitled *The Fundamentals: A Testimony to the Truth*. Milton and Lyman Stewart distributed copies free of charge, with the intent of reaching every pastor, evangelist, missionary, theology professor, theology student, Sunday School superintendent, and Y.M.C.A. and Y.W.C.A. secretary in the English-speaking world.

Los Angeles, and Biola more specifically, became the western headquarters of American evangelicalism. Reuben A. Torrey, an associate of Moody's and his chosen successor, went to Biola as dean in 1912. And Frank R. Keller, eminent medical researcher and veteran C.I.M. missionary, was also temporarily loaned to the school by the mission. These two men not only had a decisive impact on the institute itself and on evangelical churches through their writing and teaching; they also helped establish, through the financial backing of Milton and Lyman Stewart, the China chapter of Biola, the Hunan Bible Institute.

All of this history, encompassing many decades and several countries, is the hidden backdrop, the divinely ordered prologue, to the story of The Firs Bible and Missionary Conference. The Firs' own first chapter begins, in the same era, as a family history, apparently unrelated, but in God's ultimate purposes intimately connected, to these larger movements and developments.

# 1

# Migration (1851–1911)

"O God, You have taught me from my youth; and to this day I declare Your wondrous works . . . O God, do not forsake me, until I declare Your strength to this generation."[1]

THE WHIPPLE FAMILY, WHOSE name was for many years almost synonymous with The Firs, traces the American portion of its venerable and colorful lineage all the way back to the Mayflower era. Captain John Whipple, born in England during the turbulent reign of King James I, was only four years old when the first fleet of pilgrims charted a course to the New World in 1620. As a young man he too chose the colonies as his adoptive homeland and set sail for New England where he was to settle, marry, raise a family, and eventually die, in Providence, Rhode Island, at the age of 69.

Among the nineteenth-century descendants of Captain John and his pilgrim bride Sarah, our attention is quickly drawn to Orin Palmer Whipple, born in 1851 into the home of William Crouch Whipple—a stone mason and builder in Galva, Illinois—and his wife Hannah (née Geer). Although sixth-born of eleven children, Orin was one of the first to live to maturity: an older sister had died at nine; none of his three elder brothers saw their twenty-fifth birthday. From the cradle, it seemed, he had an instinct for survival, a keen independence, and an amazing capacity for adaptability.

1. Ps 71:17–18.

As a lad, Orin showed signs of his father's penchant for building, but once out of school he set out to seek his fortune in the booming post-war economy of the Midwest. A brief stint of vocational training at Bryant Stratton and Co. Business College in Chicago enhanced his native resourcefulness and he soon found the opportunity he was looking for. At twenty, he started his own small dairy business near Kansas City, Kansas. Then, whether the challenge proved insufficient or youthful restlessness simply got the best of him, a year later he was diverted back into an academic setting, accepting a position as instructor of algebra, trigonometry, calculus, and astronomy in a Kansas City military academy. The same year, he struck up a correspondence with his wife-to-be Nancy Jane ("Janie") Headrick, also a teacher, living in Corning, Iowa, not far from the Adams County home where Orin's own family had relocated.

Janie's was a pioneering family of English and Irish extraction; her father, Charles McLain Headrick, retained vivid childhood memories of a 400-mile wagon train migration from Bartholomew County, Indiana to Davis County, Iowa. It was, moreover, a devout and godly family, with denominational affiliations in the Disciples of Christ church. One of Charles Headrick's uncles preached in the Disciples Church in Indiana for forty years; a cousin, Adelaide A. Pollard, penned the well-known hymn "Have Thine Own Way, Lord." Janie's maternal grandfather, Meshach Hale (with brothers Shadrach and Abednego), bore in his name an unmistakable identification with biblical heritage and parental faith.

On May 1, 1873, about a month before her nineteenth birthday, Janie exchanged vows with Orin Whipple in a small ceremony at her parents' home. The next day she and her new husband moved to the Whipple family home near Quincy, in Adams County, Iowa. The girlish spunk which had captivated Orin are evident in Janie's diary entries from the early months of their marriage:

> May 7th—It is raining a little. Orin and I went home a horseback to get my cow. When we got there, they laughed at me for coming along when it was raining, to help drive a cow. But they said it was just like me, and no more than they expected. We started back at two, got here about six, had a good time driving the cow.
>
> May 8th—Orin and I are going to town to have our pictures taken, and then go to Pa's and stay all night. That will only make three times that I have been home the first week. I think that is doing well for a beginning.

> May 14th—It turned cold, and in the evening rained a little. I went out to the blacksmith shop where Orin was making some devices, and stayed about an hour, and like to froze, and had my eyes smoked out in the bargain, but I didn't mind it too much after all.

In a more reflective mood, some weeks later, the young bride wrote:

> This is the first day of July and I have been married two months, yet I can scarcely realize that it is true. Time passes swiftly by and doesn't wait for anyone . . . I am determined to make better use of my time . . . I want to study the Bible more than I have ever done before, for this world is but a place for us to prepare for the next.

Here, for all its simplicity, is a wonderfully pure distillation of the devotion and discipline which characterized all of Janie's life. "Redeeming the time" assumed for her a practical, even homely aspect.

Orin farmed for a time, returned to teaching briefly, and then took up his father's trade of building and masonry in earnest. In 1874 he and Janie moved to Corning where, the following March, their first child, Otis Grant, was born. An immediate delight to his mother, Otis profited from her lively intelligence and early instruction. A diary note from May 1879 records that he was, at age four, "most through his first reader." He was to do well enough throughout his school years to go on to the University of Nebraska in Lincoln and pursue a legal career. But he displayed also an early affinity with his father in the Whipple knack for building and took a college minor in architecture. In 1899, when he decided that the legal profession was not, after all, for him, since "he didn't want to be talking and thinking about people's quarrels all the time," he apprenticed to Orin and soon joined him as partner in masonry work. By that time the family had grown to include six children and was settled in Canon City, Colorado.

Other relatives, including Janie's parents and two of her sisters, Alice and Ella (married to brothers, Lewis and Edd Booker), had moved even further west, to Whatcom (now Bellingham), Washington. In 1901, Otis followed them, joining Ella's husband, his uncle Edd, in his masonry and construction company.

He had no way of knowing, of course, that Bellingham held for him also a lovely bride named Julia Cole. Nor could he have anticipated that the essential task to which he was being called in the Pacific Northwest was something more than another construction job—that God had in mind for him a ministry to be known eventually as The Firs Bible and Missionary Conference.

Julia's own background was a wonderful complement to Otis's. Born in New Orleans in December 1876, fifth of six children, Julia had, like him, enjoyed the benefits of a consistent Christian upbringing. Her father, a Baptist minister who had been preaching since he was seventeen, served as a Union chaplain during the Civil War, then moved west in the 1890s to become pastor of the First Baptist Church in the little port community of Bellingham. Her mother and namesake was an equally profound spiritual presence in young Julia's life. Like Janie Whipple, she had married in the last month of her eighteenth year; like her, she had conscientiously kept a journal. Indeed, the similarity between the spiritual convictions, yearnings, and commitments of the mothers of Otis and Julia is strikingly evident in their respective writings. On her nineteenth birthday, the elder Julia Cole reflected:

> Long ago I gave my heart into the Saviour's keeping. And though I have wandered from Him times without number He has ever been the same loving, gracious parent to me. And I would not this morning give up the trust, confidence, and security I feel in Him, and the hope I have of gaining Heaven through His blood, for any consideration whatever.
>
> Next to my conversion comes my marriage. We have been married almost a month and I think we can both truly say it has been the happiest of our lives . . . Today is my birthday. I am nineteen. How rapidly time passes, and how little advancement I make in my Christian life. Oh, for more grace, more true piety! I have endeavored today to begin anew, to consecrate myself more entirely to my Saviour. But oh, how weak I am, how utterly useless it is for me to make these new resolves without the help of my heavenly Father! I seem to realize it so fully today and have prayed much and earnestly for His guidance and blessing.

Young Julia was deeply touched by her mother's heart. Her spiritual inheritance was manifest in her own tact, wisdom, and uncanny sensitivity to those for whom God had given her a particular concern. A graceful partnership of humor and serenity was her greatest asset; she lived by prayer. As one of her many spiritual children said of her, "She never trusted to her own strength and I'm sure that's the reason she was often wonderfully victorious."[2]

It was only a matter of months after his arrival in Bellingham that Otis met Julia for the first time. She was collecting rummage for a fund-raising venture at her father's church when she came to the home of Edd and Ella Booker, where Otis was staying. Whatever was donated for the church-sponsored project has long been forgotten, but there seems to have been an immediate spark of interest between Otis and Julia. Soon after, they met again at a church party. Their initial friendship blossomed into romance, and they were mutually drawn toward a lifelong partnership. On June 17, 1903 they were married by Julia's father in the Cole family home. It was doubtless observed that day, as it was so often in their later life together, that "they were so absolutely one, and so complemented each other, that you did not get the full benefit of the Whipples until you knew both, and knew them together."[3]

Otis's wedding gift to his bride—a small summer cabin tucked in amongst magnificent evergreens near the shore of Lake Whatcom—became their honeymoon cottage and first home. The site was soon christened "The Firs"; those who visited in the early years remembered the name spelled out with fir cones above the fireplace.

During the early years of their marriage, Otis and Julia lived for much of the year in nearby Bellingham, where Otis continued to work for his uncle Edd Booker.[4] Each summer, however, saw them back at The Firs, which before long became something of a family campsite. Julia's brother Tom had bought several adjoining lots and another brother, John, later built a cabin there. Otis's mother and his sister Edna spent the summer months with them the second year. Edna later recalled her own wide-eyed, ten-year-old infatuation with the beautiful wooded setting, giving us an early description of the cabin and grounds:

> The kitchen was in one corner, the bedroom back of it, and the living room, with fireplace at one end, along the side. There was a porch along the kitchen and living room doorway side and it extended around the corner. The dining room was on the porch. Otis had built a small frame room off the porch at the corner by

2. Kuhn, "My Spiritual Mother," in Brown, *Work of Faith, Labor of Love*, 209.

3. Kuhn, "My Spiritual Mother," in Brown, *Work of Faith, Labor of Love*, 219.

4. The firm was responsible for the iconic B&B Furniture building, Bellingham's first reinforced concrete structure, as well as the Y.M.C.A. building and Eden's Hall on the campus of Washington State Normal School (now Western Washington University).

> the kitchen for my mother and me. I well remember my playhouse under that room, by the big stump.
>
> Grandma and Grandpa Cole had a small cabin just back of the main cottage, with a tiny room along one end where Uncle Tom slept. It seems like I can still see Grandpa Cole resting in a big chair on their porch. At the other end of the lot was another cabin John Cole had built for his family. The tall fir trees were everywhere.
>
> I often walked over to the lovely spring back in the woods across Cable Street. We would sometimes have a watermelon and Otis would go over there to get it, where he had put it to cool. Julia ironed on the porch by the kitchen . . . I have often thought about one evening when Uncle Tom came home from work in Bellingham (then called Whatcom), his arm around Grandma Cole, skipping along and half singing "This is the way Carrie and I go." This was before he and Aunt Carrie were married. It was such a happy summer.

Otis's father Orin and the rest of the family had intended to come west as well, making Bellingham their new home as soon as the house in Colorado sold. Mr. Whipple died, however, before his plans could be realized; in September 1904 the vehicle he was driving was struck by a train, killing him instantly. Janie Whipple stayed in Canon City for a year and then, the following September, shipped all her household goods west and came to Bellingham to live.

Comfortably surrounded by extended family, Otis and Julia settled into the first years of their new life together. Their combined talents and energies were poured into the work of First Baptist Church as well as a variety of community endeavors. From the first, their home was generously shared; it soon became not only a favorite gathering place for their many friends but also a welcoming haven for those whose greatest need was warm Christian hospitality. For more than a few, including young Isobel Miller and Doris Coffin, the Whipple household was to prove a home away from home and first portal to their own spiritual pilgrimage.

A new season of joy came into the lives of Otis and Julia when Elden Cole Whipple, their firstborn, arrived in May 1905. Nearly two years later, on March 6, 1907, a daughter, Lois, was added. Otis Grant Whipple Jr., on whom the mantel of his father was eventually to fall, was born on February 1, 1911, by which time the family was living in Vancouver, British Columbia. Grant's arrival coincided, in fact, with the birth of a new commitment and new dream on the part of his parents.

# 2

# Seeds (1911–1920)

"We rejoice in our sufferings, knowing that suffering produces endurance, and endurance produces character, and character produces hope."[1]

SUCCESS AND PROSPERITY HAD taken the Whipples to Vancouver. Otis had been made a full partner in Booker, Campbell, and Whipple Contractors and business was flourishing on both sides of the border. As material resources flowed in, Otis and Julia maintained their habitual pattern of generous stewardship. Their commitment to Broadway West Baptist Church, of which they were charter members, and their involvement in the Christian community in Vancouver was not only a source of blessing to those whose lives they touched but also an unknowing investment in the later work of The Firs. The foundation of a sizeable Canadian constituency of The Firs Fellowship was laid in the hearts of these early friends and acquaintances. The rigors of faith, however, and the preparation of their hearts for the ministry to which God intended to call them were yet to come. This new phase of their Christian experience was introduced to them rather unexpectedly in the form of a book, the biography of James Hudson Taylor.

*The Growth of a Soul*, the newly published first volume of the Hudson Taylor story seems almost to have sought the Whipples out. It was brought to their door in a satchel, along with a number of other books, by a returned missionary from the China Inland Mission, who found a continuing ministry in selling Christian books door-to-door. Attracted

1. Rom 5:3–4, ESV.

by the lady's demeanor and by the evident spiritual quality of the literature she carried, Julia purchased *The Growth of a Soul.* As she and Otis read chapter after chapter aloud to one another, tracing the testimony of Hudson Taylor's life of faith, God seemed to be speaking directly to their hearts.

The Whipples had heard of George Muller and knew fleetingly of his remarkable experiment of dependence on God alone in the Bristol orphanage work, but Taylor and the C.I.M. were entirely new to them. Julia's letters record the impact:

> At that time the Lord was blessing us financially. He was prospering the work of Mr. Whipple's hands. Everything was rosy for us. When we finished the book, we were thrilled. It was a searching message to our own hearts. I said to Mr. Whipple, "Is this kind of life only for missionaries?" Mr. Whipple said, "No, it is for anyone who will pay the price." As we read the story of Hudson Taylor's growth in Christ we felt the touch of that man's life on our hearts. We knew the Holy Spirit was speaking. We told the Lord we would pay the price.

Otis and Julia had no idea, when they expressed their willingness to sacrifice even the good gifts of God for a life of greater dependence, how much the biography of this man of God was to affect their own history, how much the principles of faith he demonstrated and advocated were to shape their own life story. Gradually, however, through utterly unforeseen changes in their material circumstances, the Whipples' trust began to be tested and refined.

> Everything went on for a year comfortably and happily . . . but then things became difficult, so it was decided to cease work in Vancouver. The office was kept there for years, but business was conducted in Seattle. The Lord was so gracious and the change came gradually. He led us step by step, but we began to realize that something was happening. All at once the Lord said, "Didn't you say you would pay the price? Aren't you willing to try Me; aren't you willing to prove Me?"

There is no better witness to the growth of a soul through all the discomfort and disappointment, financial hardship, and physical suffering of the next several years than the diary of Julia Whipple. She speaks not only for herself but also for Otis and the three children as she reflects on the lessons of faith—many of the same lessons that had challenged and governed the lives of George Muller and Hudson Taylor:

September 1916. This first year in Seattle and in this home has been wonderfully marked by the conscious presence of the Lord Jesus and the definite leading of the Holy Spirit. So many direct answers to prayer have come during the year. We regret we have not kept a record of them all. These last few months, and especially weeks, we have been so shut up to God that we learned what *faith* and *trust* are as we never did before.

The business has been unsuccessful and a sore trial through the entire year. Many times, when the monthly bills were due and we had no way of meeting them, the Lord so definitely made provision. On one day in particular, when three bills were due and we were so burdened, a check came for $65.00. The Lord has for years blessed us with so many direct answers to prayer—yet until this year we have never known what it was to *live by faith*.

During the summer we became conscious of sin in *failing to tithe* our income. Finding it so hard to meet expenses, we began robbing the Lord. We do so praise His name that He showed it to us. We confessed the sin and are by His help "bringing all the tithes into the storehouse."

Then He has definitely shown us the sin of being in debt. We have prayed much about it and feel He has brought us to the place where we dare not incur any more. We *believe* He will help us get out from under this load, though we see no way out. We have been brought to the place where we must go all the way with the Lord. It has meant hours and hours in prayer for we have been so conscious of the power of the Adversary. Some days have been dark—yet the Lord has never failed, and we have been strengthened and comforted . . . He has held us in the everlasting arms and we are safe.

September 15, 1916. Morning reading, 1 Peter 4:7: "But the end of all things is at hand."

It seems literally so in regard to all of our affairs. Business at an end, household supplies, food, and clothing all at an end. The children's shoes are worn through, telephone bill including two long distance calls amounting to $6.03, and other bills due. (We are praying to get out of debt and keep out of debt.) After the noonday prayer and great exercise of soul, the precious promise from the Promise Box was from Zephaniah 3:17: "The Lord your God in your midst, the Mighty One, will save." *God's word cannot fail.*

September 16. No help yet. The "end of things" hadn't really come as we thought. During prayer it was made plain the taking of milk must stop unless paid for each day or in advance. We had decided we couldn't run a grocery bill any longer. A small bill running from the first of September to the 15th we owe. Just as we had finished prayer the milkman came. We felt the matter must be decided at once. The precious gold dollar given to me by my dear mother eight years ago—her last gift to me—was used in buying a dollar's worth of milk tickets. *God alone knows what it cost.* I had always kept from using it and know now the Lord's hand was in it to help me learn the lesson of obedience to "owe no man." It was with some difficulty I persuaded the milkman to take it. He said he would always keep it, and I begged him to let it be a reminder of the little talk we had, and of the tract, and that someone was really interested.

September 18. A quiet morning and consciousness of the presence of the Holy Spirit. This Word from the Promise Box: "Now may the God of hope fill you with all joy and peace in believing" (Romans 15:13). It surely has wonderfully strengthened, and God is giving joy and peace in believing. In the afternoon a man from a secondhand store came to look at some old furniture we had in the basement. After some conversation we agreed on $4.00, a very meager sum. Elden was distressed on coming in from school, for he needed fifteen cents for a school paper. So, I gave him that amount for the paper and five cents to buy some Magic yeast. (On Friday I woefully fell by going in debt two cents for some compressed yeast. The Lord showed me my mistake, for the yeast proved a failure.) The gas bill was due and amounted to $3.60. Besides the $4.00 just received, ten cents was all we had. That evening Otis discovered that we had not tithed the $4.00. Oh, how ashamed we were! We saw then God's provision. There was just enough to pay the gas bill and lay by forty cents tithe money. We took out the forty cents and prayed for forgiveness.

September 19. Though the way is so dark, yet Romans 15:13 is being verified. The God of hope is filling us with all joy and peace in believing and we are abounding in hope through the power of the Holy Spirit. A letter was received from Mr. H.C. Hunt who is just recovering from his serious operation. He said that he and his wife were greatly burdened in prayer for us this morning and wanted to know the occasion. We feel now, after the fearfully hard day on Saturday when the struggle was almost more than we could bear, that we could understand the peace of mind and heart we had on Sunday, with such dear saints interceding for us. *Praise the Lord for such friends!*

September 20. Our provisions are getting very low—potatoes and all green vegetables practically gone—sugar nearly gone—one egg—have had no coffee for days—and the butter is gone. The children have been sweet in making the best of things. We know the Lord has not forgotten us, and we are surely hanging on *in faith.* Otis took with him this morning four three-cent pieces that he has had for a number of years, and four Canadian cent pieces. He found a place where he exchanged the three-cent pieces for sixteen cents to buy provisions. He brough home ten cents worth of potatoes and ten cents worth of tomatoes. Elden came in with his fifty cents earned and turned it all over. *We took out the tenth first.* Otis started out with forty cents to buy one-half pound of butter and one pound of lard. We gave back five cents to Elden. A gift of four huge peaches, with a can of oysters which we had in the house and the fresh vegetables made a most sumptuous meal, for which we truly thanked our heavenly Father.

September 21. This morning we were greatly touched by an act of Elden's. He had five cents out of his half dollar that he earned and last night slipped out after dinner and bought five cents worth of coffee, because he knew his mother had been missing her coffee these mornings. He got enough for five cents to do two mornings. Elden's unselfishness and sweet thought have been such a comfort these testing days.

September 22. Yesterday the burden seemed almost heavier than I could bear. Otis was kept in perfect peace and was such a comfort. I knew he was in constant prayer. The depression lasted through the night and was with me in the morning. We were out of nearly all our provisions, including the provision for milk. At morning worship, the burden was lifted through the morning reading, Psalm 55:22: "Cast your burden on the Lord, and He shall sustain you." On the margin of the little book my dear father had written eighteen years ago, "For me today, I thank Thee, Lord. 1898." The same message was used to lift us both *out of ourselves* and *into Him.* All of the "joy and peace in believing" came back and Saturday was a most triumphant day. Otis took with him a piece of silver ore he had had a great many years. He received $2.00 for it. After taking out the tenth and paying the electric light bill, he had $1.20 to buy provisions for over Sunday. *The Lord did provide!*

A break seemed to come in late 1916 when Otis received a new building contract. But despite heightened expectations that now, at last, God would restore some measure of temporal security, the two years that followed were characterized by accentuated failure and frustration, and brought Otis to the gates of death when a worldwide influenza epidemic brooded over Seattle and the Whipple home.

It became increasingly clear that not only the principles but also the practical outworkings of the life of faith were to govern Otis and Julia's experience for the rest of their lives. While in Seattle, their contact with the China Inland Mission was strengthened. The Whipple home was, as always it had been, open to a great company of neighbors; a monthly prayer meeting for the friends of the C.I.M. began to be held there, and it became a frequent occurrence for missionaries, many of whom sailed to and from the Orient via Seattle, to enjoy the Whipples' hospitality. "God has so enriched our lives through the China Inland Mission," wrote Julia in 1919, through "the great privilege of having in our home the dear C.I.M. missionaries":

> Mr. and Mrs. Fairclough and Christopher; Mr. and Mrs. Saunders—he blind and she deaf as a result of the Boxer movement in 1900, yet their wonderful message of the "peace that passes understanding"; Mrs. and Mrs. Miller; and dear Mr. D.E. Hoste, the General Director of the C.I.M., on his way back to China—each one leaving a special blessing and testimony.

The winter of 1918/19, which brought Otis's extended battle with influenza, also provided much of the necessary strength to meet it through the fellowship of men and women associated with the mission, among them several members of Hudson Taylor's family. On the night in which her husband's health was initially threatened, Julia received a telephone call from Ernest Taylor, asking if he and his family might be taken in.[2]

> The soft English accent and rather high-keyed voice struck to the depths of my heart. As my eyes were closed and the ears strained to catch the message because of the imperfect working of the telephone, I saw only a vision of the Lord Jesus Himself standing at the dock, seeking an abiding place. Having just

2. Ernest Hamilton Taylor (b. 1875) was the son of Hudson Taylor and his second wife Jane ("Jennie"), née Faulding. Howard Taylor (b. 1862) was Ernest's half-brother, son of Hudson and his first wife, Maria, who died in 1870. Howard and his wife Geraldine (née Guinness) were the principal biographers of Hudson Taylor and historians of the China Inland Mission.

recovered from influenza, not at all strong, and my hands more than full at the moment, I arranged with friends to take them to their home, and we would call for them within a few days when our own house guests were gone. That evening Otis had a hard chill, and an attack of flu set in. It looked at first as though it would be a light case, but infection of the kidneys developed and for nearly six weeks he was very ill.

At the beginning of the illness Dr. and Mrs. Howard Taylor arrived, on their way back to China, just having completed *The Growth of a Work of God.* The messages they delivered in Seattle were direct from God Himself. The first, given by Mrs. Taylor at an afternoon meeting, was from II Kings 13:15–19: "The arrow of the Lord's deliverance." We were all profoundly impressed and little knew how soon we were to put into practice that God-given message. A few days later another message was given to a little company gathered in Mrs. S.L. Bowman's home: "Three Avenues into God's Holiness." The first through chastening (Hebrews 12:10) pressed overwhelmingly home to me. Later, the other two: through the Word (the exceeding great and precious promises), and through the Holy Spirit (the love of God shed abroad in our hearts) came with forcefulness.

It was a great disappointment that Otis was unable to get to any of these services, but the Lord blessed us in sending Dr. Howard Taylor out one afternoon for tea. The fellowship was precious. The burden of our heart about a center in Seattle for the C.I.M., and a place for conference and prayer, was laid before him that he, in turn, would present to Mr. Hoste for prayer and thought in Shanghai.

Shortly after the departure of the Taylors, Otis grew sicker. Severe attacks came more frequently. The last day of February he grew decidedly worse and the doctor wanted a consultation. On Saturday Mr. Henry Bidlake, who two weeks previously had anointed Otis with oil in the name of the Lord with Mr. and Mrs. J. Addison Campbell, again came to pray with us. Mrs. Campbell brought a beautifully dressed chicken and five dozen eggs. That afternoon they called the league to prayer on Otis's behalf.[3] Relief came. Otis grew quiet, the fever abated, and he slept fairly well. Sunday, though there was some temperature, he seemed better till toward evening, when the fever went up to 104. My own strength seemed exhausted and hope almost

3. The Bidlakes and Campbells, friends from University Presbyterian Church in Seattle, where the Whipples attended, were later among the charter members of The Firs Council.

> gone. Otis asked the children and me to sing a song of praise for him. It was a pitiful attempt, with our hearts just crushed. While attempting it, Mrs. Campbell telephoned. To her inquiry about Otis, my only reply was a sob. She understood and said, "Take courage, we are right on the job." My own heart flew back to Mrs. Taylor's message, "The arrow of the Lord's deliverance." Mrs. Campbell too felt the time had come to smite till deliverance came. She again called the league to prayer. Within a very short time—an hour, perhaps—my own strength and courage returned with such peace and assurance, and the fever rapidly went down so that Otis slept quietly.
>
> At 2:00 a.m. Monday, Otis called me saying a chill was again coming on. We both felt it a direct attack of the Adversary at that hour of the morning when the friends would all be sleeping. Proverbs 18:10: "The name of the Lord is a strong tower; the righteous run to it, and are safe" came to us and we truly found the strong tower sufficient to protect against the work of the Evil One, for while in prayer claiming the Word, the answer came: the chill stopped and no fever came on, nor has it returned. Strength has returned marvelously quick; in a week he was up and dressed.

The period of convalescence which followed once the immediate danger to Otis's health had passed allowed for reinterpretation and renewal of the couple's commitment to "paying the price" of faithful service. They reread *The Growth of a Soul* and were able for the first time to read *The Growth of a Work of God*, which the authors, Howard and Geraldine Taylor, had left with them as a gift. As many as their own needs were (Otis's sickness had cast them into even greater dependence on God for day-to-day provisions), they still found ways to minister to those around them. Their hospitality never flagged; indeed, the witness of their many friends of those years was that the less they had materially the more generously they shared. It was Otis's saying, and their mutual conviction, that "one saves only what he gives away."

As they waited for new leading, the paradoxical challenge of Isaiah 54—which was to become almost a theme chapter for the Whipple family—came to them for the first time: "Enlarge the place of your tent, and . . . stretch out the curtains of your dwellings; do not spare; lengthen your cords, and strengthen your stakes." This directive, which they felt clearly to be a word from the Lord for them, was bewildering. Where were the means to enlarge, stretch forth, lengthen, and strengthen? When Ernest

Taylor, during a stay in Seattle, felt compelled to walk a great distance one afternoon to bring the Whipples a specific encouragement from Isaiah 54, and when its verses seemed to come to them again and again in Bible study, Otis and Julia responded willingly but unwittingly to the Lord's calling into a new work, which was to begin, of all places, at a long-neglected and half-forgotten cabin called The Firs.

# 3

## Planting (1921–1924)

"The kingdom of heaven is like a mustard seed . . . the least of all the seeds; but when it is grown it is greater than the herbs and becomes a tree."[1]

It was not until the summer of 1921 that the riddle of Isaiah's exhortation and God's further direction to the Whipple family began to come clear. Julia was at first a reluctant hearer of the Word, as she herself acknowledged:

> Mr. Whipple was in Bellingham doing construction work. At that time the China Inland Mission group was holding a prayer meeting in our home. Mr. Whipple had written asking me and the children to come to Bellingham for the summer. He asked whether we should open The Firs or rent a house. I told him that I couldn't go to The Firs; it would be too much work to put the place in order. He looked for a house but could find nothing. In the meantime, we had the prayer meeting, which Mr. J. Addison Campbell was leading, and at the beginning he gave a word that struck home to my heart: "What is that in your hand?" (Exodus 4:2). The friends left after the prayer meeting. Then I had one hard wrestle with the Lord. I argued and argued with Him. It was about two in the morning before I went to my rest. The next morning, in obedience to the Lord, I wrote Mr. Whipple that I would come to The Firs.
>
> I learned later that it was the thing Mr. Whipple was anxious to do. He wrote for us to come up over the 31st of May. The place was so grown over that it seemed hopeless to think of

1. Matt 13:31.

> getting anything ready . . . There was a thrill to think of going to work, but the Adversary was busy from every angle . . . Then the Lord gave us this word: "Though briers and thorns are with you, and you dwell among scorpions, do not be afraid" (Ezekiel 2:6).
>
> Mr. Whipple was working in town, so the work he was able to do at The Firs was accomplished in the early mornings and the evenings. The children were our only helpers. How I longed to be able to wield a hammer and drive a nail.
>
> The Lord did not promise to remove the thorns and briers. It seemed at times that we were knocked off our feet, but it was just one of the precious personal lessons. Do you know that the fir tree stands for the strength of the Lord and the myrtle for the fragrance? We learned not to ask the Lord to remove the briers and thorns but to use them to make firs and myrtle trees.
>
> How many times this word was brought to our minds in the irritating and trying things that kept coming up continually. On one occasion when the Adversary seemed to be getting the upper hand and the heart-cry was, "Oh Lord, deliver us from these thorns and briers!" He so sweetly gave the word in Isaiah 55:13: "Instead of the brier shall come up the myrtle tree, and it shall be to the Lord for a name, for an everlasting sign that shall not be cut off."

The thought of asking thirty or more additional people into the humble, hastily renovated, and already crowded cottage on Lake Whatcom would not have occurred to many, but it was Julia's heart's wish from the time she was certain of being called back to The Firs that summer. Family friends in Vancouver, Seattle, and Bellingham were invited to share a few days of Bible study and fellowship and to hear missionary speakers—as few or as many as God saw fit to send them.

And so, for five days in July 1921, at the little cabin where the Whipples' love had blossomed eighteen years earlier and where several seasons of family holidays had been shared, some thirty-five people gathered to meet the Lord and strengthen the ties of an extended household of faith.

The Whipples knew little, if anything at all, about the conference movement that had taken hold elsewhere in North America by this time. Their get-together could only really be called "the first Firs conference" in retrospect, after the pattern of annual meetings was established. There was no organization or administration to speak of, and no charge was made for food or lodging. Julia was the cook; others who came provided some help in the kitchen and washed up after meals. Nearby cottages were borrowed from neighbors to accommodate guests for the five-day period. Singing was a matter of participation rather than performance. Those who brought biblical teaching or missionary testimonies to the little assembly in the beautiful natural auditorium under towering firs had not been commissioned by chair or committee; they simply came bearing a message laid on their hearts by the Holy Spirit. Dr. Jessie McDonald, a C.I.M. medical missionary who was home on furlough, offered the first missionary challenge to be heard at The Firs. Rev. Walter Ellis, principal of Vancouver Bible Institute (an evangelical Anglican, whose scholarship and preaching, combined with his gentle demeanor, had won the confidence of a somewhat befogged and rebellious student, Isobel Miller, later Isobel Kuhn, the same year) opened the Scriptures.[2]

Before the company parted at the conclusion of the five-day session, many expressed a desire to come again the following year. Otis and Julia were hesitant to make plans until clear direction from the Lord was given. The next spring, however, the word came to "go forward," and a summer conference was held again, this time for almost twice as many people. Then, as Julia recorded, "at the gathering around the fireplace the last evening of the second conference, it was almost the unanimous expression that a third year's conference should be decided upon and announced before we separated." Otis was unsure, as he had not yet sensed a clear, specific "Thus says the Lord." Rather than engaging in further discussion, the company knelt in prayer, each one laying the matter open to a hearing and a speaking God:

> As Mrs. Cole prayed that a word would be given to Mr. Whipple which would assure him of the Lord's will, a Scripture which he had read that day, but which had not then impressed him, the Holy Spirit applied to his heart. It was from Proverbs 24:6: "In a multitude of counselors there is safety." And he realized that with all in the room then counselling that the conference be continued, it must be God's will, and this word was the assurance of it. So, the third conference was announced.

One of the notable guests at The Firs in the summer of 1923 was Isobel Miller, who had been on the hearts and in the prayers of the Whipple family since their first meeting in Seattle the previous year. In her autobiography, *By Searching*, Isobel recalls being met at the Bellingham pier and

2. For more on Walter Ellis and his significant impact on the Christian community in Vancouver and the Lower Mainland, see Burkinshaw, *Pilgrims in Lotus Land*, chapter 3. Rev. Ellis was an outspoken supporter of interdenominational ministries, notably the China Inland Mission and Intervarsity Christian Fellowship.

driven to the conference grounds by Elden Whipple and his bride-to-be, Evelyn Watson:

> It was a twisting labyrinth to me, but finally we turned into a path, drew up among tall fir trees, and there was dear Mrs. Whipple coming to meet me. Her radiance, rippling laugh of joy, and overflowing hospitality was something to cuddle down into. I was duly hugged and kissed, then shown into a big firelit room. Older people sat on chairs, and the younger ones on the floor before the big, crackling open fireplace. The flames threw a golden light over all faces, and the young people pulled me down on the floor to sit with them while the evening devotional service continued. Though always shy and reticent with strangers, here I was soon at home and filled with a wonderful contentment. The atmosphere was charged with the presence of the One whom I was learning to know and adore, and He was the center of everyone else's attention too.[3]

Otis's sister Edna, who had been married while serving as a missionary with the Disciples of Christ in China, returned to The Firs that summer as a widow, her husband Ellis Gish having drowned while rescuing a fellow missionary.[4] Edna was Isobel's cabinmate for the duration of the conference, and led the young people's meetings, setting aside her daily heartbreak at enormous personal cost to be a "cheery, radiant Bible teacher." Edna herself remembered the gathering fondly: "We met outside under the trees, wrapping up in steamer rugs for evening sessions . . . The youth group met around a long table in the open, near the front of Grandpa and Grandma Cole's cabin."

1924 saw James Outram Fraser of the China Inland Mission as one of the principal speakers. His challenge to a life of intercession and reflections on spiritual warfare left a deep and lasting impression on many. Attendance at the conference had increased dramatically; already, news of the Lake Whatcom meetings had spread throughout the Pacific Northwest and it was apparent that this venture which had begun so simply was taking on a continuous—if not yet permanent—character. Julia Whipple was able to say after the 1924 season had come and gone:

3. Kuhn, *By Searching*, 50. Isobel's first encounter with the Whipples was arranged by her father, who knew the family. Though initially resentful of this imposition, Isobel was loved into the kingdom by Julia, whom she referred to ever after as her "spiritual mother."

4. For an unpublished retrospect of her five decades of missionary service, see Gish, "A Missionary Life."

> We praise God with hearts overflowing with gratitude to Him for taking the "thing that was in our hand" and using it to His own glory. How wondrously He has worked in sending His own chosen ones to break unto us the bread of life, bringing His servants from the ends of the earth to minister unto us. And we do praise Him for those who have come to hear the messages and been blessed. There probably will be thorns and briers, but our prayer is that the fir trees and the myrtle trees will be greatly increased. And we know that to each one who had a share in this work of whatever nature it may be, if it is done as unto the Lord, there can only be blessing multiplied manyfold.

More surprises were in store, however. When the family returned home to Seattle from the conference in early August, a cable awaited them from Nanchang, China. Its unexpected message and subsequent confirmation that God was leading them to respond to it, were to radically reshape the lives of Otis and Julia and their three children, and to introduce a new phase in the ministry of The Firs.

# 4

# Branching (September, 1924)

"Therefore pray the Lord of the harvest to send out laborers into His harvest."[1]

To the amazement of many, and only after much wrestling with their own misgivings and doubts about the sudden turn of events, the Whipple family sailed out of Vancouver in September 1924 enroute to Shanghai—answering a call for short-term missionary assistance with the Chinese Methodist Mission. It had been years since Otis and Julia had first learned of the needs of "China's millions" and the vision of Hudson Taylor for ministry among them. Since then, numerous members of the China Inland Mission and of Taylor's own family had come into their lives. But that they should themselves be led out to this strange and distant land, particularly at a time when their role at The Firs seemed so essential, and that the call should come not through the C.I.M. but unexpected channels: little wonder the Whipples were, at first, somewhat taken aback. Otis described his own and Julia's hesitation, and the events leading up to the final decision and departure, in a lengthy epistle written aboard ship:

> Our hurried departure made it impossible to say good-bye to many whom we dearly love and whose prayers we long to have. Especially to those with whom we have been privileged to work at the Lake Whatcom conference and to other friends, we desire to write this good-bye and to tell in part how it has come about that the whole of this Whipple family is enroute to China.

1. Matt 9:38.

We have gone because God has convinced us that it is His will. We have been slow to believe and reluctant to see, but in the end He has responded to our mite of faith and willingness with an overwhelming assurance as to His will. Though in looking back we can see the working of God in many things leading up to what has taken place, an incident in March, this year, would seem properly to start this story. In bidding good-bye to my sister then returning to China, I told her, only half in earnest, to find me something to do and I would come out to China too. But it was altogether serious with my two sisters out there and they immediately began to inquire where there might be a need for one whose business was construction work; for though I had long wished to be used more directly in the Lord's work, His leading had been to "remain in the calling in which I was called." Several times during the intervening months letters came telling of possible openings, but it was not until early in August, returning home to Seattle from the Lake Whatcom conference, we were met by a long cable from China offering a position to me superintending the construction of a mission hospital, and for Mrs. Whipple to teach English in the mission school at Nanchang, the capital of Kiangsi [Jiangxi] Province. Expenses while there and transportation both ways for a ten-months engagement were offered. Nothing was said about the children.

An answer to the cable offer was sent indicating that we would consider a proposal for the whole family. In the meantime, we were much in prayer, seeking to learn directly from the Word and the leading of the Spirit what God's will for us was. Having just returned from the Lake Whatcom conference, where our hearts had been made full to overflowing by the blessings the Lord had given there, and as He had so clearly led us in the work by most plain directions in the most important matter from the written Word, we expected more than ever a clear "Thus says the Lord." We laid the whole thing before Him in prayer and awaited His leading.

A second cable from China repeated the former offer. The questions uppermost in our minds were: Was the offer of God, and if so, did He mean to separate the family? While we knew immediately that the finances would be a most important consideration in deciding these questions, for they were equally important whether the children went or stayed, we felt assured from the start that God would take care of the finances after we had gone as far as we could ourselves. So our chief concern was to learn His will . . . We had figured as carefully as we could and found it would take two thousand dollars, perhaps more, to make the proper arrangements at home and go for a year with a family of five, even without considering how we should get back.

Mrs. Whipple's niece, Mrs. Hollis, who was with us at the time, wished to provide $500, and later more. But we would not consider her offer, a considerable part of all she had. It did not seem to us that the Lord would be working that way: besides, what would others say or think? A dear missionary friend with whom we were advising, however, cautioned us to be very sure it was not the Lord's provision before we refused, both for our own sakes and the sake of the one who offered the $500. She had received most plain directions from the Lord as to her course. In answer to her prayers as to what He would have her to do, He said to her from Matthew 21:2–3: "Go . . . loose . . . bring . . . And if anyone says anything to you, you shall say, The Lord has need of them." But while we recognized His leading for her, we felt it must be that, like Abraham when called upon to offer up Isaac, the Lord would have her willing to give but would not in the end require her sacrifice. Besides, it was only a fourth enough; it would possibly be all right to accept it if it were the last part necessary to make up the whole.

From the first, others seemed to receive more clear leading about our going than we ourselves. While we were willing, if it was His will, we had our own idea of how we wished to be led, [which] caused us some weary extra hours.

Mrs. Hollis and Miss Margaret McCausland, both living with us, were our constant prayer helpers from the beginning. One afternoon Miss McCausland was led to pray that if it was God's will we should go, that He would give us a token to indicate it. If only our hearts could be assured, we could then go forward with the preparation. This time just before we all went to prayer, someone went to the Promise Box and took out a promise, from Jeremiah 33:3: "Call to Me, and I will answer you, and show you great and mighty things, which you do not know."

Our hearts were directed this day to seek prayer from another friend, Miss Doolittle . . . That evening after prayer meeting at the church Mrs. Whipple and I went to see her, and Mrs. Whipple remarked before our going, "I believe if the Lord means for us to go to China, He already will have been talking to Miss Doolittle about it." We had not more than started to tell her what had been happening when her face lighted up and she exclaimed, "Isn't that wonderful! Why, the Lord has been talking to me about Mr. Whipple doing building work in China." Though we had not seen her for months, the Lord Himself, for our guidance, had brought that knowledge to her. And Jeremiah

33:3 had been given to her in connection with our going! The three of us knelt to pray together, having in mind especially the need to know the Lord's will regarding the children. I had little more than begun to pray when Miss Doolittle interrupted with an exclamation that we must stop for the Lord had already given the answer to our prayer. Apologizing for interrupting, but being sure, she said, "Just wait and I'll show you the visible evidence of the answer."

Going into the other room, she returned with a small pasteboard box and taking from it a little travelling case of some plush material and filled with small travelling necessities, she said to Mrs. Whipple, "This is for you," and another similar one, "This is for Lois"; then one of a little different character for Elden and two similar to this, one for Grant and one for me, five in all. Then she explained how strangely she had been led in making these little articles, how insistently the Lord had impressed upon her that she must. First it was only one for Mrs. Whipple, then in turn for each of the others, and though she could see no special need for them, the Lord would not let her have peace until she had completed them all. They had been done in only a few days. He had told her they were to be for use "on the boat and on the train." A token had been asked for and was not one given? Clearly, all five were to go.

Our whole household, and all the friends to whom we told the story of the tokens given to Miss Doolittle, were impressed that it must be the Lord's will that we should go. And yet, personally, I was uncertain . . .

The date September 11 was the latest sailing we could take and arrive when the cable stated we were needed. We sent for passports and made application to the steamship company for passages.

We had told some of our relatives and friends, but all the time there was the absence of an assuring, direct "Thus says the Lord" to our own hearts, and there was the large financial gap. With but a few exceptions, those who felt free to express themselves thought the Lord would have us go, and we felt the same way. But we also felt that we must have this direct leading, something more plain than we then had.

One morning Mrs. Whipple, her niece, and I were together praying and again asking for this direct guidance from the Word, when the phone rang. On going to it, Miss Doolittle answered, stating that the Lord had given her a word to give to Mr. Whipple from Ecclesiastes 7:18: "It is good that you grasp this, and also not remove your hand from the other; for he who fears God will come forth from all of them" and also a warning from II Kings 7:18–19: "So it happened just as the man of God had spoken to the king, saying, 'Two measures of barley for a shekel . . . shall be sold tomorrow about this time in the gate of Samaria.' Then that officer answered the man of God, and said, 'Now, look, if the Lord would make windows in heaven, could such a thing be?' And he said, 'In fact, you shall see it with your eyes, but you shall not eat of it.'"

Plain as this word was, it was not what we were asking—a word direct from the Lord to ourselves—or it seemed not. This came through another. So we went back to prayer, and shortly the phone rang again and again it was Miss Doolittle saying that the Lord had given her another word, especially for me. It was Luke 12:35–36: "Let your waist be girded, and your lamps burning; and you yourselves be like men who wait for their master, when he will return from the wedding, that when he comes and knocks they may open unto him immediately."

No directions could have been plainer than these, and the circumstances of their being given while we were in the very act of asking should have left no doubt, but I was not satisfied. But also about this time we began to glimpse that the Lord might be doing something else besides just telling us if we were to go to China. We began more to appreciate, more to feel our need of an intercessor. Time after time because of our own perplexity we were driven to this intercessor, and never without relief because of some word given through her. Directions we felt we should have had ourselves directly were given only through another . . . We were confident we must have the direct word ourselves and no one between God and us. But we became convinced we had been mistaken.

One most helpful word that He did give to us directly was Philippians 1:28: "And not in any way terrified by your adversaries: which is to them a proof of perdition, but to you of salvation, and that from God." This word was our mainstay in many a hard attack.

And Proverbs 24:6: "For by wise counsel you will wage your own war, and in a multitude of counsellors there is safety" had become one of our strong anchors. It was after this last word was given that we asked a number of friends together, told them of the situation, and sought their counsel.

In the afternoon before these friends met, the steamship called for a deposit on the reserved passages. Still unwilling to accept the $500 from Mrs. Hollis, which she had gone after, brought, and given as God had directed her, she paid a $200 deposit herself, thus securing the passages, and refusing to accept back the $300 change from the $500 check, left it with me. I put it in the bank and left it there. That evening, in telling friends of the situation up to that time, it was told that the passages were secured, but no mention made of how or by whom. This was partly because Mrs. Hollis did not wish her name known. But during the night the Lord spoke very plainly to me because no mention had been made of this act of love and faith which, to all who knew of it, was so plainly of God. And though we had not in our hearts accepted it, still the deposit had been paid. The Lord spoke to me in these two Scriptures: Luke 24:25: "O foolish ones, and slow of heart to believe all that the prophets have spoken" and Mark 14:9: "What this woman has done will also be told as a memorial to her." The next morning, I asked if she were willing that it be told, and she gave her consent.

We continued preparations, each day readjusting the schedule of what must yet be done. Always the question: Were we going? Always the puzzle why we were not able to get more clear leading, until finally we knew on the last Sunday night . . . We realized how much was yet to be done—purchasing, packing, dozens of details concerning many things, and only three days to complete it all and go. Had it not been for Philippians 1:28 I think we might have been overwhelmed. Sunday morning, September 7, Mrs. Whipple and I took the children to Bible school and then we went to pray with Miss Doolittle.

This dear friend had been spending a considerable share of her days and nights in prayer on our behalf. And this Sunday morning, though she brought to us only words of assurance that it was God's will for us to go and that the supplies would be sent by Him in time, we left her house with heavy hearts.

We had begun to see where possibly we had missed the Lord's will. Was the way to be clearly and fully opened only after we were ready? And that meant the $300 in the bank, which we had been unable to bring ourselves to accept, would have to be used. Was it the provision God had made two weeks before the necessary purchases? And we, especially I, had been the ones to whom the Lord had been speaking these two weeks in Luke 24:25: "Oh foolish ones, and slow of heart to believe." Was anyone ever more so?

Mrs. Whipple went home and to bed that Sunday afternoon, and that night was very ill. But by morning we saw what the Lord would have us do. And we did as best we could, the next day, the purchasing we had been given two weeks in which to do. Monday night we packed far into the morning hours, and on Tuesday morning I went downtown to complete a few purchases and spent the last of the $300 and came home.

Many times the words had been in mind, "According to your faith let it be to you." Looking back over the weeks of preparation and that final day of purchasing, how little faith there seemed to be. It was more as if some outward compelling force had taken hold of us and we could do nothing else but what we did. And toward noon Tuesday, when I reached home, the Lord had been there first. During the morning the phone had brought a message that there was a check for $1500 waiting for me to come and accept!

Another night of rush and confusion because we had been so slow to believe, but finally all was done. We have been surprised at the fewness of the things that were undone . . . There was the provision of someone to take the house, someone to see about the gas, lights, phone, etc., the setting to rights of the things in the house after we were gone, the burden of caring for the preparations for next year's Lake Whatcom conference, the China Inland Mission prayer circle meeting. Everything necessary was provided for.

And then, as the last good-bye was being said in Seattle, there was put into our hands from three unknown sources, a little over $500 more. We had prayed for $2000 or more if it was the Lord's will for us to go to China; He answered with the more. We knew God was leading.

One question will be in many minds: Why are we thus being taken to China? We cannot answer now. And it may be a long time, if ever, before we can fully answer it. We have only glimpses of reasons why. We cannot see clearly ourselves, but we are satisfied that it is God's will for us now, and we are content to go forward, confident that it will all be made plain, at least a step at a time.

We are on the sea today bound for China largely because of intercessors. Is He not seeking for those who will make a business of prayer? Definite, believing, thankful prayer? And might it be, possibly, the time is so short, and the laborers prayed out so few, that He must use any who are willing? Pray ye therefore.

Affectionately yours in His service, Otis G. Whipple

# 5

# Firstfruits (1924–1930)

"Where there is no counsel, the people fall;
But in the multitude of counselors there is safety."[1]

STRANGELY—OR SO IT SEEMED at first—it was the very year in which Otis and Julia were called to China that they had been most surely convinced of the continuance of the ministry of The Firs, not only for another season but for the foreseeable future. Clear confirmation had been given from Isa 46:10: "My counsel shall stand," and all previous hesitations were prayerfully and joyfully relinquished. Only after the decision to embark for the Orient was finally made, however, did the pertinence of their scriptural promise become evident, for this was also the year in which The Firs Council was to come into being.

Henry Bowers, a close friend of the Whipples who had just retired as manager of Sears Roebuck in Seattle, graciously offered to oversee all the details of the following summer's conference. He and his wife Edith intended to renovate their own Lake Whatcom cabin sufficiently to spend most of the summer there, making necessary arrangements.

The burden of preparation had increased proportionately with the size and duration of each successive summer's gathering (conferences now met for ten days). Everything from readying the grounds themselves to sweeping and scrubbing cabins, some of which were cobwebby and dusty from months of inactivity, to stuffing tick mattresses with straw, planning meals, purchasing provisions, chopping firewood, and corresponding

1. Prov 11:14.

with inquirers had to be done before the first guests arrived. The task was enormous, but largely hidden; few paused even to consider it during their stay at The Firs.

The Whipples had prayed earnestly for some relief, but being as disinclined to solicit help as to solicit funds, waited for the Lord's provision. Now that they were leaving, others recognized the need and felt prompted to commit their support so that the work could continue. On the first days of November 1924, just over a month after the Whipples sailed for China, a loosely constituted group of friends convened for a time of counsel and prayer at The Firs.[2] Henry Bowers was elected chairman of the group, which determined to meet on a regular basis throughout the year, and Margaret McCausland, who had lived with the Whipple family in Seattle, became secretary-treasurer. One of the first items of official business recorded by The Firs Council was a motion to retain the faith basis of the work entirely, charging no conference fees and looking to God alone for the supply of all material needs.

At the next meeting, a month later, Miss McCausland presented the first treasurer's report. It read, very simply: "Amount received—$10.00; Amount on hand—$10.00." The lessons of faith were starkly practical; as Hudson Taylor had memorably insisted, "We can afford to have as little as the Lord chooses to give."

God had clearly demonstrated his concern for the needs of the Whipple family; now it appeared he would tutor others as he continued to oversee the work begun through them. The "little" increased slowly toward the summer when expenditures for food and other supplies were necessary. Work was distributed, counsel and prayer shared, and on June 25 a small circular was sent out to those who had attended the conference in previous years, assuring them that "Though Mr. and Mrs. Whipple are many miles away from their delightfully quiet summer home—The Firs—the conference has been made possible for the coming season."

The Whipples themselves received the news with delight and joined their distant friends in prayer for the Lord's blessing on the work they greatly missed. Already it was clear that their departure had been God's means of raising up the essential help they had sought for the Lake

2. The original members of The Firs Council included: Mr. and Mrs. Henry Bowers, Mrs. Henry Bidlake, Mrs. Charles H. Black, Mrs. Wm. H. Clark (née Antoinette Black), Mr. and Mrs. J. Addison Campbell, Mr. and Mrs. Thomas Cole, Miss Margaret McCausland, Mrs. Bernice Paddock, Mr. George Satler, Dr. Georgia Satler, Miss M. Belle Sperry, Mr. and Mrs. C. Ernest Walsh.

Whatcom ministry, and for this they were deeply grateful. Otis's two sisters, Maude and Edna, were both home from China that summer; they were able to provide a Whipple presence at The Firs and to convey the family's warm personal greetings to the conference group.

The year in China, with all of its adjustments, was exciting and fruitful. Upon their arrival in Shanghai, the Whipple family had been privileged to stay for a time in the local C.I.M. home, renewing their acquaintance with Dr. Dixon Hoste, Hudson Taylor's successor as director of the mission. Dear and familiar faces proved to be numerous. In this remote land, many missionaries were able to return the hospitality they had enjoyed in Otis and Julia's Seattle home. But new friends awaited them as well, among Chinese nationals and in the various mission societies the family was to encounter.

From Shanghai, Otis and Julia Whipple went on to Nanchang, where Otis supervised construction of the Methodist Mission Hospital. Elden, Lois, and Grant settled in Nanking (now Nanjing) on a Presbyterian compound several blocks from the school in which their Aunt Maude was teaching. Lois and Elden began language study; Grant was in his freshman year in high school. There were weekend sightseeing expeditions to look forward to and endless novelties to discover. One of the comical highlights of Grant's year was a visit to a little town near Nanking during spring vacation. The only vehicle in the community was a Model T Ford which had not been running for some time. Somehow, Grant managed to get it started and paraded up and down the main street, to the amusement of friends, before a cloud of less than enthusiastic local witnesses.

Later in the year, Elden went to the Hunan Bible Institute in Changsha, a newly established affiliate of the Bible Institute of Los Angeles, which the interest and financial support of Milton and Lyman Stewart had made possible. Elden, who had studied at Biola, felt immediately at home in the college environment, perhaps nowhere so much as in the company of a winsome and hospitable couple, Chester and Helen Rutledge, with whom he stayed during the visit.

Biola graduates themselves, the Rutledges had come to China at the invitation of the school's board (and with the personal blessing of Lyman Stewart, who christened them his "ambassadors to China" and provided them a lovely collection of books to start their overseas library). Chester recalled being approached by T.C. Horton after a class meeting one day in his senior year, and asked to consider the position of Business Manager at the new school. He and Helen spent many hours in conversation and prayer before making their decision. But when, finally, they returned with a "yes," they were met with a delighted "Praise the Lord! Your passage has been booked for six weeks."

It did not take long for Chester to learn that Elden's father was a builder; he was soon in contact with Otis, asking if he would be willing to oversee construction at the Hunan Bible Institute after his project in Nanchang was completed. So, in September 1925, the Whipple family was reunited and took up residence in Changsha. They found precious friends in the Rutledges, little imagining the depth and intimacy of fellowship that would flourish years later, back at The Firs.

Biola China brought into the Whipples' lives many other cherished and longstanding friends, among them Dr. Frank Keller and his wife Elizabeth. Dr. Keller had been a close associate of Hudson Taylor in the latter part of the elder missionary's career, and had, on more than one occasion, attended to Taylor's physical needs. Chester Rutledge recalled the day that Dr. Keller led him, without explanation, into an unfamiliar and rather nondescript building in downtown Changsha, through dark, narrow corridors until in the doorway of a little room he pointed to one corner and then confided, "There, just over there, is where Hudson Taylor died."[3] It seemed to Chester that he should remove his shoes, for the overwhelming presence, not of Taylor himself but of the one who had so animated his life, seemed still to linger in the room.

To Otis and Julia, the experience of living among the friends and acquaintances of this man who had had such an impact on their lives, of laboring alongside Chinese Christians to whom he had brought the gospel, and of ministering to others among the unreached millions for whom he had borne such a Christlike passion was a deeply satisfying experience. As they witnessed and celebrated the ongoing growth of a work of God, they became themselves part of its continuing legacy.

Political uprising and the outbreak of civil war in China intervened to bring the Whipples home in 1927. As they recrossed the ocean in refugee ships very different from the *Empress of Australia* on which, two and a half years earlier, they had arrived, they pondered the uncertainty of the future. Would they be back? Construction at the Hunan Bible Institute

3. Having turned over direction of the mission to Dixon Hoste and mourned the passing of his wife Jennie, Hudson desired to travel from England to China one last time; in the summer of 1905, the Kellers invited him to stay with them in Changsha. Soon after arriving, he died peacefully while reading correspondence in his room; he was 73.

was left unfinished and other building opportunities awaited Otis if he elected to return once the political crisis had passed.

Elden, now engaged to be married, intended to return with Evelyn and serve with the China Inland Mission, as did Lois. Grant, still in high school, anticipated following a similar course. Their parents, however, were less certain, and waited prayerfully, patiently, as so often they had, for the way to be made plain. Because their Seattle home had been rented, they went directly to The Firs, unsure of whether they were on an unexpected furlough or entering into a new phase of ministry at the Lake Whatcom conference.

Henry Bowers offered to turn direction of the conference back to the Whipples, but consented generously when they asked him to retain his role for the 1927 season. The Firs Council, which had been formed in 1924, would continue to share responsibility for the work, at least until Otis and Julia had direction regarding their own ongoing role. When, in 1928, the Lord clearly indicated that they were to stay at The Firs rather than return to China, the relationship of The Firs Council and the Whipple family to the work was clarified. As Otis wrote in a family letter:

> The problem of whether or not we should ourselves continue the management of the conference or accept the group control finally was decided in our minds by two things. First was the word from Isaiah 54:2: "Let them," and then the acceptance of a new rule by the whole group that we would do only those things in which we were all agreed. We felt that, although the Lord uses individuals as leaders and to start things, His desire is to gather others. The larger a group who will learn to work together, who will yield their own will, the nearer we become to what the Lord desires.

Consensus was not always quickly or easily attained. When the need for a dining hall became apparent, ten years of earnest prayer and discussion passed before there was agreement as to a suitable site. And not until full accord was reached did God send in the necessary funds to begin construction.

Otis's son Elden was to reflect, many years later, with respect to the commitment to oneness on the council:

> Trusting the Holy Spirit to do His work in the other person . . . As I think about it, I realize that from my earliest childhood right to the present, so many of my own loved ones and friends have had that attitude towards me. Not having confidence in me,

> but showing me that they were trusting the Holy Spirit to lead me aright and to cause me to grow in the knowledge of the Lord. I believe that right here is the secret of successful group work for the Lord. It is what the Lord has given us in an unusual degree in The Firs Council. It hasn't meant that we always think the other's point of view is right, but that we are completely confident in the Spirit's power to fulfill His office. As I told our group here last night, I consider my training in the council group at The Firs the greatest help I ever had in the matter of working together with others in the Lord's service.

Otis and Julia were added to the membership of the existing council, Otis as its director. On June 7, 1929, the Lake Whatcom Bible and Missionary Conference was officially incorporated under the laws of the state of Washington. For the first time, the two essential principles of the conference work—faith in the Lord's provision for all needs and oneness of spirit for all decisions—were formalized as "policies." "In the early years," Otis recalled, "we did not call them by name. We just did what we felt would glorify the Lord in the way in which He led . . . He provided the finances, He provided the program, He answered prayer. We tried to let Him both will and work in us." He went on to say that "our policies are a means of testing us, whether we will give ourselves or God first place":

> If the Lord is given His place, He is the one to have the glory. To help achieve that is why we have policies. In my estimation, the Lake Whatcom Conference was not founded to preach the gospel, absolutely necessary as that is. The gospel is the power of God unto salvation to everyone that believes. The Firs' emphasis in the beginning was to *help people believe*. When they see the Lord working and not us, He becomes real—someone they can believe in. Our policies touch two fundamental hindrances to people believing: finances and unity.

Here, in a single phrase, is a large part of the meaning of The Firs: *helping people believe*. Preaching, yes; teaching, yes. But above all, demonstrating in humble and practical ways the presence of the God of glory in miracle-working power.

This most radical and least self-interested of all commitments allowed remarkable liberty and a spirit of generous hospitality that was itself an eloquent witness to the presence of Christ at The Firs. As one said of the conference she attended in the late 1920s, "The thing that always used to impress me, perhaps more than anything else, was that you would go to The Firs and you'd just be talking away to someone like I am to you, and you'd never know. It might be an Anglican or a Presbyterian or a Baptist. It never crossed your mind what church they went to." Another echoed, "We came from many churches but were never aware of our denominational backgrounds or differences, but rather of our common allegiance to the Lord and his work."

In order to appreciate the miracle of such a fellowship, one has to remember that denominational strife was rampant in the 1920s and to reflect on the intensity of the controversies that were sapping the spiritual energy of many and fracturing denominations, seminaries, training institutes, mission societies, and, it might be added, Bible conferences. These were years of open antagonism within the strongholds of Protestantism, of famous sermons devoted less to the gospel of Christ than to human pride and the casting of stones, of the celebrated Scopes "monkey trial," which won a temporary reprieve against the teaching of evolution but paraded prejudices as well as Christian convictions.

The issues raised in the confrontation between conservative and liberal church spokesmen were, of course, issues of genuine significance, and one could not dismiss the evident harmony and lack of controversy at The Firs as an indication of naivete or quiescence on the part of the Whipples or the council. Otis and Julia numbered among their friends some of the most eminent proponents and exemplars of conservative evangelicalism. The doctrinal statement that all members of the council agreed to was fully consistent with the principles outlined in the Niagara Declaration and *The Fundamentals*.[4]

The one "fundamental" that dominated the life and work of The Firs, however, was that expressed on the sign which, each year, hung between two trees in the outdoor auditorium: "All One in Christ Jesus." His banner over them was love.

Love dictated the style of ministry, much as it characterized the welcome one received, or the fellowship shared around crowded tables at mealtime, or the quiet conversations so often enjoyed with members of The Firs family under the fragrant evergreens or near the tottering fence at the far edge of the woods. Love cast out fear, allowing the ministry to be generous rather than defensive or judgmental.

One recognized, for example, almost immediately, that the stress was interdenominational without being anti-denominational. "It is our

4. For details, see the Prologue, above, and Appendix A.

desire and earnest prayer," states an early pamphlet, "that the Lord sends only those of His choosing to attend the conferences and that He will send them back to their churches quickened in spirit . . . and better equipped to service." Speakers seldom identified their own denominational affiliation, but consistently affirmed the importance of commitment to the work of the local church. The interdenominational character of the conference was, in fact, one reason for its financial policy. Otis felt strongly that no money should be diverted from attendees' home congregations, and that this would inevitably happen if an offering was taken.

It was evident, moreover, that although the ministry was necessarily personal (helping people believe meant bearing testimony of God's faithfulness in one's own life), it was not highly individualistic. The conference platform was always shared, never dominated by a single personality. A dynamic speaker or nationally known evangelist was not necessarily to be preferred before any pastor or missionary to whom God had entrusted teaching gifts.[5] Contentiousness of any kind was avoided. The Bible and missionary emphasis took precedence over any address to contemporary issues (and divisive controversies in particular); a thorough grounding in biblical principles was deemed sufficient and considered necessary for any and all specifics of belief and conduct. Separationist "dos and don'ts" were not heralded, nor were any particular doctrinal positions, however worthy, allowed to dominate. A balanced ministry and insistence on the integrity of Scripture as a whole was carefully safeguarded. Thus, The Firs, which might have become a Keswick conference, a Baptist or Presbyterian conference, a prophetic conference, a C.I.M. conference, or a vanguard of any number of fundamentalist positions, remained true to itself—a labor of love, conceived in prayer and conducted by faith.

The place of prayer at The Firs cannot be overstated. It was the most compelling expression of love and source of blessing to all who attended conferences. One fairly sensed it as he or she came onto the grounds. Isobel Miller (later Kuhn), who was "adopted" for a time into the Whipple household in 1928, recalls a powerful movement of the Holy Spirit

5. There exists no comprehensive list of conference speakers at The Firs. Perhaps the most prominent among those who attended during the 1920s was Arthur Harries, an evangelist from Wales who had been an associate of Evan Roberts in the turn-of-the-century Welsh Revival. It was Dr. Harries who first introduced Keswick teaching, with its strong emphasis on personal holiness, to The Firs. He was a speaker in 1925 and again in 1929. Howard Guinness, member of the C.I.M.-connected Guinness family in Ireland, spoke at a youth conference in 1929 while on an extended sojourn in Canada (see note 10, below).

which came during that summer's conference as a direct and immediate response to prayer:

> The Conference that summer (1928) was the most blessed I had ever known . . . For one thing, Mrs. Whipple had prayed that every young person attending the conference should yield to the Lord before going home. One evening during the service she was impelled to go to the girls' dormitory and there she knelt by each bed, claiming for Christ the occupant of that bed. Needless to say, every evening there were decisions made. Toward the last evening there were a few who still hung back from full surrender, so the staff called us leaders of the young people to pray all during the evening service. I can never forget that prayer service. The spirit of the Lord came down upon us as in apostolic times and we all started to pray simultaneously out loud. As for myself, I was not even conscious of the others. So lifted up was I into the Lord's presence and so burdened for the souls that were hanging back that it was not until a break came that I suddenly came down to earth and realized that we had all been praying aloud together. From the upper room where we prayed, down through the treetops, we could see the open-air auditorium. As we prayed, one after another of the recalcitrant ones got up and went forward in surrender. The very last, a girl for whom I had held little hope, has now been for decades a most faithful missionary on a foreign field. Very truly it was the work of the Spirit of God.[6]

The number of young people coming to The Firs each summer was by now substantial: carloads, then caravans, from Seattle and the Lower Mainland of British Columbia became frequent. Isobel herself, through her work with Corner Club,[7] was responsible for some of the Vancouver contingent. Others came from churches where the Whipples had personal acquaintances. An increasing number were being invited by friends who had been to past conferences and considered it the highlight of their summer. Even those who had longstanding church connections

6. Kuhn, *By Searching*, 186–87.

7. Corner Club, a businesswomen's club in Vancouver, was one product of the evangelistic campaign conducted by French Oliver in that city in 1917. Frances L. Neth, from Biola, who had directed women's ministry for the campaign, met with a number of local women after a final meeting to encourage continued evangelism among their friends. A club was formed that sponsored weekly evening meetings and daily noon-hour fellowship and outreach. Isobel Miller Kuhn, who was superintendent of Corner Club from 1927 to 1928, describes her role in *By Searching*.

were powerfully impacted by the unique quality of their experience at Lake Whatcom. Why? No single explanation is sufficient. The boundless warmth of the Whipples and their extended family; the dedication and enthusiasm of the speakers; the beauty of the grounds themselves; the humor and intimacy of communal living (Tent City, an encampment of large canvas tents, each of which housed eight people, was a great favorite for some, while others preferred to sleep on the spacious porches of "El Nathan," the first residence purchased by The Firs); the scriptural games and treasure hunts; Bible studies in various corners of the woods; joyful, spontaneous singing, especially of choruses such as "Wide, Wide as the Ocean" and "One Door and Only One" which had just come into vogue: all this and more captured the hearts of high school and college students. "It was a foretaste of heaven to me," recounted one young attendee of her first conference. "I'd never met young people with such zeal. Everything was very new. The whole atmosphere, the whole concept of The Firs was such that you felt you were constantly in the presence of the Lord."

Adults were no less enthusiastic. Many out-of-town friends, unable to attend the full ten-day conference because of work or family responsibilities, thronged to the grounds on weekends. Numbers at Sunday services often exceeded six hundred. Year after year, good weather permitted the crowds to gather outside in an evergreen sanctuary, with its "beams of cedar and rafters of fir" (Song 1:17). Many, reflecting on those early days of outdoor meetings, sensed a still, small voice murmuring in tree boughs and knew the Spirit moving over their bowed heads. As hymns and choruses, unrehearsed and frequently unaccompanied, ascended from overflowing hearts, heaven seemed very close. Countless minor distractions and discomforts notwithstanding, these were unforgettable, live-changing occasions for many conference-goers.

There were some in those vast assemblies who came out of sheer curiosity, who had not been to church for years but wondered what this strange new religious phenomenon at Lake Whatcom was all about. There were rumors of great blessing, yet (as in George Muller's case) no visible means of support; one never heard mention of an offering. So they arrived anticipating confirmation of their suspicion that the whole operation was underwritten by wealthy donors or by the Whipples themselves. What they found, instead, was a work of faith, endowed, as Chester Rutledge loved to say, by Almighty God.

More than a few from the immediate neighborhood and nearby Bellingham were influenced by contact their children had with The Firs, either in Sunday School classes conducted by "Aunt Carrie" Cole or in the annual Vacation Bible School held on the grounds. Bible classes for young people had run simultaneously with The Firs summer conferences ever since 1923, when Antoinette ("Tony") Black[8] oversaw the program and Edna Gish (Otis's widowed sister), among others, assisted in the teaching. We have already met Isobel Miller at that conference: one of the others present was a young teacher whose acquaintance with Belle Sperry (a member of the council) and Carrie Cole had led her to The Firs. Vivian Gunderson's vivacious temperament and no-nonsense approach to learning made her a splendid teacher, but she also had a heart for the salvation of each young life entrusted to her. Some years later, when Tony Black went to the mission field, she stepped in, extending the outreach to neighborhood as well as conference children.[9]

From a great store of memories of those early years in V.B.S. one incident stands out in particular, and is indicative of an oft-repeated pattern at The Firs. A little boy from the Geneva community responded enthusiastically when Miss Gunderson came by with an invitation to her Bible classes—much to the surprise of his mother, who insisted that he was an "outdoors boy" and wouldn't be interested. The truths of the gospel reached into his young mind, and he committed his life to Christ. Toward the end of the V.B.S. program, it was stressed that the children should continue to meet regularly at church and Sunday School to learn more about Jesus. When classes ended, this youngster went back to being an outdoors boy. Not long after, however, when he and his family were preparing to leave for a long-anticipated trip to Birch Bay, someone happened to mention that he hoped the Sunday crowds wouldn't be as bad as usual. With a start, the child asked, "Is this Sunday?" "Why yes," responded his parents. "Then I have to go to Sunday School." Somewhat

8. Tony Black was granddaughter of Charles H. Black, Sr. and his wife Nettie, church friends of the Whipples from their Seattle years, 1916 to 1921. Several generations of the Black family have been active and generous contributors to The Firs through the decades, serving on council and board and providing strategic assistance in various ways; a great grandson of Charles and Nettie, Phil Wegener, with his wife Pam, was on resident staff from 1986 to 2000. Tony Black, mentioned here, was to marry Hal Clark and serve with him in China until 1950.

9. Vivian Gunderson had a fifty-year teaching career, was instrumental in founding two churches (Hopewell Community Church in Everson and Evergreen Community Church in Ferndale), and began a publishing house in 1960 to provide low-cost Christian materials for children. She was a lifelong fixture at Firs conferences (see chapter 13, below). She died in 1999 at the age of 95; her epitaph reads: "Led many to our Savior Jesus."

taken aback, they replied gently that he could go next week. "But I must go this week. I don't want to disappoint the Lord Jesus," he blurted out, and his eyes filled with tears. The man who finally consented to drive his son to Sunday School, having been solemnly assured that it was more important to him than a day at the beach, began his own search for whatever it was that so captivated the child's affections. The whole family ultimately came to faith.

Such individual stories reflect a focused outreach to unchurched young people in the immediate neighborhood and beyond. Volunteer help allowed the beginning of a weekend boys' conference in 1928, and the response was overwhelming. The next year, with funding and encouragement from some local businessmen, The Firs sent Christian college students into the poor and rundown neighborhoods of Bellingham to invite teen boys to a "free weekend in the mountains." Among the youngsters who responded was fifteen-year-old John ("Jack") Murray, a self-described "filthy-minded, foul-mouthed, dirty-faced" street urchin from a broken and dysfunctional family, whose days often consisted of stealing food from delivery trucks to take home to his mother and siblings. He was attracted to the idea of being in the mountains for the first time and his mother was happy about having one less mouth to feed for a few days. The speaker was Irish student evangelist Howard Guinness, scion of a prominent evangelical family with strong ties to Hudson Taylor and the China Inland Mission.[10] Guinness was on a fourteen-month sojourn in Canada, laying the groundwork for the establishment of the Canadian chapter of Intervarsity Christian Fellowship; he agreed to drive down from Vancouver to spend a weekend sharing Christ with the boys.

The first night of the conference, as the happily exhausted and well-fed youngsters gathered around a campfire, Howard Guinness told the amazing story of God's love for each of the boys, unfolding the gospel narrative in a compelling and winsome way. Jack had never heard this story before, and was shaken to the core. As he tumbled into his bunk that night, he pondered everything he had heard, prayed a tentative prayer of repentance and trust, and turned his life over to God.

10. Howard Guinness's father and grandfather were both noted evangelists; his aunt Mary Geraldine Guinness married Hudson Taylor's son, Howard Taylor, and with him wrote (among other books) the two Taylor biographies that captivated Otis and Julia Whipple, *Growth of a Soul* and *Growth of a Work of God*. For more on Howard Guinness, see his influential challenge to costly discipleship, *Sacrifice* (first published in 1936) and his autobiographical *Journey Among Students*.

The seed planted that weekend in the heart of a hardened, streetwise kid took hold; young Jack persisted and grew in his new-found faith and, when he was back at The Firs as a seventeen-year-old in 1931, felt a strong call to full-time ministry. He would go on, against all odds, to study at Biola and Wheaton College and then to pursue a seminary degree, after which he and his wife Eleanor (a Wheaton classmate and daughter of evangelist George T. Stevens) embarked on a multi-faceted, multi-decade Christian ministry. Among their many endeavors, the founding in 1941 of Harvey Cedars Bible Conference on Long Beach Island, New Jersey stands out—a ministry that was in many respects modeled on The Firs and that continues to this day.[11]

So it was that the work grew, lives were transformed, and entire families entered the kingdom of God. Two things became clear in those busy, blessed, exuberant years at the end of the first decade of conference ministry. The work was expanding well beyond initial expectations, and new staff would have to be added in order to meet the needs. Otis and Julia began praying that the Lord would send someone willing to join them on the resident family of The Firs.

11. Jack Murray also pastored four congregations, including Bible Presbyterian Church in Philadelphia, served as President of Shelton College in New Jersey, established Clearwater Christian College in Florida and Biblical Theological Seminary (now Missio) in Philadelphia, hosted a Christian radio broadcast, and led an itinerant evangelistic ministry for more than thirty years. He kept in contact with The Firs and returned as a guest speaker in the 1960s. I am grateful to his son George Murray, a co-laborer with his father for many years and scion of his evangelistic ministry, for sharing the details of his father's conversion and life story. For more on Harvey Cedars, see https://www.hcbible.org/history.

The original Whipple honeymoon cabin, “The Firs” (1903).

Otis and Julia Whipple, with their firstborn, Elden, on the porch of The Firs (1905).

Outdoor auditorium at an early Firs conference.

The Firs dining porch with conference guests.

# 6

# Nurture (1931–1936)

"God shall supply all your needs according to
His riches in glory by Christ Jesus."[1]

IN THE FALL OF 1931 Doris Coffin arrived at The Firs ready to serve and willing to share in the life of faith. She was no stranger to the Whipple family. As she later recounted, "From the age of nine, she and Lois [Whipple] were inseparable chums. It was 'Aunt Julia' who led Doris to the Lord. One day after school she called her into the dining room and there by the corner of the big square table they knelt to pray—and another soul was born again. Lunch box in hand, she went on home, a shining-eyed babe in Christ."[2]

As a teenager, Doris attended C.I.M. prayer meetings held in the Whipples' Seattle home and then, when the Lake Whatcom work began, she became a regular part of the summer conference family. A close friend of Tony Black, Doris was another of the early Vacation Bible School team. Now, having studied both at the University of Washington and Biola, she welcomed the commencement of a new phase of training.

A weekly children's class and numerous speaking engagements filled Doris's calendar in her first months at The Firs, but she was also prayerfully preparing and looking forward to a new venture—a month-long Bible school to be held during the winter season. When the invitation was extended, many came, including Ruth Walter, a friend from Biola,

1. Phil 4:19.
2. Aldrich and Whipple, *Firs of The Lord*, 58.

who was the college's dean of women as well as a teacher of missions. No charge was made, although funds were low and supplies scarce; these were Depression years. As specific needs for food and other provisions were met on a daily basis, many were helped to believe and to commit themselves more fully to the Lord they encountered in the pages of Scripture.

Ruth Walter had never seen anything quite like the life of faith demonstrated at The Firs. But she had read about it only a few months earlier when prompted, in preparation for teaching her missions class, to take up the biographies of Hudson Taylor and George Muller, as well as the early books of Amy Carmichael, who founded the Dohnavur Fellowship in South India.

Doris, unaware of all that her friend was pondering, was herself heavy in thought and prayer. She needed a co-worker; there was so much to do. But how could she approach Otis and Julia? Already, slim resources which had kept two were being distributed three ways. She waited what seemed an interminable few weeks, then, taking courage from Jer 1:7–9 (God's assurance of calling to a young and hesitant prophet), came to her dear spiritual parents. The Whipples responded warmly to her concerns and agreed to pray that someone else might be added to the conference family.

Although Ruth came to mind repeatedly, Doris didn't mention the matter to her for some time. When she finally confided her wish, she was amazed to learn of Ruth's own inclination toward just such a role. No decision was made immediately. Ruth went home to Los Angeles, sought counsel from her parents, and reevaluated her position at Biola. When she returned in the summer to help with the annual conference, the way seemed clear, and in October 1932 the resident staff of The Firs was expanded to four.

Not long after this addition to the household, Julia came to the girls, Bible in hand. As Ruth recorded in her diary:

> Early that morning the Lord gave her in her reading Proverbs 27:27: "And you shall have enough goats' milk for your food, for the food of your household, and for the nourishment of your maidservants." She remembered that goats' milk is richer than cows' milk. Then we christened our work the Modern Maidens Missionary Movement. After that the special treats, or a supply of extra fine quality, became known as "goats' milk." Many were the times we recognized God was giving us just that.

Many were the times, also, that the whole family, but Ruth particularly, would have to lean hard on the strength of that promise. More than once the common purse was empty and they had to learn, as Julia Whipple so often said, to be "pliable in the hands of the Lord." When Ruth's mother came to visit for a week-end, there was only $2.50 on hand. She never knew; part of Ruth's commitment to the life of faith was a decision never to mention her needs to her parents.

Although no one complained, it became evident to Ruth that there had never been such a sustained period of testing since the Whipples had come to live at The Firs. It was she who carried the explanation to Otis's and Julia's unspoken questions; she felt sure that this was the Lord's means of training her—a kind of crash course in the life of dependence on Him. (When this pattern repeated itself time after time as new people were added to the staff, the Whipples became convinced that she had been right, that this was the way God chose to refine those who came and to solidify the fellowship in faith and love.)

One summer, Doris went through an entire ten-day conference with only one dress. Although she was a featured singer and in front of people regularly, she bravely dismissed her embarrassment, varied accessories each day, and translated, in simplicity, the beauty of holiness. Ruth experienced her own lessons about God's provision of "raiment," recounting at a prayer meeting how a single pair of old shoes she had worn daily, unable to afford replacements, had somehow held up.[3] The Whipples, whose wisdom was born of fifteen years' experience of God's faithfulness, relied on Jesus' counsel to "seek first the kingdom of God and his righteousness," confident that their Father would take care of material needs.

> At the beginning of the work at The Firs, the Lord gave the Whipples this word: "Do not fear, for you will not be ashamed" (Isaiah 54:4), a promise that He would protect against those times of being embarrassed before others because of lack of supply. One such incident was in 1933, when we were at the literal end of money and food. The sugar barrel was empty, the flour was nearly gone, the funds were exhausted, and the cupboards held enough food for only two more meals, according to our calculations. At noon we used the remaining jar of home-canned

3. This incident is reminiscent of another shoes story. Mrs. Whipple, just prior to the 1923 conference, was given some money by her sister-in-law Carrie Cole to purchase badly needed shoes. But Julia's thoughts flew to a young friend in Victoria; she went without new footwear in order to help pay Isobel Miller's passage to her first conference at The Firs (Kuhn, *By Searching*, 47–48).

> salmon for chowder. It was on the table when a knock came at the door. Two friends to spend the night! We hurriedly took the soup from the table and redistributed it (added more liquid). We had the remainder of the roast for dinner and it was sufficient. We watched the rapidly dwindling supply of fresh bread, our last, disappear; but before the vanishing point was reached, all appetites were satisfied. For breakfast Mr. Whipple used the last of the flour for some of his excellent pancakes. The guests left before noon, without knowing the state of affairs. At lunch, while eating the odds and ends, the mail came and in it was a blank sheet of paper folded around a ten-dollar bill—the human donor unknown, but the heavenly Giver well-known.[4]

Together, the "Modern Maidens" shared experiences and learned lessons that would shape the course of both their lives.[5] They added, moreover, new depth and breadth to the outreach of the conference. Ruth taught a young people's Bible class each Wednesday evening, while Doris continued her children's classes and began a new ministry with high school students. As others in surrounding communities heard of their work, invitations to teach and speak began to come in. Within a year, they had a circuit of classes from Blaine to Seattle.

It was evident that more could be done, that the fields for many miles around were ripe for harvest. In 1933, Chester and Helen Rutledge, now home from China and in frequent contact with the Whipples, began to wonder if this task might be theirs.

Having been forced out of China the same year Otis and Julia came home, Chester and Helen returned, broken in health, to California. When invited that summer to share in the young people's work at the Lake Whatcom Bible and Missionary Conference, they responded cheerfully, delighted to renew fellowship with their China friends. Thereafter,

4. Aldrich and Whipple, *Firs of the Lord*, 62.

5. Doris Coffin later became Doris Coffin Aldrich, wife of Willard Aldrich—co-founder and long-term president of Multnomah School of the Bible. Many of her fond memories of The Firs and of lessons learned in the life of faith appeared in *The Doorstep Evangel*, a publication of Multnomah, and in her popular "Out of the Mixing Bowl" column in *Moody Monthly*. Ruth Walter, after leaving the conference for ten years to be dean of women, first at Whitworth College in Spokane and then Multnomah and Westmont, returned to become the second Mrs. Otis Whipple in 1946, Julia having died ten years earlier. She became a regular contributing editor to *The Firs Fellowship*. When Doris Aldrich died before writing her intended continuation of *The Firs of the Lord*, Ruth, who had collaborated with her on so many ventures, took up the project and brought it to completion. For more on Doris's life, see the biography by Belva Atkinson Murphy (sister of Bernice Whipple), *Mommie of the Mixing Bowl*.

Chester became director of Christian education at Glendale Presbyterian Church and was active in Christian Endeavor—an interdenominational youth ministry. In 1929, the Rutledges returned to The Firs to assist again with the young people's program. 1931 saw them in Colorado, where they shared responsibility for youth ministries in what was at that time the largest Presbyterian congregation in the United States, Denver Central Presbyterian Church. The work was challenging and its rewards gratifying. Both Chester and Helen, though, had a hankering after some form of rural evangelism, and as they poured their energies into one of the busiest churches in North America they prayed for an opportunity to serve those who were out of reach and out of touch with a thriving urban fellowship of this kind.

In the summer of 1933, another call came from Otis and Julia, and God opened a new door. As Chester recalled:

> When we were invited to have part in the program at the conference in July 1933, we had no thought that it was the beginning of a longer ministry in the Northwest . . . While at the conference, requests came to us for services in this area and faster than these services were completed other requests came in . . . As time went on, I became more and more impressed with the fact that this was to be our place of ministry. As I waited (while busy as could be) for the Lord to give a confirming word, the message that came to me constantly was: "This is the way, walk in it" (Isaiah 30:21). I could not get away from this word, but . . . we both felt certain that God would not give just one of us a clear call to a work. He had called both of us for Christian service before we ever met and He had led us as one during the years of our service together. So we waited patiently for Him to make His will known to us both. How well I remember the day Mrs. Rutledge came to me and said, "It is all settled, this is where the Lord wants us, so we might just as well write for the storage company to send our things on." Now, I am perfectly certain that this does not mean that I was more sensitive to the Lord's leading, for I look back and thank God for those days of waiting . . . I believe it is absolutely necessary for the Lord's servants to be agreed on any such important move, if they are to expect his full blessing in the undertaking.

The Whipples, who well remembered their own experience leading up to their move to The Firs in the summer of 1921, were in full agreement, and all the more grateful when Chester and Helen responded with a heartfelt shared "yes" to the call to Lake Whatcom.

The principles and policies of the China Inland Mission with respect to finances were familiar to the Rutledges; they were in a measure prepared for the adjustment from a comfortable, dependable salary to reliance on a common purse and an unseen provider. Still, recalled Chester, "I had never really known what it was to live by faith." The refining process was again severe: "There was nothing, absolutely nothing in the way of worldly goods. If I hadn't been here and gone through it, I would not have believed it possible."

All that the Rutledges had, they brought. And as Doris Coffin—who had seen this before—recounted, the Lord began immediately to school them in the life of faith: "He sent in no further provisions until all their funds were used. It could not have been easy to see the money disappear, but how graciously it was given to maintain The Firs family during that time. And what a peculiar testing for the Whipples as they . . . exercised the grace of receiving while Chester bought the supplies."

One might have thought that after the extraordinary pace of youth work in a thriving church in a major American city, nothing—least of all a quiet conference center six miles from a modest port town—would seem to pose a major challenge. But Chester and Helen found themselves drawing upon all their accumulated skills and experience in Christian service as they settled into responsibilities at The Firs. Chester became head of the young people's department and was soon involved in an ever-increasing number of weekend conferences for boys, girls, high schoolers, and University students, as well as casual get-togethers for neighborhood youngsters. There were, additionally, invitations to speak at schools, to fill pulpits, and to conduct evangelistic meetings at many nearby centers. Helen taught Bible classes for women and filled the new and necessary position of conference registrar. In 1935, remembering perhaps the gift of Lyman Stewart to them, the Rutledges began a new venture, The Firs Bookroom.

As for the grounds themselves, these were the days, Ruth recalled, when "everyone did everything." Total property now exceeded fifteen acres, and flower beds, lawns, vegetable gardens, cottages, young people's quarters, campgrounds, water systems, all with constant need for repair and upkeep, presented endless chores for the resident group. Chester even found himself setting charges and supervising blasting of stumps to clear land for building—a skill he had acquired in a summer job as a teenager, and which had seemed irrelevant ever since. Added to this were all the normal responsibilities of home and family (the Rutledges' son Don was three years old when they came to The Firs). Grant Whipple, looking back years later, commented that with fuel to gather for a woodburning stove and supplies to buy on an almost daily basis, since that was the way the funds most often arrived, "a lot of time was taken up with just living."

The rural evangelism ministry that was, from the beginning, the Rutledges' first love, commenced soon after their arrival, then was given added incentive when Chester was made extension secretary of Christian Endeavor. The third autumn after their move to The Firs, Chester engaged in mission trips to British Columbia, Idaho, Oregon, and California, as well as myriad towns and rural districts throughout Washington State: "Churches, school houses, grange halls, town halls, club buildings, and homes have furnished the meeting places for some three hundred services during the past year. The message has also gone forth over five different radio stations. The driver's seat of a Chevy has been the pulpit from which many heart-to-heart talks have occurred."

Chester seldom traveled unaccompanied. Rural outreach had been a shared dream, and Helen entered into its actualization, going with her husband as often as other responsibilities permitted. Pastors and teachers often joined him; while they exercised their own gifts of ministry, Chester gave himself to visitation—extending invitations, sharing the gospel on doorsteps, encouraging the faltering, strengthening ties of fellowship. Otis, after going out with him on one itinerary was moved to remark, "I doubt if there are many roads in our part of the country that Chester hasn't traveled to see someone he knows. He is a true pastor who is responsive to people's needs and who gives wise counsel. People all over Washington, Oregon, Idaho, and Montana look forward to his coming."

Soon after these pilgrimages began, Chester started to mark, on a large colored map, all the places he visited in his extension work. The boundaries eventually extended north into the interior of British Columbia, east over the Rockies into Idaho and Montana, south to the California border. By the 1970s, large portions of the map would be completely obscured by clusters of little pin markers—an amazing witness to decades of joyful, self-sacrificial labor.[6] Each marker had special significance for Chester; he loved to recollect individual narratives, pointing to various small corners of his well-worn map: here, he would recall, a man who

6. Chester would later put the tally at more than 2300 meetings in over 296 towns in the years of his itinerant ministry. *Bellingham Herald*, August 6, 1983, 4.

had been for years bitterly hardened against the gospel and resentful of his wife's profession of faith, bowed his head in humble repentance and spiritual surrender. Or there, moving his finger slightly, he and Ralph ("Pop") Riley had the privilege of ministering together to a little gathering of thirty, one wintry day. The roads had been treacherous and bad weather kept many away, but when an invitation was given, fully half the congregation responded to the message and committed their lives to Christ.

"You will never know," wrote one pastor, "how much we in these outlying districts appreciate this ministry of The Firs." And there is a sense in which much of the fruit of Chester's rural evangelism will always remain hidden. As in every such work of faith, one sows, another waters, and seeds grow secretly until the Lord's increase is made plain. So, it came as a special joy, once, when a man approached the Rutledges after a meeting near Penticton, British Columbia, to say, "You won't recognize me, but I was one of the three who were here last year. When I got home, I knelt by my bed and gave my life to Christ." Chester thought back, recalling his hesitation to proceed with that service, since so few were present, and his later misgivings that anything at all had been accomplished. This word came as a reminder and an encouragement of the Lord's blessing even when "results" are not immediately apparent.

One indication of blessing that did become evident through these years was a growing attendance at the summer conference of people who had been reached first in Chester's travels to rural communities: The Firs' constituency expanded steadily through the 1930s. Otis and Julia watched with joy as the work prospered and some of the responsibility was shifted to younger shoulders. Their selflessness allowed them to share what they had never, since the dedication of their small honeymoon cottage, considered theirs. "He must increase, but I must decrease" was a way of life for them. Yet their participation never diminished, and their labor never slackened. Edna Gish recounted a touching remembrance of her sister-in-law from the summer of 1935:

> One day in the dining room at El Nathan, Julia was going over with me the things she wanted to get done before Conference opened in a few days. She pointed to the drawers under the china cabinet and said, "I must clean the silverware and straighten those drawers." That is one of my last memories of Julia, working untiringly as long as she had strength for the Lord's work at The Firs, where she and Otis had committed their all to Him.

Many there were who wept when they heard, in May 1936, of Julia Whipple's passing after a painful struggle with cancer. Once, in those last hard days, Carrie Cole, who was like a sister to her, sat at her bedside. Sensing Julia's pain, and seeing moisture gather at the corner of her eyes, she leaned over to comfort her: "Dear sister, weeping may endure for a night, but joy comes in the morning." The reply came in a little gasp, from faltering lips and a tranquil heart: "He gives joy now."

Otis, staggered with loss, and seeking direction as to his own continuing role at The Firs, elected to spend a year away, visiting his two eldest children, who were with their families ministering with the C.I.M. in China. The direction of the conference was turned over, for the duration, to his youngest son Grant.

# 7

## Scion (1936–1946)

"Acknowledge those who work hard among you, who care for you in the Lord and who admonish you. Hold them in the highest regard in love because of their work."[7]

HAVING COMMITTED ENTIRELY TO the Lord the need for staff at the Lake Whatcom Conference, Otis and Julia had refrained from influencing anyone, even their own children, to join the resident Firs family. Grant's early intention to return, with Lois and Elden, to China had won their heartfelt blessing and approval. But as Grant began to prepare, first at Biola, then at Wheaton College, for Christian service overseas, the Holy Spirit began nudging him gently toward consideration of a field much closer to home and bringing influences to bear on his life that would later be regarded as a kind of matriculation to full-time work at The Firs.

Training at the Bible Institute of Los Angeles was not precisely a foregone conclusion for Grant, but the family's long association with the school and Elden's and Lois's previous study there made it a logical next step after high school graduation. Although he stayed only a year (1930–1931), Grant formed many lasting friendships, one of the most influential of which was with a classmate, Dawson Trotman, who later founded The Navigators. Trotman's biography, *Daws*, records a particularly daring extracurricular activity in which he and Grant occasionally indulged, the kind of hair-raising diversion now associated with extreme parkour: "They would get a running start on the roof of a thirteen-story

7. 1 Thess 5:12–13, NIV.

building, jump to the waist-high ledge rimming the roof, and from there to the roof of the Mayflower Hotel."[8]

What drew them close, apart from these exploits, was a compatibility of spiritual influences and aspirations. Dawson had been profoundly affected by reading the lives of Hudson Taylor and George Muller, and adhered personally—and later, organizationally—to the faith principles they espoused. He was passionately committed to the integrity of the Word of God and thoroughly convinced of its power to change lives. And the heartbeat of his evangelistic zeal was a dedication to leadership training. Paul's exhortation to Timothy, "The things that you have heard from me among many witnesses, commit these to faithful men who will be able to teach others also" (2 Tim 2:2), set the agenda which his own and Grant's later ministries would exemplify.

During the same year, Grant became acquainted with a lovely, engaging young woman from Vancouver, who was in her second year at Biola. Bernice Atkinson had been introduced to Grant the previous spring when he visited the campus to see his sister Lois. The possibility, however, that they had actually met as children during the Whipples' Vancouver days, when both families spent a good deal of time at the home of mutual friends, the H.C. Hunts, prompted amused speculation.

Bernice's parents were active in the Plymouth Brethren assembly of Mount Pleasant Hall (now Granville Chapel) and in many areas of Christian service in Vancouver. Her father, Dr. John T. Atkinson, a successful osteopath and co-founder of the Canadian Osteopathic Association, had served on the committee of the French Oliver Evangelistic Campaign in 1917 and, with his wife Mary, lent leadership and support to numerous Christian organizations. The Atkinsons' lovely Shaughnessy home was a haven of hospitality for many, including members of Intervarsity Christian Fellowship, whose meetings were held there from the early 1930s until Dr. Atkinson's death in 1961.

The friendship that blossomed between Bernice and Grant was one of many that grew out of an informal fellowship of Biola students from the Pacific Northwest, most of whom, unlike Bernice, had attended conferences at The Firs. The more Bernice spent time with them in classes, listened as they chatted over lunch in the cafeteria, and met with them in weekly prayer meetings, the more her own interest in The Firs grew.

8. Skinner, *Daws*, 53.

In the summer of 1931, she and her sister Belva attended their first Firs family conference.[9]

September took Grant to Wheaton College, where he found time for football and baseball in addition to a demanding course of study. Bernice went to the University of British Columbia and entered a pre-med program, with her sights set on a career in medicine. She returned frequently to The Firs, helping out in the conference kitchen and elsewhere as she was needed—displaying the capability, thoughtfulness, and cheerfully unstinting hard work that would so characterize her later role—and generally endearing herself to the conference family. Continued correspondence with Grant assured both that a lifelong commitment was in store; when Grant came home at the end of his freshman year at Wheaton, he brought a ring.

Thinking that additional biblical training would be more of an asset to her future husband's ministry than further medical studies, Bernice transferred to Wheaton and looked, with some trepidation, she admitted, toward mission work in the Far East. An unspecified dread of China and insecurity regarding the teaching role she would doubtless be expected to fulfill ("Maybe I could do it in China, but I certainly couldn't do it here," she claimed, after a distressing practicum) had to be yielded up.

It began to come clear in her second year at Wheaton, however, that the Lord's intention for her and Grant was that they should return to the Lake Whatcom Conference. Grant's changing sense of direction began to emerge through a series of realizations while he was visiting the C.I.M. home in Vancouver in the summer of 1932. He began to wonder if his mission field might actually be in the Pacific Northwest, that a place of familiarity could be a setting of a whole new area of responsibility and blessing. Several passages from Isaiah seemed to speak directly to him, as he pondered: "Do not remember the former things, nor consider the things of old. Behold, I will do a new thing . . . I have made you hear new things from this time, even hidden things . . . I, even I, have spoken: yes, I have called him, I have brought him, and his way will prosper" (Isa 43:18–19; 48:6, 15). Bernice, meanwhile, was led to a passage in the book of Revelation: "I have set before you an open door, and no one can shut it;

9. Belva was one of the founding members of the Fundamentalist Society at the University of British Columbia in 1926, which became in 1928 the Varsity Christian Union and later merged with Intervarsity Christian Fellowship. She helped organize a high school outreach (to be called Interschool Christian Fellowship) in 1931, and later that year invited youngsters to her parents' summer home on Hollyburn Mountain for I.S.C.F.'s first camp. In 1934, Belva married Intervarsity staff member Maurice Murphy.

for you have a little strength, have kept My word, and have not denied My name" (3:8). While neither was sure exactly what "new things" awaited them through the door that God was opening, both became convinced that their place of service was to be The Firs.

Grant's Wheaton experience culminated shortly before graduation in the spring of 1934 with a series of evangelistic rallies that he and a group of fellow students conducted in surrounding communities. Some of the details and initial reactions were conveyed home in an exuberant letter:

> At 6:30 we all went up to the church for a fellowship supper, and then at 7:30 the rally of all the neighboring churches began. We had a good song service and the quartet sang, the fellows played their instruments, and we all gave testimonies. Harvey [Chrouser] closed the meeting with his testimony and, being in his home church, he broke down, but the power of the Spirit was there; many hands were raised for prayer, and two girls accepted the Lord . . . When we left, we felt as though there was much accomplished that we knew nothing about, and after we got home a letter came from the pastor of that church with the following report: at the close of the Sunday morning service the invitation was given because the Spirit seemed to be lingering over from the night before, and fifty came forward, fifteen for salvation and the rest for consecration.
>
> We left Stratford at 3:30 a.m. in order to get to Green Bay by 7:00 a.m. where we were invited for breakfast at the reformatory before our meeting. After breakfast we went to the chapel and then all the fellows marched in; I guess about 300 were in our service. We gave our testimonies and the fellows sang, and we made the way of salvation just as plain as we could, then Harvey asked for those to raise their hands who wished to be prayed for and many raised their hands. He then felt led to have those come forward who wished to accept Jesus Christ as their Savior and oh, I wish you could have been there to see the Lord work. Our friend was the first fellow on his feet, and without hesitation came right straight forward. We were told about 125 came forward to accept the Lord. Just to see those great big fellows, nearly every one of them crying, with their hardened hearts softened, was a sight none of us will ever forget . . . They have given us permission to send testaments up to them and to write, so we are praising the Lord.

Brimming with enthusiasm for evangelism, Grant returned to The Firs that summer. Bernice spent the year in Vancouver working in her father's medical office until she and Grant were married in May 1935. After a honeymoon trip through the eastern states and Ontario, she settled in with her new husband and his parents in El Nathan.

"It was an indoctrination for me," recounted Bernice with characteristic self-effacing candor. "I had no idea what living in a communal household would be like, where you didn't just do what you felt like doing but fitted in with everyone else's plans. It was a new experience for me to see every penny going to buy food. I used to wonder what was going to happen when my trousseau was worn out and all my nylons were gone. We never suffered; the Lord was good to us. But there was never a feeling of security. I learned a lot, and had a lot to learn."

Grant's indoctrination was of a different sort, but similarly rigorous. He joined Chester Rutledge in programming young people's meetings and conferences and traveled with him on numerous speaking engagements throughout the area. When at home, he helped with all the myriad tasks the ministry required, including everything from housekeeping and maintenance to landscaping and building improvements. Since his role was not sharply delineated, he had to be something of all things to all facets of the work. If the lack of definition was at times frustrating, it was also an invaluable preparation for the position of acting director which came to him in 1936.

Grant's first major responsibility after his father left for China following Julia's death was to conduct—with Bernice, Doris Coffin, Ruth Walter, and the Rutledges—the 1936 summer conference. A rather staggering assignment, approached, as a council member observed, with real fear and trembling. Yet, as Belle Sperry reflected after it was all over, "It was like our Lord that the conference was an unusually blessed one":

> First, there was sunshine every day and not a drop of rain. One of our speakers was unable to come, but just two weeks before the opening of the conference the Lord gave us Dr. Lewis Sperry Chafer, who ministered to us in the power and fullness of the Spirit . . . [10] There were 633 registered during the conference, of

10. Dr. Chafer was the co-founder and first president of Dallas Theological Seminary (serving from 1924 to 1952), an eminent theologian and influential evangelist who was also deeply involved in the Christian conference movement. Like the Whipples, he was drawn to the faith principles pioneered by George Muller and Hudson Taylor, though his initial efforts in the 1920s to impose them on the fledgling seminary were somewhat misguided and ultimately abandoned. (He eschewed direct solicitation of

> which 515 came from out of town. A large proportion of young people were in attendance . . . [of whom] several were born again during those ten days. The climax of the conference came on the last evening when nearly a hundred promptly responded to the appeal for preparation for the service of the Lord Jesus Christ.

Miss Sperry's report was circulated by means of one of the "new things" that Grant initiated, *The Firs Fellowship*, a quarterly brochure designed to keep an ever-growing constituency of friends abreast of conference activities. The first issue appeared in December 1936, and the *Fellowship* was subsequently sent free of charge to everyone on the mailing list and anyone who requested it. Free will offerings, specially designated, paid production and mailing costs.

As news went out and links were maintained and strengthened with the Christian community throughout the Pacific Northwest, the conference grounds became increasingly a center of Christian hospitality for out-of-town guests. An open-door policy prevailed, as it had in Otis and Julia Whipple's home. El Nathan and the Rutledges' cottage were always open to callers, as were the Bowers's home, Miss McCausland's and Mrs. Black's residences, and even Miss Sperry's tent.

Neighbors in the Geneva community who had not actually attended conferences watched with curiosity all the comings and goings at this quiet lakefront retreat. There was much they didn't understand. The people who lived at The Firs were always busy at their incomprehensible tasks. None were on a payroll or a nine-to-five schedule. They held classes for children and young people; even adults met to study the Bible with them. Now there was a steady stream of visitors from parts unknown. But the resident staff, for the most part, were neither especially socially outgoing nor active in community affairs.

One family of near neighbors to the Rutledges publicized its suspicion of and hostility toward the work. It became widely known that if they ever sold their property, they'd certainly see to it that "that religious bunch" at The Firs didn't get hold of it. Chester's contact with the family was minimal, but his neighborly warmth was unassailable. When he discovered the gentleman tinkering unsuccessfully with an old ruin of a car one day, and learned that he and his wife had no other means of getting to a family funeral in Seattle, he offered to drive them down and back. The

---

funds, but was willing to incur significant debt, thus depending, as a staff member observed ruefully, on "the grace of creditors"; faculty salaries were constantly in arrears.) See Hannah, *Uncommon Union*, 22–23, 111–15.

man refused gruffly at first, obviously embarrassed to accept "charity" from people he had so openly abused. But at Chester's insistence, he finally acquiesced. The trip allowed for unhurried conversation and a quiet testimony of God's presence in Chester and Helen's lives. While nothing appeared obviously to change after they returned home, the family's outspoken opposition to conference activities was noticeably quelled. Then, not long afterward, the neighbor was at the Rutledges' door with news that he and his wife were considering moving and he wanted to give The Firs first option on the property. Startled, Chester took the story to the council. Prayers were offered, money flowed in from several sources, and the home was purchased. As a result of thoughtful, obedient stewardship of the love of God, hard hearts were softened. The Firs is full of unmarked memorials to those whose sensitivity to God's ways rather than insistence on their own allowed participation in a quiet adventure of faith.[11]

The spirit of hospitality and communality always overflowed at conference time. The summer of 1937 saw the largest conference on record. Among those registered, 365 stayed on or near the grounds, eating on the covered porches of the expanded honeymoon cabin and El Nathan. Nearly seventy camped nearby and provided their own food, and an additional 482 attended meetings only. Still others came but did not register. Such numbers seem, retrospectively, almost inconceivable, but it was reportedly a remarkably ordered, joyful company. Where one might have expected irritability due to the discomforts of crowding, a sweet spirit of intimacy and good humor prevailed. Of the "auto camp" recently added to the grounds, one person's enthusiastic comment was: "What a grand vacation, camping and conference at the same time!"

Otis Whipple had returned, rested and spiritually refreshed, to The Firs for that summer's conference and assumed directorship once more. Grant and Bernice were now fully conversant with all aspects of the work and well established in their long-term affiliation. It was Grant's unspoken desire, however, to further his theological training at seminary. He and Bernice had no resources for such a pursuit and wondered if and how it would ever be possible. On the last day of the 1937 conference, Tony (née Black) and Hal Clark approached Grant to ask if he had ever

11. A less happy incident occurred decades later. In 1987, a longtime local resident and much-loved member of Geneva Community Church left her home to The Firs in a bequest. She was single and without natural heirs, but an estranged sibling, upon learning that the home would not revert to the family, sent an unsigned poison pen letter with angry accusations of religious "brainwashing" and theft.

considered going back to school. When he replied in the affirmative, a smile came over their faces; their heart's wish was to provide him with the necessary funds. So, the matter simply and wonderfully resolved, Grant left for The Biblical Seminary in New York[12] (a school the Clarks themselves and other friends, including Doris Coffin, had attended), just days after his first child, Anne Adele, was born. Bernice followed shortly afterward with the baby.

In addition to carrying a heavy class and study load, Grant served a half-time pastorate in a Dutch Reformed church in Brooklyn and continued to be active in youth work. His vision for a significant outreach among young people in the Pacific Northwest grew, as did his own and Bernice's affection and concern for the overall ministry at Lake Whatcom. In a letter home that obviously meant much to his father, Grant remarked, "I've been thinking about you a good deal and have longed so many times to be with you. My heart . . . is there in that work and a good deal of my time is spent thinking about it and praying for it. I just naturally relate everything I'm studying here in terms of the work [at The Firs]."

While the method of Bible study taught at his New York seminary was the finest he had ever encountered, Grant became concerned, during the year he was there, about an undercurrent of skepticism with respect to the authority and reliability of Scripture. That the Bible *contained* the Word of God was never at issue; that it *was* the Word of God in its entirety, however, was openly questioned—and by some openly denied. After prayerful consideration and many hours of discussion with members of faculty and administration, Grant elected to transfer the following year to Dallas Theological Seminary, where Lewis Sperry Chafer, who had spoken at The Firs summer conference in 1936, was president.

The single most important contribution of Dallas Theological Seminary to his ministry, in Grant's view, was an utter confidence in the inspiration and authority of Scripture. But it was here, also, that another contact of deep and lasting importance was made. Jim Rayburn, a fellow student, discovering Grant's interest in youth evangelism, invited him to help out in a high school program then called Miracle Book Club, which met with students in school classrooms for after-school Bible classes. The work was fruitful. Jim's greatest burden was for unchurched teenagers—those who would be least receptive to normal channels of Christian ministry—and a classroom, one step removed from a church building,

12. In 1966 the school was renamed New York Theological Seminary.

attracted some who might not otherwise have been exposed to the gospel. Still, school was "establishment" territory. He began to wonder whether it might be even more effective to have an evening get-together at one of the students' own houses.

Gradually, a new concept and a new strategy of youth work began to take shape in Jim's mind and those of his close associates. It was actually more missionary-oriented than typically evangelistic, for it involved conscientious penetration into a culture quite foreign to most church-going Christian adults. Jim felt it was crucial to translate, without compromising, the Christian message into youthful idiom, as well as to win the confidence of natural leaders (athletes, student reps, cheerleaders) who would in turn influence others and set a process of indigenous evangelism in motion.

The idea took on definitive organizational shape in 1940. Grant was among the first of Jim Rayburn's club leaders in the Young Life Campaign. There was immense mutual benefit in their relationship and their shared ministry. Jim's creative approach to programming and indefatigable fervor for high school work were decisive in shaping Grant's whole attitude to young people's ministries in Bellingham, while Grant's long experience in conference work at The Firs aroused Jim's interest in Christian camping.

In 1941, Jim asked Grant to head up what he called a Young Life convention, which would bring kids into Dallas from surrounding areas to stay at homes and meet in a church for combined club meetings. Grant proposed trying a conference rather than convention format. When Jim asked him to explain, he drew on his experience at The Firs to suggest getting kids out of the city into a relaxed, informal setting, with stretches of time for recreation and relationship forming a context for the teaching ministry of one or several leaders. Jim agreed, and permission was secured to use two campsites at Bachman Lake, northwest of Dallas. Young Life's first conference was both popular with kids and spiritually fruitful; several similar ventures in later years would be held at The Firs. Young Life went on in subsequent decades to establish rural camps in Colorado and seventeen other states, and to promote a conference-type camping philosophy for which the Bachman Lake experiment set the precedent.[13]

13. In contrast to Intervarsity Christian Fellowship and Camp Firwood (see chapter 9 below), Young Life maintained a highly centralized, speaker-and-leader-oriented camping program. In addition to its American sites, Young Life currently has camps in British Columbia, the Dominican Republic, Scotland, Armenia, and France.

Back at The Firs, Grant's father received word of this new ministry with interest and offered thoughtful and sympathetic encouragement: "Pioneering never can be easy. But we claim the promises for you and hold to God's faithfulness." As far as the Lake Whatcom Conference itself was concerned, Otis kept Grant and Bernice informed by means of weekly letters. A minor identity crisis, provoked by renewed suggestions that The Firs identify more specifically and exclusively with Keswick,[14] had led to reassessment and reaffirmation of the founding principles of the work. In an October 1941 letter, Otis commented:

> We need a basis so that we and prospective workers, the council, and the public all know exactly how things are . . . I confess the details are not yet clear to me. But I cannot conceive of any other than a real faith basis that everyone can recognize as that. I am fully convinced that the principle of Matthew 6:33 ("Seek ye first the kingdom of God and His righteousness, and all these things shall be added to you") has been the Lord's teaching for this work . . . I cannot but feel my chief part has been, as Mother's was, in demonstrating the truth of that verse.

A test case came sooner than expected. Both the faith basis and emphasis of the ministry and its financial policy were challenged and reaffirmed when two couples, Paul and Margaret Toms[15] and Mr. and Mrs. Edwin Rogers applied to join The Firs staff. A committee formed to consider their applications dealt prayerfully with the question of how to incorporate and how to finance such an increase in personnel: "If the Lord is moving these couples to this work, the Lord has work for them to do and will make ample provision for them. The Conference was started on a faith basis and without doubt we are unanimous to have it continue that way, but in order to have it [do so], it is imperative that any new workers be of exactly the same mind."

14. Keswick "holiness" teaching had, from the first decade of the Lake Whatcom Conference, been a significant part of its ministry emphasis. Some had periodically suggested a greater formal identification with Keswick, but it was felt that the distinctive character that God had ordained at The Firs should not be changed.

15. While Paul Toms was kept busy with buildings and maintenance on the conference grounds, Margaret established a successful kindergarten program for local families that occupied The Firs dining room Monday through Friday, between weekend conference gatherings. Paul Toms Jr., who grew up within The Firs family, would succeed Dr. Harold Ockenga as pastor of Boston's historic Park Street Church in 1969, serving in that role for twenty years.

Both couples agreed. The Rogers assured the council that "the whole program of The Firs Conference appealed to us primarily because it is a work of faith. Remove that element, and it would lose much of its attractiveness." The Toms shared the same feelings. The Lord, through severe testing very similar to that experienced earlier by Otis and Julia Whipple and subsequent members of the resident staff, had begun to speak to them about "changing our means of provision from that of independence to that of entire dependence upon Him," providing scriptural assurances from the book of Isaiah.

The committee unanimously agreed that "any new workers that are added to the staff should share equally the funds available in the maintenance fund for resident workers." Once again, provisions were broken and multiplied, and the needs of an enlarged staff wonderfully met. Grant and Bernice, with daughter Anne and their first son, Bruce, arrived to join it in the summer of 1941.

The Whipple family itself had passed through recent sorrow with the death of Elden's wife Evelyn in 1940 of cancer, while home on medical furlough and not long after giving birth to the couple's daughter Julia. Elden returned to China with his four young children later that year; he married fellow C.I.M. missionary Marian Carleson in June, 1941. Then, in December, an unanticipated and unimaginable series of events caused the lives of both Elden's and Lois's families overseas to be threatened. The journal of Lois's husband, Nathan Walton, composed aboard ship after the nightmare had passed and all were returning home, describes the day it began:

> It was early morning, December 8, 1941, and I stood on the verandah of the Stam Memorial Home in Tsingtao, overlooking the peaceful waters of the bay, little dreaming that news would soon be flashed over the radio to startle most of the world into active participation in World War II. To the north, Lao Shan, the Old Mountain, had already lifted its rugged head above the morning mists to greet the golden rays of dawn, and now fast motor launches sped out to sea in search of "enemy" craft. This was the usual morning activity and I no longer lifted the binoculars to see it.
>
> The unusual, however, arrived two hours later in the form of a dozen Japanese Marines, armed to the teeth, declaring a state of war to exist between their country and ours; on which grounds they promptly seized our car, motorcycle, radio, telephone, and camera, and made off with them all. Elden Whipple,

> my brother-in-law, had only just returned with the car, having succeeded in getting past the naval guards on the highway, who by that time were stopping all cars.
>
> The sudden appearance of the Japanese soldiers was a decisive victory for them, for on such short notice we had to agree to the terms of unconditional surrender! Unresisting, and in fact with smiles, we also accepted the humiliating restrictions of a three-hour daily freedom within certain limits. No one seemed excited or disturbed but the Japanese as they busied themselves in plundering. For our part, we would continue to abide under the shadow of the Almighty.[16]

Halfway around the world, Otis received first news of the Pearl Harbor attack with amazing peace. A letter begun early that morning, before the events unfolded, reveals how graciously the Lord had prepared him:

> My dear family: The sun is shining, outside and in! I have been praising the Lord for all his many blessings. These days, things around here tend to make me feel like Jacob. Let me find it and quote: "And Jacob their father said to them, 'You have bereaved me: Joseph is no more, Simeon is no more, and you want to take Benjamin. All these things are against me'" (Genesis 42:36). And yet none of the things he feared were true. If God be for us, who can be against us? One needs the sunshine once in awhile to remind one . . . But this morning I am very conscious that all things do work for good to us who love the Lord, who are called according to his purpose.

Later in the day, he would return to his unfinished correspondence:

> Nearly 10 p.m. Sunday night, Dec. 7. I reached home from church before hearing the news that Japan had attacked Honolulu and Pearl Harbor. And a good share of the time since has been spent at the radio. Bernice asked me to be there for dinner. And I stayed until nearly dark. I have thought a good many times of what I wrote this morning, and I know the Lord is on the throne. He is keeping peace. The news of what is happening in China or what has happened will come in the Lord's time. The radio had the news here in Bellingham four minutes after the bombing began. Of course, we wonder if you have been evacuated from Tsingtao and if those in the interior have gone further in or have come out as well. Christmas! Where are the Chefoo

16. Printed in *China's Millions*, a publication of the China Inland Mission, February 1944. An extraordinarily detailed, firsthand account of the Whipple families' internment and repatriation may be found in Black, *Heritage of Faith*.

> kiddies? And a rush of questions come to mind. We remain in prayer and are trusting.

It was two long years before the family was reunited. Christmas 1943 was "a day of joy and thanksgiving at The Firs," read a note in *The Firs Fellowship*: "Mr. Whipple sat down to dinner surrounded by all his family, not one missing. How we praised our faithful Lord who, after the trying months of internment, has brought Elden's and Lois's families safe home. They are now settled in our two missionary cottages and beginning to get the rest they greatly need."

The missionary cottages were new additions to The Firs, the fulfillment of a long-cherished dream. Since 1939 "Bonnie Cotte," a cabin owned by Mrs. Black, had been used by visiting missionaries, but when funds became available, two log buildings to be set aside as furlough homes were constructed. The Waltons and Whipples were among the first to use them.

Little more than a year after receiving its new occupants, however, one of the cabins was tragically destroyed by fire. The Waltons, except for son Tommy, had been away in Vancouver for two days when a fire set in the stove in preparation for their homecoming flared out of control and set the building ablaze. Returning home from school, Tommy found a great throng attempting unsuccessfully to quench what was by then a towering sheet of flames. Nate and Lois, well-tutored in adversity, responded gently, shunning what many might have considered a natural response of bitterness or self-pity—thankful for their son's safety (especially, he later recalled, after they had established that he wasn't the culprit!) and that God had "counted us worthy to suffer once more the loss of material things." Even the children shouldered the disaster bravely: Barbara, who was eleven, reflected with disarming matter-of-factness, "If someone had to lose things, I'm glad we were the ones; we're used to it."

The Waltons relocated in other conference facilities until they were called to the C.I.M. American home office in Los Angeles. One of the unanticipated blessings to result from the fire was the provision of material for another conference residence, a much-needed home for Grant and Bernice. "A fireman remarked to Grant, as they stood by the charred heap of debris, that such a loss automatically gave them top priority for necessary materials to rebuild. Investigation verified this and also revealed the new house did not have to be put upon the site of the burned one."[17] Post-

17. Aldrich and Whipple, *Firs of the Lord*, 89.

war restrictions on the purchase of building materials were thus strangely bypassed and, with a $4,000 dollar gift that Bernice's father had provided for construction of a permanent home on the grounds, Grant and his father began planning and building. Other funds came in as supplies diminished, and work progressed unhindered, without a cent ever being drawn from the conference treasury. In 1946 the family, with two new additions—Richard Grant (Dick) and John Douglas (Doug)—settled into their new quarters.

Standing, left to right: Ruth Walter, Doris Coffin, Bernice Atkinson (Grant's fiancée), Helen Rutledge, Grant Whipple, Chester Rutledge; seated, Julia Whipple, Otis Whipple; on grass, Jack Hollis, Don Rutledge (1933).

Early cottages at The Firs retreat center.

The Firs dining hall, facing Cable Street (1947).

Conference guests at dining hall entrance (1950s).

Youth conference at the retreat center (1950s).

# 8

# Second Spring (1940s and early 1950s)

"Your old men shall dream dreams, your young men shall see visions."[1]

RESPONSIBILITIES HAD INCREASED DRAMATICALLY for Grant and Bernice since their return to The Firs. Immediately upon their arrival from Dallas, Grant was made director of the young people's department. (Chester Rutledge's hands were more than full with his itinerant ministry and The Firs Bookstore, by now occupying expanded facilities in downtown Bellingham.) His experience working alongside Jim Rayburn soon bore fruit in the establishment of several Young Life-type clubs in local high schools. By December 1941, nearly one hundred young people, many from non-Christian backgrounds, were meeting weekly in five different area homes. Once the clubs were established, the students were eager for a name so they could advertise and get the word out to friends. Eventually, after prayerful deliberation, the name "Beta Sigma Fellowship Clubs" was adopted. Beta being the first letter in the Greek word for "life" and Sigma the first letter in the Greek word for "saving," the clubs were thus, collectively, the Life-Saving Fellowship. The coded name appealed to its young adherents.

Grant felt particularly strongly about the "fellowship" aspect of youth ministry, knowing how important it was for youngsters, especially unchurched youngsters, to be in a comfortable relational setting where they felt free to ask questions. The groups grew steadily; Bellingham High

1. Joel 2:28.

School opened up its school assembly on the morning of Halloween to club leadership, and that night 150 students attended a Beta Sigma rally, followed by a hugely successful party in the main dining hall at The Firs.

The time was ripe and interest exceeded all expectation. Combined club attendance grew from an average of 115 in the first year; between 150 and 300 were coming out regularly in 1942. At a special rally in October of that year, five hundred jammed the Bellingham Hotel lounge, while others were turned away for lack of space. A weekly half-hour Beta Sigma broadcast over a local radio station extended the message even further. The blessings were more than just numerically apparent, however. Each week, club leaders (beside Grant, these included Ted Deibler and Ralph Hetrick[2]) saw teenagers turning to Christ in definite believing commitment, and going on in the faith.

Jim Rayburn came to Bellingham at Grant's invitation in 1942 to conduct a series of meetings that culminated in the regular spring young people's conference at The Firs. More than 250 were on the grounds for that final weekend and it proved to be one of the most memorable conferences to date. Jim himself recounted that the group included "many splendid Christian young people, a fine number of 'babes in Christ' just beginning to get going for the Lord, and a large crowd of wild kids from all over the Northwest":

> Saturday night I felt that I had to limit the testimony meeting in order to give the new kids a chance, so I said, "No one but first-timers and only those who are less than one year old in the Lord." Before the words were out of my mouth a little girl from Bellingham High, five or six months a Christian, with as radiant a testimony as I ever have witnessed, was up there by my side, pouring out her heart before those kids in genuine adoration for "the Lord Jesus Christ who died for me." For almost an hour they came . . . Several said, "It was right here in this room one year ago now, at our spring camp." Some said, "six months." But actually, most that came, moment by moment through that amazing hour, said "I have known the Lord twelve days!" or "I

2. Ted Deibler and Ralph Hetrick, both Dallas friends of Grant and Bernice, came to the Pacific Northwest at Grant's suggestion, serving successive pastorates at the United Presbyterian Church in Burlington, Washington and assisting in Beta Sigma clubs. Ralph Hetrick later served for a time on the staff of Young Life Campaign and then, after pastoring a church in Yakima, accepted a call to Calvary Church in the Pacific Palisades on the west side of Los Angeles.

> closed with the Lord three weeks ago tonight" or "It's just been a week since I found the Savior."[3]

The campaign received wholehearted support from the entire Firs family. In a letter full of Beta Sigma news, Otis informed friends that "It is my part to see that the young people of the district get in to the evening meetings. I have rigged a canopy for the truck. I carried fourteen last night."

The spirit of revival was unmistakable. Hundreds professed their new faith in Christ and their willingness to follow him in a life of obedient service. But the situation was not unique to the Pacific Northwest. The 1940s witnessed the most dramatic phase of youth revivalism in American and Canadian history as, almost simultaneously and apparently spontaneously, new programs and organizations burst into flower. In addition to Young Life, Jack Wyrtzen's Word of Life rallies and broadcasts, Youth for Christ, King's Teens, Child Evangelism Fellowship, Intervarsity and Interschool Christian Fellowship, and Nurses' Christian Fellowship, to name only a few, noticeably reshaped and quickened the evangelical youth culture in North America.

Late in the decade, spiritual renewal penetrated to the heart of Christian campus life as successive prayer revivals (some of which lasted for several days of continuous confession, supplication, and praise) swept over Baylor University in Texas, then other Southern colleges, and eventually Bethel, Wheaton, North Park, and Asbury, as well as several major schools in the west.[4] During a college conference at Forest Home in the San Bernadino hills near Los Angeles in 1949, a young evangelist named Billy Graham—president of Northwestern Schools, Minneapolis and former vice-president of Youth for Christ—entered a new phase of ministry; the four-week evangelistic campaign he had planned for Los Angeles was extended to eight, and hundreds of attendees, including some notable Hollywood celebrities, responded to his invitation to publicly declare their newfound faith in Jesus Christ. Such events received front-page treatment in the nation's newspapers.

The demands of follow-up and discipleship were, in the wake of such revival, enormous. Grant shared with other youth leaders a deep concern for the continued spiritual growth of new believers. As he reflected in

3. *Firs Fellowship*, December 1943.

4. For autobiographical reflections on the college revival movement in the 1940s, see McIver, *Riding the Wind of God*.

a *Firs Fellowship* essay in 1943, the need had been apparent also to Jim Rayburn:

> Through contact with the Navigators in Los Angeles and after much experimenting with their detailed materials designed to make the young Christian study the Word and witness for Christ, the Young Life Campaigners have perfected the very thing we have been praying for. As a result of much consideration and prayer while the Rayburns were with us, it was decided to make the Beta Sigma clubs a part of the Young Life Campaign and to use the material the Campaign had developed.

Grant became area director for Young Life in the Northwest region. In the summer of 1943, he asked Jim Rayburn to share his organization's strategy for reaching youth at a Christian workers' conference hosted by The Firs. Both Jim and Dawson Trotman came to the grounds for a similar gathering the following year, bringing their leaders and sharing also a joint Young Life/Navigators staff conference.[5] Dawson later expressed how much all the participants were encouraged by the ministry of Dr. Jack Mitchell of Central Bible Church, Portland and Multnomah School of the Bible, and of Dr. Wilbur Smith from Moody Bible Institute in Chicago, both of whom conducted seminars. "God sent them and they fed us. We did not realize how empty we were and how much we needed the Word. We came home with new spiritual vigor."[6]

This was the first visit of the Navigators to conference grounds; they were not long in returning. The Firs hosted a Navigators retreat in 1946, which brought Dawson Trotman, Lorne Sanny, Harold Chrisman, and eighty trainees for a weekend of intensive study and memorization. A relationship of mutual cooperation and support was quickly established.

Youth work was one of the most prominent but not the only aspect of The Firs' ministry claiming attention in the 1940s. Expansion in programming seems, in fact, to have been the keynote of the decade, and the complexity of the work proliferated as much as its volume. Added to the regular summer family conference and various young people's weekends

5. Jim Rayburn maintained a frenetic schedule throughout his life, though he suffered debilitating migraine headaches; the medications he was prescribed caused devastating side effects, including chronic insomnia. At a point of near-despair in his later years, looking back over decades of ministry, he recorded in his journal that he could remember only three times in his life, since founding Young Life, that he had experienced true rest. One was on an extended overseas sabbatical with his wife. The other two were at The Firs. Rayburn, *Diaries*, 445.

6. Skinner, *Daws*, 252.

were Christian workers' conferences, Christian teachers' conferences, business and professional women's conferences, and in 1949 the first couples' conference.

Grant, with the blessing of his father and the council, assumed more and more of a director's role with respect to all of this activity. He was also carrying a pastoral ministry—first at the United Presbyterian Church in Burlington and then at Broadway United Presbyterian in Bellingham—and teaching courses at Multnomah School of the Bible in Portland. In 1946 he reluctantly stepped down as Young Life area director in order better to cope with his other responsibilities. At Jim Rayburn's request, he retained an advisory role on the board of directors; he maintained, moreover, close ties with the organization and its leaders, continuing to encourage Young Life's use of the grounds and the contribution of club leaders to regular Firs conferences.

1946 was a year of celebration in the Whipple household, as Otis married Ruth Walter, whose love for the family and the work of The Firs went back to the days of the Modern Maidens' Missionary Movement. Ruth had been away from the grounds for ten years, serving as dean of women at several Christian college campuses. "Although domestically inclined," she was, by her own admission, "not domesticated by any means." And initially it "filled her with dismay to think of taking on a home and husband. But love won out and her gentle, patient, and long-suffering husband helped her through the crucial period of adjustment to being a housewife and acquiring a ready-made family, complete with grandchildren":

> Materially, they had little . . . When the newlyweds began housekeeping, their only furniture was a nest of teakwood tables from China and their wedding gifts. They had no car but rode blithely in the conference pickup. They settled down in what was expected to be temporary quarters (Bethany, a small missionary cottage) among the odds and ends of chairs, tables, and beds . . . Fortunately, happiness does not depend on costly or even harmonizing surroundings, which was well, for nothing matched. They had the Lord and each other, and it was fun and satisfying to do things together.[7]

Otis's intention was to begin construction of a new home on the grounds, using a wedding gift of money from friends on the council. He was

7. Aldrich and Whipple, *Firs of the Lord*, 82–83.

reluctant to prolong occupancy in housing that had been designated for missionary use. As plans were drawn and sites examined, however, the health of Ruth's mother, living in Portland, failed badly and both Otis and Ruth, who had intended to have Mrs. Walter come and live with them, now felt it was imperative that she join them as soon as possible. Getting a new home built would mean a long delay; some suggested that they stay instead at Bethany, remodeling and expanding it for their needs. The council and donors of the gift approved the revised plan and on Christmas day, 1947, a familiar Scripture was brought to mind with new forcefulness: "Enlarge the place of your tent." So, with a sense of joyful freedom, Otis settled down to his drawing board and another dream began to be actualized.

There were many blessings associated with the enlargement of Bethany, not the least of which indicated God's concern for the desires as well as the needs of his children. Both Otis and Ruth wanted a fireplace, but since it seemed a luxury rather than a necessity, they were reluctant to use any of the designated funds for that purpose. They created a wish list for God's eyes only, on which they wrote "fireplace"; any extra, unspecified personal gifts of money were put into a special envelope. "The day came when a decision had to be made so a place in the building could be prepared for it. Otis estimated the cost, without labor, as he intended it to be a do-it-himself project, and Ruth counted the money. He said, $175.00. She said $176.00."[8]

Furnishings were provided through friends and family, a miscellaneous collection that somehow came together to create a tasteful and harmonious décor. Some older pieces that badly needed refinishing or recovering were transformed by the generosity and expertise of Stanley North, a professional upholsterer from Vancouver. Other staff residences also benefited from Mr. North's skills, as did the many conference guests who were housed in the new conference dormitory, Sperry Lodge.[9] With borrowed sewing machines set up in the lodge's attic, he and his wife Winnie painstakingly made over old mattresses with new ticking and covers before the 1948 summer conference.

8. Aldrich and Whipple, *Firs of the Lord*, 86.

9. Named for Belle Sperry, one of the original council members and a faithful supporter of the work until her death in 1947. The legacy she left to The Firs allowed for construction of this spacious dorm facility, which had been on the drawing board for several years.

Among God's choice gifts to The Firs in 1948 was the addition of Doug and Helen Anderson to the resident staff. Biola graduates and friends of the conference for many years, Doug and Helen had already been offering frequent assistance in family and children's conferences. Out of their close association with the work grew a desire to commit themselves in a full-time way.

The Firs held an important place in Helen's heart, since it was here that she had as a teenager yielded her life to Christ. Subsequent summers had brought her back to the grounds to help in the conference kitchen. She and Doug met in Vancouver and attended Biola together; they were married in 1940, a year prior to their graduation. Youth ministry with the British Columbia Evangelistic Mission claimed much of their attention when they returned to Vancouver, while Doug resumed his employment as a florist, a position he had held for eight years before going to Bible School.

When the Andersons settled at The Firs, Helen took over registration responsibilities, freeing Helen Rutledge to give more time to her women's Bible classes (known as Maranatha Club) and the busy conference bookstore. Doug joined the bookstore staff for a time, but it was not long before his penchant for carpentry, his electrical and plumbing skills, and his scrupulous concern for building quality were put to good use on the grounds crew. He worked with Paul Toms on building and maintenance projects until Mr. Toms's death in 1951, then was put in charge of the department.

"Work, Uncle Doug-style" soon became something of a legend around The Firs. Doug's skills were many, and those for which he lacked formal training he soon learned by practice. His life's refrain was that "God is not looking for ability, but availability," a principle expressed in one of his favorite biblical texts: "Whatever your hand finds to do, do it with all your might" (Eccl 9:10). In this spirit he entered into the work of The Firs: no job was too big or too small, whether it entailed construction, remodeling, landscaping, wiring, or even directing Junior High conferences.

Physical work on conference properties always involved aesthetic as well as functional consideration. Otis was a lover of beauty, particularly the natural beauty with which God had so abundantly furnished The Firs. His letters are full of unabashed delight in the towering evergreens that had initially attracted him to the site, and in the seasonal concert of shrubs and flowers that dotted the landscape: "I have been wandering around the grounds a little. I found four dog-tooth violets. The trilliums are plentiful and the wild currants and daffodils and fruit blossoms are out. The 'snow on the mountain' along the walk west of the house, is also in full bloom. Canterbury bells are coming out, [along with] roses, snapdragons, sweet William, calendula, and many others." Doug, with his experience as a florist, was similarly appreciative of the natural aesthetic of the property, and eager to accentuate it. And in 1949, Ralph ("Pop") Riley brought to the conference, in addition to many other skills, an exceptional gift for gardening and landscaping.

Inside conference buildings an affection for simple artistry was similarly cultivated. While extravagance was out of the question, creative attention to detail and colorful touches were everywhere evident. As hostess of the conference dining room and later director of all food services on the grounds, Bernice Whipple was a gifted practitioner of the hidden art of planning, serving, and contextualizing meals with grace and thoughtfulness. The attractive array of good foods to which conference guests were treated deserved the appreciation so often expressed, and fresh-cut flowers in season or simple, decorative accents were the added signature of Bernice's love and hospitality. The humblest gesture of creative service presented itself as a gesture also of worship, "something beautiful for God."

When each conference ended, it was Helen Anderson's responsibility to oversee all housekeeping chores, making certain that accommodations were clean and ready for next arrivals. But registration tasks occupied most of her time. During her first year at The Firs, there were twelve scheduled conferences. A decade later, there would be as many in the spring quarter alone. But not all of these were at the Geneva conference center. By then, The Firs had grown to include three properties.

# 9

# Growth (1953–1958)

"Lengthen your cords, and strengthen your stakes,
for you shall expand to the right and to the left."[1]

THE STORY OF HOW FIRWOOD, the first of the two additional properties, came to The Firs can be seen, retrospectively, to have its beginnings many years previous to its actual purchase, in the conference's long association with Intervarsity Christian Fellowship. As far back as the early 1930s The Firs played host to Christian fellowship groups from various centers of higher education in the Pacific Northwest, including initially the University of British Columbia (Vancouver), and the University of Washington (Seattle); these were at first simply university conferences, since Intervarsity (which was imported to Canada from the U.K. in 1928) was not incorporated in the United States until 1941. From that point forward, except for a hiatus during the war years, Intervarsity and Interschool Christian Fellowship groups used the grounds regularly for youth gatherings and leadership training seminars. It was through these contacts and the close association of Bernice Whipple's parents with Intervarsity in British Columbia that Grant and Bernice came to know Cathie Nicholl, who was northwest regional director for the Canadian chapter of I.V.C.F.[2]

1. Isa 54:2–3.

2. Here again, a China connection is notable. Cathie Nicholl was born in China to Scottish missionary parents in 1910. She studied at Chefoo School, a Christian boarding school in Shandong Province, established by the China Inland Mission, until she was eighteen, then moved to Toronto and began what would become her life's work

In December 1953, while visiting the Atkinsons in their Vancouver home, Grant was invited to sit in on an Intervarsity camp committee meeting at which Cathie and a group of staff workers were present. Pioneer Pacific, Intervarsity's Thetis Island camp, had not yet been purchased, but a fact-finding study had verified the desirability of such a move.

"As I sat listening to all they'd been doing and to their whole philosophy of camping," Grant recalled, "I heard things I'd never heard before." The only camping which had been done at The Firs to this point was merely an extension of the normal summer conference program. The Firs had no recreational equipment to speak of, owned no boat, and had nothing in the way of a developed strategy or program for youth camping. Excited by the possibility of extending The Firs' ministry in this way, Grant shared his findings with the council. Cathie Nicholl herself made a lively, slide-illustrated presentation at a council gathering shortly thereafter and the idea began to take fire.

In the spring of 1954, not knowing really what they were looking for, Grant, Pop Riley, and Jessie Rogers (a seasoned leader with Camp Fire Girls, who was specifically enlisted for the enterprise) rented a boat and set out to reconnoiter Lake Whatcom. The whole of the twelve-mile lakefront was beautiful, but nothing particularly striking in the way of a potential campsite property was visible until the trio passed through a narrow channel between the lake's only island and a scenic wooded point jutting out from the west shore, where they discovered a magnificent sheltered bay. The motor was shut off and the boat drifted in: Pop stepped out on the white sandy beach and led the others in exploration of the point and the rugged, heavily wooded bluff that would one day be called Fircliff. While the property was not topographically well suited for residential use, it seemed ideal for an outpost camp. On the opposite side of the point from the beach, there was a sharp drop-off, perfect for boating and moorage. Between the point and the shaggy cliff was a level shelf, large enough to accommodate tents and a makeshift dining and eating area. The scenic off-shore island looked promising as well. For their own part, the three explorers were convinced: they had no idea who the owner was, but knelt together while Pop led in prayer that the Lord would make the property available to The Firs.

---

with the then-fledgling Intervarsity Christian Fellowship. For more on Cathie Nicholl, see the memoir edited by Wickett, *Cool Waters Beckon Me*.

Inquiry led Grant to the owner, Glen Corning, who gave his permission for The Firs to use the property for a two-week period during the summer. So it was that in July 1954 a group of thirty junior high campers and leaders set out from The Firs in rented canoes, paddling down the lake to what they called "White Sands." In the solitude and the rustic comforts of tent and tarp and campfire cookery, a good-natured camaraderie was formed. New skills were learned, as well as the disciplines of interdependent communal living. Barriers came down and dialogue between campers and leaders took on a depth and honesty that were in many cases unfamiliar to both. As camp came to an end, one youngster expressed aloud the desire of many: "Wouldn't it be great if the Lord gave this property to The Firs?" Another suggested that they pause and ask him. Heads bowed and camper after camper prayed—forthright, believing prayers. When the resident staff heard of the little company's faith, they added their own petitions. There was nothing further to do except wait, and certainly no funding with which to initiate any negotiations regarding a purchase. The answer, however, was not long in coming.

> In August of that summer a friend and supporter of The Firs heard about the camp and the campers' prayers. The story moved him to write to Grant, asking him to approach the owner of the property on his behalf to see if it might be bought. Surprisingly, Mr. Corning was willing to sell. Not surprisingly, the price seemed hopelessly out of range. The entire tract, with 2,600 feet of shoreline, could be purchased for $130,000.
>
> That price put everyone back on his heals for a bit. Because of the type of property, it seemed it would have to be all or none. There were several conferences between Mr. Corning and Grant, representing The Firs' friend. This friend had authorized Grant to offer $25,000. Later he upped it to $35,000. In order to sell the entire eighty-acre piece in one transaction, Mr. Corning reduced his asking price to $40,000. There the matter stood, with a $5,000 gap—and God . . . After a week of silence, Mr. Corning phoned Grant, asking him to come in to his office. There he told him how the night before his decision to hold to his price had crumbled. As he had been thinking about the matter, he was gripped by the realization of why The Firs wanted to buy this land. "I decided if there's one man in the Northwest interested enough in kids to invest $35,000 in them, I should be willing to give $5,000. So, my price is $35,000."[3]

3. Aldrich and Whipple, *Firs of the Lord*, 123.

Scarcely before anyone had time to draw breath, a whole new avenue of ministry had opened up, and one of the finest camping properties in the state was waiting to be developed, equipped, staffed, and opened up to campers. Jessie Rogers (almost immediately dubbed "Smokey") stayed on to provide expert advice and leadership in programming. Pop Riley added his long experience as a Y.M.C.A. athletics director, basketball coach, and camp leader, as well as specialized skills in archery, crafts, and recreation. Grant practiced the time-honored art of availability and learned as he went. Others came as the needs grew. Lois Spearin, superbly qualified for all phases of the waterfront program, and holding an Masters degree in counseling from Western Washington College of Education, joined the resident staff in 1956.[4] Jerry ("Unk") Wilson, who with his wife Milly was seasoned in church youth ministry in Spokane and Bremerton and an avid supporter of The Firs, served as Firwood's first camp director.

At first, Firwood was used as an outpost site for camps based at the main ground; when the wind blew from the north, gear was gathered and packed into canoes and everyone paddled. (Conveniently, such a breeze normally constituted a forecast of good weather.) The components of a "tent city" and such equipment as could be borrowed or rented furnished their stay. And when the wind changed, camp was dismantled and the return trip begun.

Construction of cabins began slowly with materials on hand and numberless hours of volunteer labor. Since there was no road into the property, all supplies and tools had to be boated and barged in each spring. By the end of 1956, six huts were built high on the rugged bluffs and roofed with cedar shakes by Doug Anderson and his crew. Plans were underway to construct a covered cooking and eating area, sturdily and inexpensively, from varnished, sized, and fitted log poles that Doug Anderson and Tom Walton scrounged from telephone and power companies.[5] But the "Longhouse," as it happened, had to wait. Doug was, from 1957 through the following year, preoccupied with yet another project—on Mount Baker.

4. Lois grew up in Bellingham as an enthusiastic proponent of outdoor sports and recreation; her involvement in the Bellingham chapter of Camp Fire Girls provided a great preparation for her many roles at The Firs.

5. Doug was famous for his creative scavenging on behalf of The Firs. Having let it be known around town that he needed timber or supplies he would sometimes get a call from utility companies about old poles they no longer had use for or simply find them along the roadside and then, with permission, salvage them for camp use. See also chapter 11, below.

"You shall expand to the right hand and to the left" (Isa 54:3) had long been a familiar and cherished passage to the Whipple family. But never had its literal fulfillment seemed so evident as in the middle years of the 1950s. The Firs staff and council had just begun to adjust to the idea of owning and operating a new eighty-acre camp facility six miles down the lake when Grant brought startling news about another incredible, unsolicited opportunity to expand in a whole new direction.

Mount Baker, a spectacular, craggy peak overlooking northwest Washington and the lower mainland of British Columbia, was well-known to conference-goers as a spot often visited during or after weekend gatherings. Only a two-hour drive from Bellingham, and paved to the summit ski area, it was easily accessible and became a favorite site for hikers, skiers, and photographers. The wider public had been slow in discovering the area, however, and in the mid-1950s the Bellingham Chamber of Commerce resolved to launch a promotional campaign that would introduce leisure crowds to their magic mountain.

In the late fall of 1955, a phone call came to Grant from a member of the Mount Baker Committee of the Bellingham Chamber of Commerce. "Has The Firs ever thought of operating a ski facility?" was the surprising question. There was a momentary pause until Grant's characteristic steadiness and composure kicked in: "No, not at all," he replied. "Might you consider building a lodge," continued the caller, "if a site was provided you at Mount Baker?" An explanation of the Chamber's objectives was offered and Grant listened quietly. What possibly could this mean? "At least give the idea some thought," was the parting encouragement offered to him as he hung up the phone.

For several days Grant thought about little else, and prayed for wisdom in meeting this extraordinary new possibility. A lunch meeting was called in which the Chamber's proposal was more fully outlined and Grant, in turn, explained a little about the history and character of The Firs, its faith principles, its financial policy, and its lack of available funds sufficient to consider construction of such a facility at this time. The men listened patiently and seemed not to be dissuaded; one agreed to make contact with the forestry supervisor about available building sites.

Several more days went by and then a call came from the forestry supervisor, who confirmed his support for the Chamber of Commerce plan and invited Grant to go up and look over the area. He would hold any site selected from within the designated building zone.

At this point, the situation was brought before The Firs Council. On the first Saturday of December 1955, Grant outlined the recent course of events. As the minutes from that meeting report:

> We have learned that there are some choice sites available to us without any charge to our organization. They seem to be very desirous of our entering into the area and are willing to hold property, giving us ample time to make plans and see whether funds would be forthcoming for development purposes. This whole project has been initiated from the outside, but in our thinking has opened up new possibilities, especially for winter usage. To our knowledge there is no Christian organization in the Northwest holding facilities for this type of recreational outlet. It might be that the Lord is wanting us to consider such a project and give Him opportunity to make provision, if this is His plan.

It was moved and seconded that Grant, on behalf of The Firs, should indicate interest in the offer, and if a promise of funds allowed for development of plans that would satisfy the forestry service, that the conference would then make a formal application.

On Monday of the following week, Grant, Pop Riley, and Doug Anderson bundled up and set off to spy out the land. As in the case of the previous expedition, when a lakefront campsite was the object of their search, the Lord led them, after hours of considering alternatives, to the recognizably perfect site. He had overseen to preserve it; the Forest Service had simply overlooked it. At noon, when it appeared every corner had been scouted, Grant asked the forest ranger if there was anything else at all that they might look at. After he paused and thought, looking out across the quiet snowscape, "Well, there might be. I don't know much about it, but there's something back by the ridge where we started."

Doubling back, they came to a rise just across the road from a small, ice-covered alpine lake which, they were told, was beautiful in summer. Wading in through waist-deep snow, they traversed a steep, semicircular ridge which hid a softly sloping valley (ideal for beginning skiers, they were already thinking), well away from the sight or sound of the road. It was protected, secluded, and utterly breathtaking: Mount Shuksan brooded over them to the southeast. "Is this a single site?" inquired Grant after they had circumnavigated the area. "Actually, I think it's three sites, said the ranger, "but I'll do some inquiring."

On Tuesday, word came that the Forest Service would be willing to release the sites as a single tract if The Firs decided to develop it. As potential barrier after barrier crumbled, expectancy grew.

Wednesday brought another amazing development. A letter and packaged arrived in the mail from a gifted architect on The Firs Council. Bill Trimble had left Saturday's meeting with his mind full of thoughts of an alpine ski lodge, and sleeplessness prompted him to spend most of the night getting his artist's conception of The Firs Chalet on paper. Finished and colored, it was posted to Grant the next day.

While things moved outwardly at an almost dizzying speed, Grant looked to the Lord for clear, specific leading. Like fresh, pure water from an unfathomable pool, several verses from Isaiah came back to assure him: "Enlarge the place of your tent, and let them stretch out the curtains of your dwellings; do not spare, lengthen your cords, and strengthen your stakes, for you shall expand to the right and to the left . . . For you shall go out with joy, and be led out with peace; the mountains and the hills shall break forth into singing before you, and all the trees of the field shall clap their hands" (54:2–3; 55:12).

So, scarcely a week after explaining to the Chamber of Commerce that The Firs was a work of faith, had no cash reserves, and moved ahead only when all were in agreement that the Lord was leading, Grant was back in the office with full council support, the promise of adequate funding, and—incredibly—architectural drawings in hand. The application was accepted and agreement formalized.

Details of construction and interior design, selection of contractors, and purchase of materials all took time. The property could not even be properly viewed until the following spring, when the snow melted. When Grant and his father drove back up the Mount Baker access road in July 1956 to survey, they found their snowy habitat transformed into a beautiful alpine heather meadow. Across the road, High Woods Lake glistened in sunlight. Shuksan, still icy, was majestic against a sapphire-blue sky. In her shadow, the first indications of the intended Firs Chalet were laid out with stakes and twine.

Building did not begin until late spring, 1957. Two Norwegian contractors, Ole Satermo and Ivar Kvernmo were selected from among several who bid for the project. Another gracious provision, for they were deeply committed Christians. The initial donation of $40,000 that had come into The Firs for the Chalet project was, it was felt, sufficient to get the shell of the lodge built and enclosed; equipment, tools, personal gear, and food were transported up the mountain and work went ahead (often from 4 a.m. to summer twilight at 9 or 10 p.m.) until the snow flew.

Material resources and volunteer help were provided in great bounty the following year. Carloads of men from the little Geneva community fellowship contributed many hours and kinds of labor under Doug Anderson's supervision. The father of a resident staff member, A.T. Wilson, built a fireplace and chimney. Ole and Ivar, once paid, gave extra labor at no cost, including construction of a four-story circular staircase, the pieces of which they precut off-site, according to precise measurements, and then took to the lodge to assemble. Staff and neighborhood women organized work parties to help with painting and cleaning and to provide meals for the workers.

In order to quell the impatience without dissipating the enthusiasm of avid skiers while the lodge was being built, and to acclimatize leaders to the prospect of winter camping, The Firs began to host ski camps in 1956. The main conference grounds provided the base of operations and bus and carloads went to Baker during the day. Dozens of used skis and boots, donated by a Seattle rental shop and repaired and refinished by Pop Riley, came as a particularly timely provision.

By the winter of 1958 the lodge was functionally complete and ready for use. A special pictorial feature of *The Seattle Times* in March 1959 described it as "a great A-frame building whose roof descends to the ground, designed to shed snow of any depth," then added details about the interior: ski shop, first-aid room, showers, and recreation area on the main floor; large lounge and kitchen on the second; and girls' and boys' dormitories on the third and fourth floors, all linked by an open circular stairway winding the entire height of the building. Members of The Firs staff were especially grateful that the article began by saying:

> A banner across a mighty beam in the lounge of the lodge proclaims, "In all thy ways acknowledge Him." That phrase sums up the purpose and intent of The Firs, a Christian camp and conference organization that is unique in the West. Behind The Firs is the idea that Christianity can and should be taught in daily living through activities familiar and loved by all ages. The ski lodge at Mount Baker is believed to be the only ski lodge in the nation built by a religious group.

In December 1958, fifty-five international students, many of whom had never seen snow before, shared a Chalet Christmas sponsored by the University of Washington's Intervarsity Christian Fellowship chapter. There could scarcely have been a more appropriate inauguration for the newest Firs facility on Mount Baker. In its thirty-five-year history, the conference had been instrumental in sending hundreds overseas in Christian service, as "witnesses to the uttermost." Now, within its own lodge, a representative company from fifteen cultures and almost as many religious backgrounds, gathered to share Christian fellowship and to celebrate the Lord's nativity.

It was beyond anything Otis and Julia Whipple could have asked or imagined as they hurriedly cleaned and renovated an almost derelict cabin and invited friends and missionaries to join them in the summer of 1921. And yet it was wonderfully consistent with all they knew of God's abiding faithfulness. Otis, who had watched the Chalet taking form, adding his own insightful comments as to detail (the massive three-story window that looked out on Mount Shuksan was particularly satisfying to him), did not live to see it completed or to hear reports of the international Christmas. In January 1958, in his eighty-fourth year, he died suddenly and quietly, without prior sickness or infirmity.

The funeral drew many friends, relatives, and acquaintances, those who had been in some way touched by Otis's unshakeable trust and selflessness. "He was a man of true humility," reflected Wilbur Smith in the *Sunday School Times*, "who never tried to promote himself." Willard Aldrich closed the simple funeral service with a challenge to all present: "This is a time when in memory of this life lived by faith, and in the presence of God, you and I should give ourselves anew to the service of the Lord Christ."

Tom Walton and his wife Patti carried the burden of those words home with them as they returned to Portland. Tom was cast back in thought over his own childhood years at The Firs and began to wonder if the Lord might have a place for him there. His current career aspirations were directed toward police work; although he and Patti had both studied at Multnomah, they had not anticipated going into full-time Christian service, certainly not, at any rate, in their own backyard. "This was the first time we really thought about The Firs," Tom remembered, "as a ministry we could maybe have a part in. Before that it had been just a place my father and grandfather and my relatives had lived. But the Lord put the thought in our minds at that time."

After much prayer and numerous conversations with Grant and the rest of the resident staff, the Waltons moved to the grounds, offering to help out wherever they were needed. A six-month provisional period was agreed upon, during which they covenanted to seek specific guidance as to the possibility of a long-term commitment to the work. The confirmation that came to Tom, after he abandoned fruitless efforts to interpret Scripture according to his own and Patti's needs, was in his regular devotional reading of the book of Deuteronomy: "The Lord your God has set the land before you; go up and possess it, as the Lord God of your fathers has spoken to you; do not fear or be discouraged" (1:21). The specificity of the directive and the assurance of God's care seemed overwhelmingly plain. Grateful that the certainty he sought had at last been given, he shared the day's revelation with Patti. "Oh those!" was her response as he pointed out the verses to her. She had read the same text a month or more before, but not wanting to influence Tom's decision, she had waited, trusting God to make the way clear to him. They shared their conviction with Grant and, with a clear sense of call, entered fully into conference activities. The timeliness of the Waltons' addition to The Firs family can scarcely be overstated. Tom was named manager of the Chalet, a position for which no one else on staff was comparably suited. With Lois Spearin, an experienced skier, he and Patti gave the Baker program outstanding leadership from the outset.

Taken together, Firwood and the Chalet represented an immeasurable enrichment of the program of The Firs. Increased capacity, an exceptional year-round schedule of camps and conferences, diversity and flexibility in programming (with potential for highly specialized ministries) were a few of the immediately obvious benefits. The new properties provided the ideal environment, moreover, for a whole new philosophy of camping and youth work that had been developing at the main grounds.[6]

Many ideas that Grant first heard from Cathie Nicholl and her Intervarsity coworkers were adapted to their distinctive Firwood form in the late 1950s. A modified decentralized program was introduced, and as such was activity-and-counselor centered rather than meeting-and-speaker centered. Camping skills and recreation were emphasized, creative adventure and fun freely celebrated. Counselors living in with a cabin of six or more campers provided spiritual instruction on a

6. While The Firs' two new properties were immediately christened Firwood and The Firs Chalet, the original Geneva property has been variously called "the main grounds," "the conference center," or "the retreat center" through the years. For that reason, these various designations are used interchangeably in this book, and without capitalization.

systematic basis through daily Bible studies, but also set the spiritual tone of a camper's experience through shared devotions, informal discussion and counsel, and personal example. A conscious attempt to eliminate sacred-secular dichotomies and to demonstrate that all things can and should be done to the glory of God gave campers a balanced, practical picture of the Christian life—one that they could take home with them.

Almost instantly, it became evident that there was in this kind of program outstanding potential for reaching non-Christian young people. Even parents without any religious affiliation or conviction were willing to send their children to a Christian camp if it was clearly a real camp. And youngsters themselves responded eagerly; Christian kids were readily able to persuade their unchurched school friends to come to Firwood. "My own idea of a Christian camp," said one seasoned leader, "had previously consisted of a baseball diamond, a couple of pine trees, a lodge, and a camp meeting area." Here, on the other hand, there was soon an excellent waterfront program, built up over the years with sailboats, canoes (including a full-scale replica voyageur team canoe), power boats, waterskiing equipment and scuba gear, as well as archery, riflery, crafts, and even horsemanship. Yet the emphasis on a genuine outpost experience was retained. Jessie Rogers set the spirit of things from the very beginning with her insistence on basic skills and basic equipment. A #10 tin can might serve as pitcher, salad bowl for gathered edible greens, or baking dish for a simple huckleberry cobbler. Overnights were a part of every camper's experience; whether they took home memories of the tent and tarpaulin encampment on Fircliff, fishing for crawdads at the "railway spot," swimming at Corning's Cove, or slipping over the smooth stones of a clear mountain waterfall into an icy pool, they remembered also the same huddled intimacy around a flickering fire that the first junior high group had known in 1954. One counselor's remarks regarding the outpost experience are typical: "I found it a highlight in my week as far as what could be accomplished spiritually. There is something about being totally away . . . out under the stars, just surviving together on simple necessities. Although Bible studies didn't always go smoothly, in the evening around the campfire there was a beautiful freedom of communication. A lot of questions and conversations about Christian things opened up."

The dynamics of such moments are always personal rather than strictly program or facility-related; as any veteran camper will tell you, "Firwood is people." People who commit their summers, sometimes at great financial sacrifice, to grow together as the body of Christ and share life with hundreds of junior, junior high, and high school students. Inasmuch as Firwood summer staff members give, however, they also receive, as do the churches and communities to which they return—better trained and equipped for mature Christian leadership.

Within a few years after Firwood's inception, applications were beginning to come in from former campers who wanted to return as members of the summer staff. These normally, if accepted, became counselors in training (C.I.T.s)—understudies to those who provided the real backbone of day-to-day ministry. In many cases though, because of their closeness in age to campers, C.I.T.s were able to penetrate barriers, build bridges, and open the way to the gospel more quickly than the older staff. They were thus given opportunity to exercise their own gifts as they learned and grew, after which many of them applied to come back as counselors.

A somewhat similar strategy of camping was adopted at The Firs Chalet, although the program itself differed considerably. Because ski camps were too short for a highly decentralized counselor-oriented ministry (many lasted only a weekend), informal meetings with a trained youth worker were the rule. Counselors, again crucial to the spiritual tone of camp, provided personal follow-up during the day and in an evening devotional and sharing time. Much of the day was left free for activity and recreation. Experienced skiers went up to the Mount Baker ski area, half a mile away, to test their skills against a variety of slopes. First-timers stayed closer to the lodge, learning a hundred ways to fall on the beginners' hill, while Tom Walton, Lois Spearin and others gave patient instruction. Still others braved an ice-crusted cliff on innertubes or toboggans, or sought the solitude of the white-blanketed forest on snowshoes.

It was anticipated and soon verified that the Chalet would have an even more significant outreach to unchurched young people than Firwood. "We've seen hundreds of kids come to know the Lord," reflected Tom Walton, "and any number of these tell us they'd never set foot in a church, but were willing to sit in on a few meetings if they could go skiing the rest of the day." Again, an effort was made to eliminate a secular-sacred dichotomy. One of the most startling revelations for many high school and college students at the Chalet was that Christians who obviously took their faith seriously did not take themselves overly seriously; they could engage in daredevil antics on the slopes, produce uproariously funny skits, and share games, meals, and conversation without holier-than-thou pieties.

In its first year of operation, The Firs Chalet was the setting for six ski camps, only one of which was sponsored directly by The Firs. The Intervarsity international house party, which became an annual event, set an important precedent for use of the lodge by Christian organizations and churches throughout the Pacific Northwest. In 1959 there were five Firs-sponsored Chalet camps of the twenty scheduled. That ratio increased somewhat in the 1960s. Each year, however, after The Firs' own program was set in accordance with availability of personnel and schedules at the other two properties, the lodge was opened up on a first come, first served basis to other groups. Thus, the blessings and the miracle of the Chalet were shared widely beyond the immediate, and by this time sizable, Firs constituency.

This was a reasonably new venture for The Firs. For many years, use of the main conference facilities had been scheduled almost exclusively by the ministry itself. Chester Rutledge's involvement with Christian Endeavor and Grant's work in Young Life, as well as personal contacts with the staff of Intervarsity Christian Fellowship and Navigators had, however, inevitably led to some relaxing of the policy. Then in the mid-1950s, just as Firwood was coming into being, it was formally decided by the council, and with the unanimous approval of the resident staff, that Christian churches and organizations would be permitted to use Firs properties, provided they affirmed agreement with The Firs doctrinal statement.[7]

7. See Appendix A.

# 10

# Fragrance (late 1950s–1962)

"Many of those who heard the word believed."[1]

THROUGHOUT THE 1950S, as conference facilities were being opened up for more extensive outside programming, the outreach of resident staff members was also, more than ever previously, being extended into the surrounding communities of Geneva and Bellingham. In 1957 Grant joined the Bellingham chapter of Rotary. The same year he was invited to serve on the St. Luke's Hospital Board. Mount Baker negotiations fostered relationships with representatives of the Chamber of Commerce and the Forest Service. Other civic organizations such as the Bellingham School Board later invited his participation. As these natural channels of cooperation and friendship with business leaders and town officials opened up, several men came to personal faith, and a men's Bible study was established.

Still other Bible classes had their beginning in the more immediate vicinity of The Firs. During the early and middle years of the 1950s, Geneva was experiencing a modest population boom. Scattered cottages and summer homes were being remodeled for permanent occupation as roads in and out of Bellingham were improved. Large lots and undeveloped tracts of land were subdivided and new houses built. What had long been a tranquil and predominantly rural community was becoming a quiet suburb from which people commuted every day to work. Among the newcomers to Geneva were several Christian women who, in expressing concern for their neighbors, decided to begin a home Bible

1. Acts 4:4.

class. Feeling somewhat inadequate to teach it themselves, and having had contact with The Firs through conferences, they asked Ruth Whipple if she would be willing to help. Ruth agreed, and the ministry was soon blessed and multiplied:

> Most of the women came at first out of politeness, secure in the assurance that they had no needs along that line. But gradually, as the Holy Spirit began to work through the Word, He brought light and life where there had been darkness and death. Then the women tried to tell their husbands, but it was all so new they had no adequate words. So, in a few months the men asked for a class for themselves so that they could know what their wives were talking about. It was formed with Grant as teacher and soon they were catching up with the women.[2]

Two years after this initial neighborhood study commenced, one of the women in the group received an unexpected appeal from a niece living in Bellingham. The young woman and a group of friends, "vaguely aware of the need to know something about 'religion' in order to answer their children's questions" were seeking direction for a course of study. Could she help? Sensing an opportunity, yet wise enough to realize that any suggestion of a Bible study as such would threaten and alienate, she simple agreed to meet with them to discuss possible approaches. Then she prayed, and took the matter to Ruth for counsel.

When the first evening gathering was held, Ruth too went along, and met a polite but guarded company of young mothers. They had not expected a Bible teacher. But as Ruth herself recalled, "Out of that jungle of their seemingly endless questions . . . emerged one that led to the heart of their unrecognized need. 'Doesn't it speak somewhere in the Bible about being born again? What does that mean?' In the give and take . . . all the other questions died away. It was a wonderful opportunity to pierce through the smog of their ignorance and unbelief."[3]

At least one woman came to understand and to experience spiritual rebirth that first night. Others followed as the class, which had been intended to last only a matter of weeks, continued for months and years. A husbands' group was formed as well, with Grant again as leader. Grant's own reflections on the emergence of these new home studies prompted him to reflect:

2. Aldrich and Whipple, *Firs of the Lord*, 113–14.

3. Aldrich and Whipple, *Firs of the Lord*, 115.

> The two men's classes seem to have come into being through a pattern that could possibly be significant in other similar situations. In each case a women's class preceded and in each case the class was predominantly non-Christian and consisted of individuals who were uninformed so far as Christian truth was concerned . . . A private home, casual circumstances, a group of men fairly well-acquainted with each other, together with a comparable lack of understanding in spiritual things, set the stage for these Bible classes.
>
> Attempts were made to follow a consecutive Bible study, but for many weeks pent-up questions dominated the class time even to the wee hours of the morning. Gradually, the Holy Spirit was able to get through not only to the minds of many of them but also to their hearts.
>
> The work of The Firs has been a real blessing to these couples, but now they in turn are being a great help and blessing to The Firs. Over and over again we have been grateful for a crew of these men who have helped out in times of special need. Dining room tables have been built, trees cut down and bucked up, materials hauled out into Firwood, and equipment to the ski chalet. All of this has been a labor of love because of a desire to see the Lord's work furthered through The Firs.[4]

The Firs' growing ministry to married couples was significantly reflected in its conference schedule throughout the 1950s. Couples' retreats had begun experimentally in 1949, but within ten years, their popularity exceeded that of almost any other conference held on the grounds. The concept, unique to The Firs at the time, was that each couple attending should bring, as guests, at least one additional couple with whom they were acquainted, whether or not they were Christian believers. In 1957 the fall couples' conference hosted 224 people at the retreat center; more than fifty couples were turned away because of housing limitations. As a result of this overwhelming interest, two identical conferences were planned for successive weekends the following spring, in order that all might be accommodated.

Meanwhile, a Young Life-styled outreach program called "Club 7-Teen" took four staff members—Lois Spearin, Bill Ogdon, and Paul ("Skip") and Renee Schilperoort (who had played an important part in the planning and design of the Chalet)—into high schools and homes in Bellingham, and to Mount Baker and Orcas Island, sharing the Christian

4. Quoted in *Firs of the Lord*, 115–17.

gospel.[5] Margaret Toms, a trained and gifted teacher, taught afternoon children's Bible classes in which fully three quarters of the local elementary school's students were enrolled. She also superintended The Firs Sunday School program and operated a kindergarten that mothers in the community had requested.

The kindergarten was a uniquely fruitful addition to the conference ministry. No one had initiated or even considered such a development but, using a regular preschool curriculum and Bible story illustrations, Margaret Toms answered the appeal and touched the hearts of many young children with Christian truth. They in turn carried these lessons home, recounting them to parents who sometimes followed up with questions of their own.

All of these activities added new strength to the little interdenominational Geneva community fellowship that had been meeting informally in The Firs lounge, with Grant as pastor, since Palm Sunday, 1952. In 1960 discussion was introduced at a council meeting about organizing a corporate body with a formal constitution and church membership. Some were hesitant at first, concerned that the conference's primary task was to serve area churches that were already established. But there had never been a church in the immediate Geneva community. Staff members whose responsibilities kept them on the grounds most weekends had for many years longed for a center of worship nearby. Now, with Geneva growing quickly and an increasing number of new believers in need of discipleship and fellowship, the time seemed right for such a venture. An arrangement was prayerfully arrived at by the council and community whereby the church would be organizationally distinct from The Firs—incorporated separately as Geneva Community Church, with its own board of directors and internal policies. A building site was provided by The Firs, through the generosity of Elden and Marian Whipple, on conference property but across Cable Street from the main hub of conference activities.

In 1962, a chapel designed by Chalet architect Bill Trimble was erected. Thousands of hours of volunteer labor as well as many generous financial gifts were contributed to the project. Doug Anderson supervised the work. The building was described in the February 1962 *Firs Fellowship* as "a simple sanctuary that will seat approximately 320 people. Its rustic design, heavy shake roof, stained glass windows, together with

5. Young Life itself had by this time phased out in Bellingham, its Pacific Northwest headquarters now being Seattle.

touches of native Shuksan rock, blend very naturally with the tall fir trees surrounding it." Long rectangular windows along the roofline let in the beauty of those beloved sentinel firs.

A year later, on February 10, 1963, the chapel was dedicated as a memorial to Otis Whipple, who had not only founded the ministry but also designed and built many of the buildings on the grounds. His son Grant continued in the role he had previously filled in the little lounge fellowship as the congregation's first pastor. Doug Anderson was named assistant pastor.

Large conference gatherings, from the very beginning, took advantage of this beautiful new facility. Even during the summer of 1962, before the building was complete, it proved providential for family conference meetings that were, for the first time in the history of The Firs, forced entirely indoors by relentless, torrential rain. The outdoor auditorium, rain-drenched, was abandoned as crowds huddled in the partially finished sanctuary across the street. "Boards were laid over the mud outside for walkways; tools, lumber, saw horses, and ladders were piled up at the rear of the auditorium; the cement floor was swept, folding chairs were borrowed and, for the first meeting, seating for over 400 was ready."[6]

6. *Firs Fellowship*, November 1962.

# 11

# Steadfastness (1960s)

"There are diversities of gifts, but the same Spirit."[1]

It is fitting that Isaiah's exhortation was not only to lengthen cords, but also to strengthen stakes, for with all the remarkable stretching and growth of the 1950s came severe testing. While those looking on saw two new properties, an enlarged full-time staff, and a year-round program as cause for celebration and a sign of unprecedented prosperity, few were aware of the day-to-day crises of faith which staff members faced as a matter of course. The maintenance fund was regularly low, with staff remittances at times four, five, even six months in arrears. The early experience of Otis and Julia—when the "Modern Maidens" and then the Rutledges joined the staff—came to mind; this seemed to be God's way of sifting, refining, and consolidating his family at The Firs.

The staff was drawn close in mutual support and prayer. There had never been a change in the "common purse" principle; the distribution of resources was solely according to need rather than rank or term of service. As in times of material blessing, so also in shortage: all met and shared as one in Christ Jesus.

The Firs Council was through these seasons bound more intimately to the fellowship. These friends knew the needs and labored in prayer while they gave of themselves in a hundred selfless, practical ways. Some could have, as many supposed they did, reached into their own pockets and made up the difference. But the clearest evidence of their own faith, and their faithfulness to God's work at The Firs, is that they too waited

1. 1 Cor 12:4.

prayerfully, responding with little or much as he directed. When gifts came in, therefore, they bore the mark of divine provision and specific, need-meeting care; sometimes, for his own reasons, the Lord seems to prefer loaves and fishes to several hundred *denarii.*[2] The Weyerhausers and the Blacks, for whom The Firs was a cherished spiritual home, were, with other members of the council family, gracious and generous stewards; their constancy in friendship and prayer was a mainstay.

It was through the administrative wisdom and foresight of Clarence Black that a new corporate structure and bylaws were created for The Firs. The need for modification of existing structures was, by the middle 1950s, more than apparent. Ever since The Firs had consisted of a few wooded lots, as many staff members, and only one yearly conference, all decisions regarding the work—from the selection of speakers to the location of a new building to the purchase of tools and building supplies—had been made by the council. Now, thirty years later, the complexity of the conference program, the legal and fiscal implications involved in stewardship of major properties, and the sheer weight of day-to-day administrative detail was such that staff and council members alike were becoming overburdened for lack of an appropriate distribution of authority and responsibility.

It was Clarence Black's suggestion, and the mutual decision of staff and council in 1954, that in order to facilitate operations the office of director and of chairman of the council should be made distinct and separate. Grant Whipple was named executive director of The Firs and vested with responsibility to administer and manage all functions of the work, within the policies established by The Firs Council, of which he was a member but not the chair.

Orderly and efficient procedural relationships began to take form. Over the next several years, Clarence Black, who was unanimously selected to be council chair, directed the process of continual evaluation and reorganization of the corporate structure with singular competence, gentlemanly tact, and quiet, Spirit-directed patience. Bylaws were drawn up, distinguishing a three-fold division of personnel: staff, council, and additionally a board of trustees.

The concept of a board was not new to The Firs, as a 1966 *Firs Fellowship* points out: "When the work was first incorporated in 1929, our founders envisioned both trustees and a membership. Because of the size

2. See Mark 6:37–44.

of the work at that time, however, these two bodies were made up of the same individuals. Each year at the annual meeting, the trustees would adjourn as a trustee board, then convene as a membership reelecting themselves as trustees for another year." In 1963 it was decided that while the council membership, with its essential ministry of counsel, prayer, support, and representation of The Firs in each member's home area, should continue to be enlarged, The Firs Board, conceived as the primary decision- and policy-making body, should be fixed at thirteen members elected from The Firs Council.[3]

Because of the reorganization of authority relationships, an unwritten principle of operation gained new significance, that of mutual submission. No longer did everyone do or decide everything: a representative group of council members, committed to the ministry of The Firs, were entrusted with that responsibility. And a spirit of humility and great faith—"trusting God to do his work in the other person"—was both demonstrated and commended by the executive director. Grant's unwavering adherence to the traditional spiritual principles that undergird The Firs and confidence that "in the multitude of counselors there is safety," combined with flexibility and openness to new leading, set the tone for board, council, and staff relationships. "We need the wisdom of our older members," he said in a 1965 council meeting, "but we cannot survive without the energy, enthusiasm, and vision of young men. We need to define and guard the distinctiveness of The Firs and, at the same time, be contemporary in our outlook."

The early 1960s brought a number of new young men and women into the ministry, among them another member of the founding family. Dwight Whipple, son of Elden and Evelyn Watson Whipple, joined the staff of The Firs in June 1963 after graduating from Fuller Theological Seminary. Main grounds operations, including editorial responsibility for all conference publications, as well as involvement in ski camps at Mount Baker, kept Dwight busy for the fall and winter months. Spring and summer were devoted largely to Firwood, of which he was named director in 1964. Under the able leadership of "DiDi"[4] (later shared with Judy Wyndham, "Putter," who became his wife in 1965), Firwood saw

3. Later increased to sixteen, but subsequently considerably reduced. At the time of writing The Firs Board has ten members.

4. At Firwood Dwight was known by the Chinese nickname (meaning "Little Brother") he acquired overseas as a boy.

increases in camper and staff capacity, new facilities, a more diversified program, and refinement of its leadership training emphasis.

An inductive Bible study curriculum developed by Don Anderson proved a tremendous asset to counselors as they opened the Scriptures to their camper charges. Don and his wife Pearl had joined the conference staff in 1962, bringing with them extensive experience in church and youth-related ministries. A graduate of Dallas Theological Seminary, Don had pastored a church in Paris, Texas and directed a Young Life club there, then moved to First Presbyterian Church in Bremerton, Washington as a youth pastor. When called to The Firs, Don was named youth director at Geneva Community Church and fitted into a variety of conference operations. Among other things, he pioneered a day camp ministry at The Firs, which was to become a major feature of the conference's outreach to children. For Firwood leaders and campers, his "Grassroots Bible Studies" may have been his most significant and enduring contribution to ministry at The Firs.[5]

In 1967 a strategic addition to Firwood's facilities and program was made through the purchase of Reveille Island, a twelve-acre, heavily wooded, undeveloped property just one hundred yards from the shoreline where Grant, Pop Riley, and Jessie Rogers had first set foot more than a decade earlier. There had long been a bit of mystery and lore attached to Lake Whatcom's only island, due largely to a fanciful narrative published by self-styled Whatcom County historian Worth Wilson Caldwell in an October 1922 special edition of the *Bellingham Sunday Reveille*. The story that, in his words, "clings like the tree moss on the evergreens," concerned the fateful demise of Anola, a beautiful young First Nations maiden and her lover Altama who, with their loyal companions, were attacked by an enemy tribe during the couple's wedding banquet on the island and chose death by drowning rather than an ignominious surrender.[6] It was,

5. Don was later founder and executive director of Pine Cove Camps in east Texas; he retained strong ties of friendship with The Firs and its leadership and returned frequently to speak at camps and conferences.

6. In Caldwell's recounting, the two tribes in question are identified as "Haidas" and "Nootkas"—neither of which has any connection to Whatcom County; he likely intended Nooksacks for the latter. It would now seem that the whole story was plagiarized and adapted (with no change to the protagonists' names) for local consumption by Mr. Caldwell from a virtually identical nineteenth-century tale from the Mississippi gulf coast. In "The Legend of Singing River," Anola is "princess of the Biloxi tribe" and her lover Altama, "chief of the Pascagoula tribe"; when threatened with enslavement by hostile marauders they sing a doleful chant and, hands clasped, wade to their death in the Pascagoula River.

like the infamous "Maid of the Mountain" yarn, too good a story to pass up, and generations of Firwood campers would hear "the island legend" recounted around an evening campfire, as C.I.T.s hidden in the woods offered their own mournful "death-song" accompaniment at a strategic moment in the telling.[7]

A Firwood camper found an arrowhead on the island shelf in 1969, and though there is little documentation of tribal encampments along Lake Whatcom, the lake was almost certainly once frequented by indigenous hunters and fisherman. The island was logged several times in the 1800s, its trees boomed and floated six miles down the lake to mills at Larson. In 1891, Reveille Island was deeded to Leslie A. Jenkins, who homesteaded on its shores. George A. Jenkins, brother of the original owner and a shrewd Bellingham entrepreneur, acquired the property with the intention of developing an amusement park and resort for well-to-do townspeople. But plans fell through and the land was turned over again "in consideration of the sum of ten dollars and other valuable considerations" to Leslie A. Jenkins.

It was many years later, when the property was owned by Lou Tusing, that The Firs first expressed interested in Reveille Island. Not long after Firwood was purchased, Grant made contact with Mr. Tusing, who had moved to Alaska and had no immediate intention to develop the property. Although unwilling to sell at that time, the owner very generously gave exclusive permission for its use to The Firs. A pattern repeated itself; the island became a popular overnight spot and the site for various special events in the weekly camp schedule. Campers prayed, much as older brothers and sisters had prayed for Firwood itself, and one counselor, certain that God would answer, began an "island fund" by contributing small regular amounts toward its purchase. Early in 1967 Mr. Tusing offered the property for sale, and through the generous gift of a friend of The Firs, ownership was secured. Subsequent years have proven how crucial was the timing of this acquisition. With lakefront property being bought up all around Lake Whatcom and a major land development corporation moving in next door to Firwood in 1972, the island provided a crucial buffer. It became increasingly easy to imagine

7. The Reveille Island legend was revisited in June 2024 by students and a videographer from Western Washington University, who produced a short investigative film, "Loose Ends: Ghost Stories of Lake Whatcom": https://www.youtube.com/watch?v=WOnOfoLw85s.

what kind of impact alternate ownership and development would have had on camp.[8]

For all of its expanded and diversified ministry to youth and adults in the Pacific Northwest, The Firs had not lost sight of its founding commitment to support and perpetuate foreign missions. In 1964 a whole new area of overseas missionary activity opened up through a letter home from Chester Rutledge's son Don, serving with the Central American Mission in Guatemala. Without specifically requesting anyone by name, Don lamented the lack of experienced laborers to build a much-needed guest house at the mission's headquarters and asked if anyone could be spared to provide short-term assistance. Chester knowingly took the letter to Doug Anderson.

The note awakened a thirty-year-old dream and unexpected opportunity to fulfil a promise. While Doug was still in his teens, he had vowed that he would go, if the way ever opened up, to a foreign mission field. But could he be spared at The Firs, and how would the necessary funds be provided? Obstacles were removed one by one as The Firs Board wholeheartedly endorsed the project and granted a leave of absence; Geneva Community Church offered financial support. Helen agreed that her own contribution to the venture would be to stay at home with the family, continuing her registration duties at the conference office. In January 1964 Doug set off on his first missionary journey. Several months later he was able to report: "With the help of a national crew, I placed the anchors for the 350' radio towers of Central American Mission's TGNA and completed the guest house foundation. I was so thrilled with the accomplishment and with the privilege of helping our missionaries that I asked the Lord to give me ten more trips."[9]

God honored Doug's prayer and prospered his labor, sending him back the next year, with an enthusiastic volunteer helper, Howard Smiley, to finish the guest house. Two Washingtonians, John Braithwaite and Lloyd Wiebe, along with George Reel from California, joined Doug in 1966 as he went back for a third time to construct classrooms for Robinson Bible Institute (now Guatemala Bible Seminary).

8. Ten years later, another strategic addition was made to Firwood when the contiguous Baker property, long used by Firwood overnight campers, was purchased from a would-be developer. For more on the "South Cove" purchase, see Appendix B.

9. Engels, "Calloused Hands." TGNA Radio was the first evangelical radio station in Guatemala and now has transmitters also in Belize, Honduras, El Salvador, and Mexico.

Then, early in 1967, a call came from Japan to help build a lodge for a Conservative Baptist Bible Camp, "Camp San," and with great cheer Doug responded once more:

> The mission agreed to have the foundation finished and I began praying for a good, husky carpenter to help me enclose the building in three months. The Lord sent me a 75-year-old retired manual arts teacher. The person who met us at the airport later confided, "I thought he looked like he needed a rocking chair more than he needed three months of hard labor in the mountains of Japan." However, Lloyd Hazelton proved he could keep up with anyone half his age and his professional knowhow was exactly what we needed.[10]

As the plane touched down at Hanada International Airport in Tokyo, Lloyd confided to Doug, "I'm seventy-five, and this is the first time I've stepped out and done anything for Jesus Christ." Others who accompanied Doug on his mission ventures expressed similar sentiments.

For Doug, one of the joys of this first term in Japan was the sense of continuity with the work pioneered by Otis Whipple over forty years earlier just across the East China Sea. With the assistance of local volunteer helpers, Camp San's lodge was erected and enclosed on schedule. The next year brought Doug back again with David Fast, a retired cement finisher, and Norm Zucati, a building contractor from Centralia, Washington, whose church provided generous financial support to the trip. In two and a half months, aided by missionaries and nationals and with tools supplied by hardware dealers in Bellingham, the three men finished the lodge—laying the last floor tile half an hour before the dedication service scheduled for midafternoon of their final day on site.

When calls for short-term missionary help continued to come and it became evident that Doug was to be given at least the ten trips he has requested (including return trips to Japan and Guatemala, as well as Indonesia), a foreign outreach department was established as part of the regular ministry of The Firs. Doug began to carry word of the prospects and blessings of this new adventure into schools, churches, and service clubs. His challenge was radical, yet eminently practical:

> I am convinced that we as laymen can revolutionize world missions by adding a new dimension to our present missionary program. We send out missionaries and support them with

10. Engels, "Calloused Hands."

> prayer and finances, but they need laymen to do physical work for which the missionary has neither time nor training . . . We need more missionaries, but we may not have time to train another generation of them. We had better help those already on the field.[11]

Even while he was away, Doug was tireless in sharing his vision for lay missionary assistance. One of his co-workers in Guatemala nicknamed him "Postcardo Anderson" in recognition of the 250 postcards mailed to interested friends over the six-week period. During his first two trips to Japan, he sent out more than fourteen hundred cards.

Response was gratifying, and the blessing redoubled. Numerous churches, catching Doug's enthusiasm, recruited and financed lay teams from their own congregations for short-term missionary projects. And among those who joined Doug on each of these trips, many returned on their own, either as short-term helpers or, in several instances, as full-time Christian workers. For Doug himself, these experiences proved enormously satisfying; he and Helen were delighted when their oldest daughter Jean, following the Lord's leading, stayed on in Guatemala permanently. Their two other daughters, Janice and Barbara, later joined her on short-term missions.[12]

During all of this time, physical work at The Firs' own properties continued apace. Indeed, each of the years Doug was called overseas proved to be extremely busy also at home. A number of new staff men were added to the buildings and grounds crew during these crucial years. Tom Walton and Ed Rogers were already very busily employed, as were Al and Belle Muench, who helped in the buildings and accommodations departments of the work respectively from 1962 to 1967.[13] Earl Moore first offered his versatile and able assistance in 1964 and Bill Knaus, an experience painter and electrician, moved with this wife Florence to The Firs in 1967. In early 1968 the Lord brought Jim and Grace Summers from Vancouver, British Columbia into the resident conference family. While Jim's specialized construction welding skills were put to immediate

11. Engels, "Let Joe do it!"

12. Barb Anderson met her future husband, Bruce Vander Meulen, on one such trip; they would in 1986 join the resident staff of The Firs, not long after Doug and Helen retired. See more on the Vander Meulens in chapter 15, below.

13. The Muenches' son Frank would join the resident staff of The Firs in 1972, following his service with the Army Signal Corps in Bangkok, Thailand during the Vietnam War. He and his wife Linda (née Rasmussen) were to serve in various capacities, notably as Firwood caretakers, for more than four decades.

good use, Grace served in the housekeeping department until assuming responsibilities as dining room hostess and coordinator of women's ministries.

An account of the Summerses' call to The Firs provides an insightful footnote to the couples' ministry which continued to flourish throughout the 1960s. When Christian friends invited them to attend a couples' conference in 1961, Grace and Jim hesitated. The idea of attending any kind of religious gathering was new and somewhat threatening, particularly to Jim. Grace was more amenable, since the chance to do some shopping in Bellingham appealed to her; they decided ultimately to come.

"We were impressed," Grace remembered, by the whole atmosphere. There was something here which we had never encountered." No special coaxing was necessary to bring them back to a later conference. Fears and reluctance vanished as they felt themselves remarkably at home in what had seemed at the outset such an alien environment. The more they learned about the work of The Firs and God's faithfulness in blessing it over the years, the more irresistible became the tug on their own hearts. They began to give up vacation time to help on the grounds. It was the unmistakable evidence of a living God at work in the lives of these people whom they were coming increasingly to love and respect that finally pierced their agnosticism: "The Chalet story impressed us tremendously," observed Jim. The breakthrough for both came at an Overseas Missionary Fellowship (formerly China Inland Mission) conference in 1965, when both responded to a speaker's call for commitment. "We hadn't discussed it. It was utterly unexpected for both of us, and very unlike us. We were amazed at ourselves."

Not long afterward, Jim and Grace began to consider making application to join the resident staff of The Firs. The likelihood of their being accepted was minimal, they thought, but they wrote and waited. Young as they were in their Christian experience, the Lord began to lead them through periods of financial uncertainty and discouragement, giving them difficult but invaluable schooling in the life of faith. The Firs responded to the Summerses' application with a conditional "yes," pending immigration clearance. Papers were sent to appropriate centers of officialdom and another period of waiting, trusting, and refining commenced. Finally, after a year of patient and prayerful seeking after the Lord's will, the Summers were summoned to an immigration interview. With no illusions about obtaining easy clearance, but with expectancy nonetheless, they met with a customs official, where the transcending of bureaucratic obstacles was breathtaking.

"What will you be doing at this place, The Firs?" asked the officer.

"I'm not exactly sure," replied Jim truthfully.

"How long will you be there?"

"We don't know."

"How much will you be earning?"

"I haven't any idea." (In order not to be influenced in their decision, they had deliberately refrained from inquiring about staff remittances.)

After twenty minutes of such questioning, the incredulous official granted clearance to the equally incredulous Summers, and the matter was settled. They arrived at the conference grounds with sons Kerry and Ken in April 1968 and set up housekeeping at El Nathan.[14]

Their new home and various other buildings on the grounds received a much-needed facelift after their arrival, when the resident staff was swelled by the arrival of forty Navigators during July and August. A six-week work and study program was one of the new fruits of Grant's long association with Dawson Trotman and the Navigators organization. Working four hours a day, six days a week, the trainees contributed over five thousand man-hours of labor. (Some preparatory groundwork had been done by members of the University of Washington rowing crew, who lived and worked on the grounds for a March training camp.) Most of the rest of the Navigators' waking hours were devoted to Bible study and Scripture memorization. This first cooperative work and study venture was so successful and mutually beneficial that the program became an established feature of the summer season schedule. The second summer program saw the Chalet transformed inside and out: the lodge was painted, walks and a patio built, and the grounds landscaped. At Firwood, the Navs' efforts combined with those of pre-camp volunteers and C.I.T. men to produce a new rifle range and swim dock, as well as to upgrade the access road into camp.

14. In the family's nearly twenty-year tenure at The Firs, Grace proved to have a special genius for programming women's conferences (with notable speakers including Kay Arthur, Elizabeth Elliot, June Hunt, and Jill Briscoe), as well as luncheons and coffee hours. She was imaginative in her planning and oversaw events with seemingly effortless elegance. In the mid-1980s, she and Jim responded to an invitation to join the staff at Cedar Springs, a Christian retreat center in nearby Sumas, Washington, started by well-loved friends of The Firs, John and Katherine Bargen. (Ironically, it was while Katherine was attending a Firs women's conference in 1974 that her husband, driving around Whatcom County on his own, first encountered the property that would become Cedar Springs.)

A narrow, steep, and twisting access trail had served Firwood's needs for many years, since virtually all food and supplies were boated to camp from the conference center down the lake. It was, however, the scene of a tragic accident in June 1966, when Bill Welch, a local tradesman and long-time acquaintance of The Firs, was leaving Firwood after a day of assisting with camp preparation chores. On a particularly steep section of the route, the tractor he was driving stalled and overturned, pinning him under it and killing him instantly.[15] He had been working with the grounds crew only three days, recalled his widow Marya, and had never been happier. His sense of spiritual peace and wellbeing were such that just days before his death he had spoken with serenity and assurance of his readiness to be called into the Lord's presence. Marya and her infant daughter Lorie retained their Bellingham residence for two years, then moved to Miami, where Marya served as a bookkeeper and secretary with the West Indies Mission, Logoi, and her local church. In 1975 she returned, almost in spite of herself, she said, but with conviction that the Lord was leading, not only to Bellingham but to the resident staff of The Firs.

Improved access to Firwood, while an enormous boon to summer staff, campers, and visitors, was also an obvious potential liability during those months in which camp was vacant each year. In 1968 the Lord answered a prayer of many years with the provision of year-round resident caretakers for the camp property and equipment, thereby alleviating fears of off-season vandalism or intrusion. Henry and Beth Baumgart, whose daughter Marybeth was a veteran Firwood presence, moved to their newly finished apartment above the Longhouse just after the 1968 summer season. When staff and campers met them for the first time in 1969, they were immediately adopted as "Mom" and "Pop."[16]

Simultaneously, Firwood came under new directorship. Dwight and Judy Whipple were led into pastoral ministry in Oak Harbor, Washington in the fall of 1969, but a replacement was ready in Jon Aldrich ("Zeke"), a member of the large "mixing bowl" clan of Doris (née Coffin) and Willard Aldrich. Jon and his wife Linda ("Zing"), both Multnomah

15. The Welch Building, part of Geneva Community Church's Christian Education complex, was named as a memorial to Bill.

16. When the Baumgarts took up ministry near Tacoma in 1975, Frank and Linda Muench moved to Firwood as resident caretakers, exchanging housekeeping responsibilities at the retreat center, which they had shared since 1972, for supervision and maintenance of camp property and buildings, a role they maintained for fifteen years. Frank was not only an able handyman but an incorrigible prankster and engaging story-teller; he and Linda were much loved by Firwood staff and campers.

graduates, came to the conference in June 1969 directly from Dallas, where Jon had earned a seminary degree. They fitted in as needed in several areas of conference programming, then spent the summer months at Firwood. Jon formally assumed his new role as director in November.

Jon's creative "boot camp" approach to leadership impressed itself upon the staff in memorable ways that first summer. C.I.T.s remembered being stunned out of a sound sleep one night toward the end of a rigorous leadership training week to perform unfinished chores. By the time everyone was convinced that the persistent airhorn alarm was not a figment of their collective imagination and managed to dress in the dark and report for duty, grim good humor turned to collective amusement. Work went ahead until daybreak, with some in the Longhouse kitchen striking up verse after verse of "I've been workin' at Camp Firwood all the live-long day," with a raucous pots and pans accompaniment.

The whole leadership structure at Firwood was considerably firmed up under Jon's direction, as was the counselor-in-training program. Outpost camping took on a new look, as extended backpacking, sailing, canoeing, and horseback trips were introduced. Additional recreational class options, including rock climbing and a popular "waterfront smorgasbord" entered into campers' daily menu. It was "Zeke" Aldrich who gave Firwood its cable slide and first proved that (a) a well-manned team canoe, and (b) sixty fleet-footed campers on shore, with rope-and-pulley contraption, could pull a water skier. But many remember also his thoughtful, probing Fireside talks, richly illustrated with his own Sugar Creek Gang-like childhood on the Aldrich family farm near Portland.

Jon's mother Doris had, on the occasion of The Firs' twenty-fifth anniversary, written regarding the faithfulness of God in honoring the founding principles of the work so dear to her own experience:

> Each worker knows that he comes to The Firs looking to the Lord alone for support. Through experience and time, a system of handling funds has been worked out. It is similar to that of the China Inland Mission. All bills for running expenses, which include utilities for each staff residence, are paid first. There is an estimated basic monthly allowance per person, and when there is sufficient, each is given that amount. But if there is not enough, whatever is on hand and not designated is pro-rated and each receives a share. Needs are mentioned in prayers before the Lord. The staff, with the council, of which some are a part, look to God for his supply and He has never failed.[17]

17. Aldrich and Whipple, *Firs of the Lord*, 72.

In 1970, as The Firs celebrated its fiftieth anniversary, the principles and practice of financial operation under which Jon and all other members of the conference staff were serving had scarcely altered. Over a period of years the board had considered, discussed, and prayed about potential changes in the stated financial policy, with the result that greater liberty was given to staff and council members to share specific needs of The Firs with those expressing interest in the work. There was some concern that the very adherence to the policy of silence had created confusion as to the faith commitment of the conference, and a feeling that the integrity of the work would be better safeguarded by some clearer public stance with respect to the manner of operations.

While the policy on paper was relaxed in this way, the underlying principles of The Firs remained firm: promotional fundraising, appeal letters, and financial solicitation were eschewed. No offerings were taken up; no work was undertaken without assured funding. And staff still came to the grounds on a missionary basis, aware that their only guarantor of material support was the Lord himself.

As Grant explained, "If our primary motivation is to get people to give, then we don't want to even mention needs. But if the motivation is to avoid concealing things or creating false impressions or having the effect of minimizing prayer, this is something else. The distinction is very difficult—so very little, still, is ever said." A board member who participated in decisions related to the revision of the policy added his own reflections, conveying something of the impact of Grant's openness and submission to board directives:

> The historic foundations of The Firs are still very much a reality, although perhaps less apparent than once they were. Observing Grant over the years, both in his staff role and as a gracious board member, one could see transparent integrity and total commitment to the fact that God's work done in God's way would never lack God's provision.[18] We have learned together, and through his example, that however much we personally may want to see a new building, program, or staff appointment we should primarily pray about it and then move ahead only as the Lord clearly led us and provided the means for its realization. We

18. This conviction, often repeated by Grant Whipple and others at The Firs, owes to one of Hudson Taylor's most famous quotations: "Depend on it. God's work done in God's way will never lack God's supply. He is too wise a God to frustrate His purposes for lack of funds and He can just as easily supply them ahead of time as afterwards, and He much prefers doing so."

> don't want anyone to feel burdened with the work or to invest anything apart from the Lord's leading; we don't want to express needs in an environment which embarrasses anyone. We would want, rather, as the Lord leads and *only* as he leads, to suggest what we may regard as needs in an environment where they might be recognized as opportunities, and where people would be joyful in getting involved.

Joyful involvement has as many expressions as participants. Some slip money into one of the unobtrusive offering boxes located on the grounds. Others send a check earmarked for camper scholarship funds. A nearby resident deeds her house to The Firs, asking only that she be allowed to live there for the duration of her lifetime. A nursery owner donates hundreds of rhododendrons and azaleas to be used in landscaping. A council member purchases new ski equipment for the Chalet. Friends offer to lend horses and riding tack to the summer camp program. In this way, as rookie Firwood staff members are reminded each year during leadership training week, every building, every piece of recreational equipment, even the ground underfoot, is a gift, a trust, from the hand of God. There is nothing ordinary or commonplace about even the least of the resources which surround you at The Firs; all has about it the fragrance of prayerful self-offering. And one learns, over time, to take little for granted, much for grace.

Some gifts seem to fall almost inexplicably from the divine treasurehouse without passing through normal intermediary channels. When the Firwood kitchen needed to have its old galvanized steel dishwasher runner replaced, Doug Anderson asked the Lord about it. Shortly afterward, stopping at a roadside restaurant while out on a round of travels, he noticed something shiny in the grass beside the building and went over to investigate. Remarkably, there it lay: a nearly new stainless steel runner, almost exactly the right size, certainly serviceable, and obviously discarded. Doug found, by asking, that it was a castoff of recent renovations in the restaurant kitchen; he could have it for a pittance. The transaction was simple and the problem of getting it back to The Firs was solved when other restaurant guests, who had a large vehicle and were heading to Bellingham, agreed to deliver it. Doug arrived home to find that it was already there waiting for him.

"After a while," observed another staff member, "you come to expect such things. When your eyes are wide open to the mercies of God you notice gifts that others overlook." So it was that glass, window sashes, doors, concrete bricks, and other materials for one reason or another regarded as worthless by companies that manufactured them were left, like sundry sea-gifts at low tide, for conference use. Those for which no immediate use was apparent were carefully stored against the day a projected building expansion project—part of a ten-year comprehensive plan being drawn up for the main grounds—got underway.

The desire for a master plan for orderly and systematic growth at the conference had been on Grant's heart for many years. Discussion at board, council, and planning committee levels remained rather preliminary and tentative until Bill Graham, a city planner from Vancouver, British Columbia, hearing of and expressing interest in the project, quietly and generously offered his services to The Firs. The expertise he brought and the hours he gave resulted in a masterful ten-year plan and a bilateral land use contract with Whatcom County—the first such agreement county planners had ever seen. The contract detailed all projected expansion, including housing units, parking facilities, and enlarged recreation areas that The Firs intended to proceed with as funds came in over a ten-year period. The quality of Bill Graham's proposal won immediate respect for him and the project in the county and the Bellingham business community; local officials sought his advice regarding the establishment of zoning regulations in the Bellingham area, and not only watched with interest but also offered generous assistance toward the realization of The Firs' comprehensive plan.

There were many who already had a high regard for operations at The Firs. Through Grant Whipple's and Doug Anderson's personal relationships with men in the downtown community, many, irrespective of their religious convictions, expressed warm interest and confidence in the work. In 1974 some watched with admiration as a crew of men led by Doug Anderson installed an internal sewer system on conference grounds.

An improved sanitation system was the one major prerequisite to furthering and upgrading facilities on the grounds; the comprehensive plan could not have proceeded without it. Although the matter had been discussed at length by staff, the final go-ahead came swiftly and decisively from without. In 1968 The Firs, as well as all of its near neighbors, received notification of the formation of a Local Improvement District. Sewers were to be installed throughout the Geneva/Lake Whatcom area by district engineers—with allocated costs being assessed to property owners. For the first time in the history of The Firs, long-term financial obligations were imposed from outside.

This new intrusion of external authority into internal policy was a matter of deep concern and prayer for resident staff and council alike. Again, there was a tremendous stretching and strengthening, as the letter of longstanding policy regarding debt was challenged. Submission was necessary and submission chosen, without any change in the spirit of commitment to "owe no man anything."

"In a way," one council member observed, "it was indicative of the Lord's sense of humor to bring us to this point by such a strange vehicle. A sewer system of all things. And something which we all were so anxious for." God's loving interest, moreover, was demonstrated in an almost miraculous outpouring of material resources. Several unanticipated bequests and gifts provided for a major portion of the materials and hookup costs. Moreover, while district engineers worked along Cable Street, Doug Anderson and a crew of staff men—with less experience than faith, courage, and commitment to perform this task "as unto the Lord"—completely installed the internal system at The Firs. One who looked on said, "As I watched that man do sewer work and listened to him share the project with us in board meetings, I was more touched and broken by what I was seeing and hearing than I can reasonably express. It was a *spiritual* job he was doing! He took untrained men in those holes with him and they did exceptional work, professionally and quickly, at minimal cost. The quality of the work and the speed with which it was completed was such that the licensed professionals expressed open and sincere admiration."

A labor of love. The kind of "Joe job" that Doug gave himself to, at home and abroad, for the sheer delight of serving his Master, and the kind of humble ministry that forms the daily routine of all who work on the grounds. Answering phones, preparing accommodations, fixing and serving meals, repairing equipment, handling correspondence, servicing vehicles, pulling weeds. Over it all, God writes the superscription, "Not in vain," which is also an encouragement: "Therefore . . . be steadfast, immovable, always abounding in the work of the Lord" (1 Cor 15:58).

# 12

# Evergreen (1970s)

"I bow my knees to the Father of our Lord Jesus Christ, from whom the whole family in heaven and earth is named."[1]

One of the oldest departments of The Firs benefited very particularly from the main grounds comprehensive plan. The Firs Bookstore, since its relocation at the conference center in 1961 (under Jerry and Milly Wilson's management), and with the addition of Hank Chamberlin's impressive administrative and marketing experience to its operation, had increased its clientele and inventory so substantially that expansion of facilities became in the early 1970s a major priority.

Hank and Betty Chamberlin's relationship with The Firs dated to the 1950s, during which time they attended the men's and women's Bible classes taught by Grant Whipple and Ruth Whipple respectively, and then became active participants in the little Geneva community fellowship. During the construction of the Geneva Chapel, Hank provided indispensable help in organizing volunteer work parties. Betty became conference bookkeeper in 1963; shortly thereafter, Hank retired from a management position at Sears in Bellingham to join the resident conference family. Together, and with the assistance of an able staff, the Chamberlins greatly increased the volume and enhanced the selection of Bibles, study and devotional aids, and a full range of Christian literature, music, and stationery available at the bookstore, making their corner of the grounds a favorite haunt both of conference-goers and neighbors in

1. Eph 3:14.

the immediate Bellingham area. The store also became a principal supplier of pastoral materials, Sunday school curricula, sheet music, and related items to churches throughout the Pacific Northwest. Enlargement of its floor and shelf-space both reflected and anticipated its increasingly significant role in the overall conference program. The Firs Bookstore was to become the largest Christian bookstore (and one of the largest independent bookstores) in Whatcom County.

It was always regarded as a ministry rather than merely a business, however. Many came in just to browse or to find a gift, while others, troubled by personal problems, were looking for Christian counsel or comfort, or simply for conversation. To meet customers with an attentiveness to their spoken or unspoken needs required a rare gift of sensitivity along with thorough knowledge of the store's holdings. Marylou Ogdon, who worked in the store for many years, was cherished for just such qualities. Every new book that came into the store she somehow found time to read; every new person she found ways to listen to, share with, minister to. Many recalled her pointing them to "just the right book" or simply taking time to converse with them about her own spiritual experience. Her heart was captive to her Lord; she loved to serve him in serving others.

In the last few months of her life, troubled by weakness, pain, and fatigue, Marylou continued to work as much as she was able. A council friend who came into the store one afternoon remembered speaking to her of her soon approaching death. There was a wonderful expectancy about her; she talked as one about to embark on a journey for which she had been preparing all her life. Two weeks later she had indeed gone home—joyful, tranquil, radiant with anticipation. Her carefully guarded savings from a life of selfless labor were left to The Firs, with an expressed desire that they be used in the simplest and most imaginative of ways, to remodel the conference snack shop as a place of relaxed, informal fellowship and conversation. A beautiful addition to the "Cookie Jar," with comfortable sunken hearth area, was built as a memorial to Marylou's lovely, animated witness and her generous stewardship of the Lord's gifts.

Such "beautiful, godly people," reflected Barb Kinloch, are themselves the priceless authentication of the Lord's living presence at The Firs. There is something compelling and challenging in the very simplicity—the unspectacular but thoroughly convincing sanctity and trust—that one associates with those closest to the conference that continually draws others, as it drew her, to identify with the ministry.

Barb and her husband Greg had both been Firwood campers and later camp and conference leaders before being accepted to the resident staff in 1971. They were, in fact, something of a Firwood institution by then, having shared the summer immediately prior to, and all three following, their marriage in 1968 with hundreds of campers who knew them only by their camp nicknames "Smudge" and "Smear."

Greg served as program director and assistant camp director under Jon Aldrich in 1969 and 1970 and then, after coming to the conference on a full-time basis, worked year-round with him in evaluating, planning, and setting guidelines for the orderly expansion and growth of Firwood. Creative programming experiments were devised to help compensate for the increasingly noticeable encroachment of civilization around the once-quiet shores of Lake Whatcom. In the fall of 1972, he and Jon oversaw production of a summer staff manual that formalized the philosophy, policies, and procedures of the camp program. Organizational relationships were clearly outlined. The counselor-in-training program was modified to allow more direct, in-cabin apprenticeship of young leaders by matching each C.I.T. with a counselor partner. A detailed but flexible leadership training curriculum was devised.

When Jon and Linda Aldrich left to take up ministry in Nacogdoches, Texas in 1973, Greg was named camp director. Barb continued to be involved with him in leadership of the summer program and spend her summers at Firwood, although she was also by this time a very full-time mother. She felt a little like Lucille Ball, she jested, having her family "born on T.V." When, on the last Friday of camp in 1972 it was announced that Jason had at last come into the world, everyone at Firwood burst into raucous applause. The youngest Kinloch was an instant celebrity. Another son, Jonathan, arrived a year and a half later, and was treated to similar fanfare during his first year at camp.

The summer staff itself, in a decade of increasing cultural dislocation, began to take on an overwhelmingly family profile. "To me," wrote a C.I.T. on an end-of-summer evaluation, "Firwood means meeting brothers and sisters, seeing campers become part of the family." A senior counselor offered simply, "For me, Firwood means a kind of second home." And as beneficiaries of each other's love, staff members ministered healing and provided models of loving Christian relationship to many for whom it was completely unfamiliar. "It hasn't been a calculated change on our part," Greg observed, "as much as a response to a change in our campers. It used to be that kids who came from troubled or separated or divorced families were the exception. Now they are the rule. They need love in a very basic way: they need brothers and sisters, and they need a counselor to be not only a friend but the kind of parent figure they may never have had. The biggest crises we have to deal with at Firwood now, as distinct from the sixties, are not related to drugs or smoking or drinking, but home and family life. Instead of rebellion we are meeting apathy, loneliness, boredom, and despair in the faces and the lives of camper after camper."[2]

Letters from adults who attended conferences on the main grounds and at the Chalet reflected similar issues: "I came with many needs. My marriage was in a shambles and my emotions on the verge of exploding. I needed concrete answers as to how to handle myself as a Christian wife and mother"; "I find it very hard to put down on paper how I feel, but I do want you to know how much this conference has meant to me. I have just recently given my life completely to Christ. It took a real shock—my husband left me—to bring me to the realization that I needed God"; "We have been through two years of varied and many problems and heartaches and this weekend has been a rewarding and refreshing and uplifting time which was badly needed."

For Barb and Greg themselves, the experience of integrating their personal and family lives with their camp life both challenged and enriched their own relationship. And Firwood's first truly homegrown campers, Jason and Jon, began to learn very early the security and blessing of a colorful and varied eternal and spiritual family. These were lessons reinforced daily in the routine of life on the main grounds. "I think of Uncle Doug," reflected Barb, "who in his quiet little ways took time with my boys, teaching them the meaning of work while offering, from their point of view, an exciting challenge: how many nails could they find hidden in the grass and stones around a building or renovation site? Or of Uncle Chester, bringing out his two-pound coffee can, letting them sift through all the beautiful agates he had tumbled."

The inheritance of such "uncles" and of a whole new family of "in-laws" was part of the experience of every staff member who took up

2. The turbulent sixties—which featured cultural revolution at home and a contentious overseas war in Vietnam, in which some Firs and Firwood personnel served—had an impact on camp, bringing the first serious exposure to alcohol and drug abuse. But mature leadership (the average ago of staff members was increased from seventeen to nineteen) and an exceptional staff/camper ratio permitted remarkable stability. The effects of the Jesus Movement and charismatic renewal were also felt in many lives; radical challenges prompted radical discipleship.

residence at The Firs. It could be a little overwhelming at first, admitted Jan Hunter, who with her husband Colin joined the resident staff in 1976. But a healthy sense of balance and perspective was fostered, and an understanding of the importance of individual as well as corporate identity. Said Jan, "I will never forget or cease to appreciate Bernice Whipple's advice to 'raise my children as if no one was watching'. She anticipated my apprehensions perfectly, and her warm, practical wisdom was exactly what I needed."

Such wisdom, extended to the whole area of family life on the grounds, in combination with the compelling presence of Christlike lives and a pervasive atmosphere of prayer and faith, hospitality and love, goes a long way in explaining the consistency with which staff children accepted, affirmed, and identified personally with all that The Firs represents. The conference was not a typical or perfect environment in which to grow up, but neither was it restrictive or insular. Many to whom the grounds were home went on to Bible school or seminary and subsequently ventured into some form of full-time Christian service. Others carried their Christian experience and conviction into a variety of secular professions. But virtually all aligned in vital personal ways with the ministry and retained deep ties of love and commitment to The Firs.

The third generation of Whipples were among the Firs-raised young adults who, with a consistent, understated witness, continued to open doors to neighbors and strangers alike. In the middle 1970s, Grant and Bernice's son Bruce and his wife Lillian were, while juggling many aspects of family and community life, conducting a Bible study in the upper floor of the Geneva Fire Hall near the conference property. Most attendees were university and college grads in some way connected to Geneva Community Church, with one notable exception.

Mike Gowan had been raised in Walla Walla, in southeast Washington State, in an Irish Catholic family. Eldest of six children, he grew up in a religion-soaked milieu: he served as an altar boy, was proficient in the Latin of the Mass, went to a Catholic high school, and then attended Gonzaga University before graduating to the life of many young rebels of that era: protest, idealism, and self-indulgence. When his father died unexpectedly at fifty-one, so did God, in Mike's mind: how could a good God permit such tragedy, leaving his mother bereft and impoverished, with young children to care for? Angry and without clear direction, Mike went back to school, this time Eastern Washington University, where his questions about the meaning of life went unanswered by his atheist professors and he began to sink into depressive bouts of drinking. The one campus group that opened a crack in his skepticism was Intervarsity Christian Fellowship. Its members reached out to him with kindness and with persistent openness to his argumentative questions. God began to reveal himself in small ways and large—initially as the "something" or "someone" behind the visible universe, and then, through a Bible study in Colossians, as "Jesus Christ . . . the image of the invisible God." Still confused but now intent on answers, Mike bumped around in several locations among various denominations, including Baptists, Pentecostals, and Seventh Day Adventists. (His mother never stopped hoping he would return to the Catholic fold.) Eventually, feeling that he needed to start over in a place he'd never been, he moved to Bellingham, where God was, of course, waiting for him. After meeting and engaging in contentious debates with local members of the Unification Church (informally known as "Moonies"), Mike became convicted that Jesus was, in fact, "the way, the truth, and the life" and that "no one comes to the Father except through [him]." In his own words, Mike at last surrendered his life, "on his terms, not mine." If not exactly, like C.S. Lewis, a reluctant convert, he was still a somewhat cantankerous one, unwilling for glib and easy answers. When he joined the Bible study in the old Fire Hall, he was introduced to the book of Ephesians, a veritable "constitution" of kingdom values and the Christian life. Bruce and Lillian Whipple were "the best, kindest, smartest, most loving, and welcoming" of interlocutors, through whom he also connected with Grant and Bernice and eventually also Bruce's brother Dick and his wife Sharon. It was in a later small group of post-college professionals led by Dick and Sharon that Mike met his wife Heather.[3] Together they would attend retreats, volunteer in a church-based project to serve local widows, and partner with The Firs in various capacities for decades to come.

Ever since Isobel Miller learned to love Julia Whipple as her spiritual mother, The Firs has been a haven of hospitality for those actively seeking the Lord and for those as earnestly running away, seeking to evade the "hound of heaven."[4] The family circle has often widened to welcome

3. Heather's faith journey was very different from Mike's. Having grown up in an atheistic/agnostic home, she came to faith as a young adult through the ministry of Intervarsity Christian Fellowship at Western Washington University and then studied for a time at the Dutch campus of L'Abri.

4. Francis Thompson's famous poem of that title bears witness to the relentless, loving pursuit of God: "I fled Him, down the nights and down the days; / I fled Him, down the arches of the years; / I fled Him, down the labyrinthine ways / of my own

"adopted" children. Grace and Jim Summers, whose sons Ken and Kerry were raised on the grounds, found themselves responding to brokenness and extending their own family in the mid-1970s by taking in a sixteen-year-old foster daughter. While seeking the Lord's specific guidance, they were led in their regular devotional reading to Luke 10 and 11. The parable of the good Samaritan and of the friend at midnight seemed to speak directly to their own and Michelle's situation, but it was a commentary note that confirmed absolutely the answer they were seeking: "If a guest comes to your house, the Lord will provide."

This was a promise believed, and proven, decades earlier by the Whipples, and written deep on the heart of The Firs. In love the loaf is offered, in faith broken. And God's sufficiency is made known to all who have eyes to see: a miracle story. As Chester Rutledge once confided, with a thoughtful smile and a gentle shake of his snowy head, "There's not a single thing I know of around The Firs that *isn't* a miracle story."

---

mind; And in the midst of tears / I hid from Him . . . "

An early cabin at Camp Firwood.

Firwood campers, outdoor Bible study (1950s).

Firwood's iconic Longhouse, before additions (early 1960s).

Firwood sailors (1960s).

The "white sands" swim beach at Firwood (1960s).

Firwood staff, 1970, including Barb and Greg Kinloch, standing, far right.

Winter view of The Firs Chalet on Mount Baker (1960s).

The Chalet in summer, with Mount Shuksan in background (1970).

Chalet campers enjoying a "cold plunge" (1980).

A full house at the Chalet.

# 13

# Succession (1977)

"We your people, the sheep of your pasture, will give thanks to you forever; from generation to generation we will recount your praise."[1]

SEPTEMBER LIGHT TOUCHED THE TOPS of evergreens and flickered over gardens, lawns, and a cluster of cedar buildings. The large summer conference crowds were gone. The happily chaotic comings and goings of Firwood campers and staff had ended with the last days of August, as all returned to classes and other fall responsibilities. There was the slightest chill in the air, subtly evoking a change of seasons.

Council members who were together for a weekend of fellowship, consultation, and prayer, carried their own thoughts about with them quietly. Impressions still lingered from the previous evening—a slide presentation illustrating more than fifty years of conference activity. Many were seeing familiar corners of the grounds with new eyes, recognizing within or beyond present landmarks the cottes and cabins, tents, and auditorium which had once comprised The Firs. The rippling laughter of Julia Whipple, the frank, thoughtful reflections of Otis, the sweet poignancy of Doris Coffin's singing, the exuberance of an un-auditioned choir, and the prayer and praise of many former staff and council members mingled, in memory and imagination, with the sound of wind in the tree boughs.

In the quiet front room of Bethany—the old missionary residence enlarged and remodeled for newlyweds in 1946—a graduate student

1. Ps 79:13, ESV. This chapter is a revised version of the "Epilogue" to *Work of Faith, Labor of Love.*

just beginning to research the history of The Firs sat chatting with Ruth Whipple. Reminders were all around them: a photo of Otis on the coffee table, his well-thumbed and heavily annotated Bible, lovely furnishings representing the gracious provision of the Lord and the generosity of many friends, the fireplace for which there had been just enough money, and books. Histories and biographies mostly. Instructive, godly memoirs that helped shape those who shaped The Firs. In answer to a question about the origins of the conference, Ruth went to a bookcase and took down three precious volumes, A.T. Pierson's classic biography of George Muller and the two-volume account, by Dr. and Mrs. Howard Taylor, of Hudson Taylor's life and labors: *The Growth of a Soul* and *The Growth of a Work of God*. She recounted how she had been led to read these books before she had even heard of The Firs, how they introduced her to, and helped prepare her for, a life of radical dependence on God as her trusted provider. Then she began to highlight some of the amazing instances of God's faithfulness during the years since first she joined the staff, many of which are recounted in the early chapters of this book.

As this conversation continued in one peaceful corner of the grounds, several cars bearing Washington, Oregon, and British Columbia license plates were pulling in off Cable Street onto conference property. By midafternoon, nearby residents and friends from Bellingham had begun to arrive as well. The hush and solitude of the day was replaced by a hubbub of welcome and reunion. The occasion? A reception to honor Grant and Bernice Whipple and express appreciation and best wishes as Grant retired from directorship responsibilities at The Firs.

Grant had been a frequent, if unassuming, recipient of recognition in the recent past. When, little more than a year before his retirement, word came from Wheaton College that he had been named Alumnus of the Year, he remarked off-handedly to Bernice that he was sure there had been a mistake. Even when finally convinced that the information was accurate, he protested that his "only claim to fame was longevity." An article in *The Bellingham Herald* the following week (June 13, 1976) offered a more realistic assessment, noting that Grant's involvement with Christian Camping International (as the organization's first president, from 1962 to 1965, and later as chairman of its board of trustees), his service on the St. Luke's Hospital Board and with Bellingham Rotary, and his role as national board chair of Bible Study Fellowship,[2] in addition to

2. Grant met Audrey Wetherell Johnson, a British-born C.I.M. missionary, in 1950. Forced out of China and living temporarily in the Bay Area of California, Audrey

his nearly forty years as a staff member and then executive director of The Firs might have had a bearing on his selection. Mention might also have been made in this article, entitled "Someone Special," of his six years on the Bellingham School Board, twenty years on the board of Multnomah School of the Bible, and twenty-five years on the board of reference for Overseas Missionary Fellowship.[3] Grant's continuing responsibilities, in fact, were sufficient to ensure him of a very busy "retirement."

Most, however, of those who gathered in the conference dining room on that September afternoon in 1977 knew Grant as a neighbor, a pastor, a servant leader, a man of vision and man of faith, a mentor, a friend. His own and Bernice's love and influence had touched them in ways impossible for any newspaper to document.

Walt Warkentin, in bringing greetings on behalf of Christian Camping International and Hume Lake Camp, spoke of Grant's quality of life and witness rather than his many accomplishments and distinctions. Harvey Chrouser, Wheaton College faculty member and director of Honey Rock Camp, whose interest in Christian camping was born at The Firs, related how Grant's personal spiritual demeanor had impacted him ever since they were classmates at Wheaton. Several board and council members spoken of the fruits of their long association with Grant and Bernice. Many others, including Vivian Gunderson (still teaching, still active in V.B.S., and still attending conferences at The Firs every year) and Mrs. Charles Hone, whose husband pioneered the boys' conference ministry in the late 1920s, likewise conveyed their own gratitude and best wishes. The Whipple family itself was well represented at the gathering;

---

traveled with a new acquaintance, Alverda Hertzler, to the summer conference at The Firs, where she was delighted to reconnect with fellow C.I.M. exiles. In 1952, she began to teach a small women's Bible study that would eventually grow into an international ministry called Bible Study Fellowship. Grant not only employed some of Miss Johnson's teaching methods in neighborhood Bible studies held at The Firs, but served on the board of directors of B.S.F., including as chair. See Johnson, *Created for Commitment*. Alverda Hertzler, who felt a call to Christian service at that same 1950 Firs conference, worked alongside Miss Johnson for three decades as B.S.F.'s administrator.

3. The China Inland Mission, after decades of extraordinary hardship and persecution as well as extraordinary fruitfulness, was forced to leave China after the Communist takeover; all C.I.M. missionaries departed the country in 1950. The following year, the mission was reconstituted under the new name, Overseas Missionary Fellowship, with headquarters in Singapore and an outreach into other East Asian countries. The continuing legacy of the C.I.M. in China is recounted by Taylor's grand-nephew A.J. Broomhall in the magisterial seven-volume series, *Hudson Taylor and China's Open Century* and the more succinct *Shaping of Modern China*; see also Austin, *China's Millions*.

in addition to Otis's widow Ruth and a healthy sampling of Lois's and Elden's families, all of Grant and Bernice's children where there, along with grandchildren. Anyone looking on and looking back had cause to be reminded how blessing, too, is often visited on the children, to the third and fourth generations. Yet none of these had been called into full-time work at The Firs. The occasion was thus historic in another sense; the responsibility of directing the conference was, that same weekend, entrusted to new hands.

Dick and Char Eley joined the resident staff of The Firs in the spring of 1974, when Dick was named director of public information and programming at the conference center. For two years they enjoyed a busy initiation to the work, focusing shared energies on the multifaceted summer schedules of day camp, adult retreats, and other ministries. In 1976, as consideration was being given to the appointment of a successor to Grant, the board named him executive assistant. In that role, he apprenticed himself both to directorship responsibilities and to the person whose temperament, commitments, and life principles had profoundly molded the corporate character of The Firs. Now, a year later, Dick stepped into a major new role as executive director of the ministry.

Like many who found their way to a place of ministry at The Firs, the Eleys were led by a circuitous route. A native of Pontiac, Michigan, Dick met Charlotte Dalke from Powell, Wyoming at Northwestern College, Minneapolis in 1959, at which time he was studying to become a music teacher. Music and sports had always occupied much of his life and he entered upon this course of study almost unreflectively. Three years into a program of music education however, misgivings about teaching prompted him to transfer to the business school. Following graduation, he found work as an accountant in a Minneapolis manufacturing firm, enjoying what he assumed was the beginning of a lifelong business career. He and Char married in 1961, and served together as youth sponsors at Bethesda Free Church, bringing their combined talents in music and recreation, teacher training (Char had studied elementary education at Northwestern), and a natural affinity for young people to the task. Their giftedness was noticed by a church board member, who suggested that Dick further his biblical training and consider a call to full-time Christian ministry.

September 1964 found the Eleys in Grand Rapids, Michigan, at Grace Bible College. In order to make ends meet, Dick took on a youth pastorate at the local Berean Church and worked part-time in a friend's company. During his final year at Grace, he interned at another Berean congregation in nearby Muskegon, overseeing Christian education, youth ministry, and music. That position continued after graduation and, with a growing family (two young sons, Todd and Brent, had by now arrived), Dick put thoughts of seminary on indefinite hold. In 1967 a call from a Minneapolis college friend who pastored a church on the west coast opened up a new opportunity, this time at Seattle Berean Church.

It was while overseeing the Christian education program with their new congregation in Seattle that Dick and Char first encountered The Firs. Accompanying kids to the Chalet on Mount Baker for a winter retreat, they were smitten with the location, the program, and the whole idea of a recreational ministry of this kind. As contact with The Firs expanded to include junior high retreats at the conference center and leadership workshops at Firwood over the next several years, the Eleys' interest in closer affiliation with the conference began to crystallize, and when Greg Kinloch visited the church for consultation with youth pastors in 1972, Dick was ready with a query: how could one become a part of the resident staff at The Firs?

Channels of communication were opened up but no position became available until 1973, at which point a call came indicating that they would now be considered. Through a series of interviews with Grant Whipple and Doug Anderson, then with the entire resident staff, the Eleys were introduced to the history and principles that gave The Firs its distinctive character. The financial policy and faith basis of the word were discussed at length. Doug challenged Char and Dick to seek specific leading from Scripture so that they would be able to discern a clear call of the Lord; their faith would need to be tested and validated at the outset, he suggested, if they were to be sure of their readiness for the countercultural adventures and trials of a faith ministry.

The Eleys prayed and wrestled honestly with their doubts and hesitations: were they really ready to give up the privilege of owning their own home and the security of a dependable monthly income? In March 1974, following the counsel of Prov 3:5–6 ("Trust in the Lord with all your heart, and lean not on your own understanding; in all your ways acknowledge Him, and He shall direct your paths"), they arrived with Todd, Brent, and their youngest, Jeff, to take up residency at The Firs. They came to appreciate the wisdom of having a clear call early on; for several months, there were insufficient funds to pay staff remittances. The Eleys' savings drained away and the temptation to second-guess their decision was at times overwhelming. A hard but good process, Dick later recalled, since it knit his family into the fabric of the work and taught them firsthand something of the experience of those who had labored here before them. "It is essential to the future of The Firs that we not just dwell in a philosophy but actually live on our knees," he observed:

> We need to be growing in our prayer life, to be entering into a deep sense of prayer partnership with one another. And above all, giving the communication of our concerns with the Lord himself far greater priority than any discussion of them with people. We must plan intelligently and steward gifts responsibly. We must be ready to adapt our resources to changing demands . . . God is asking us to be faithful, as he always has. Our tradition, passed on to us by Otis Whipple and Grant, is that of Taylor and Muller—a tradition which teaches that no work like The Firs can ever belong to a person, a staff, or a board but only to God himself.

# *Endurance in Hope*
# 1978–2025

# 14

# Transition (1978–1984)

"And we know that in all things God works for the good of those who love him, who have been called according to his purpose."[1]

IN STEPPING INTO HIS new role of executive leadership at The Firs, Dick Eley brought a young man's energy and vision, as well as a background in business. He followed Grant Whipple's example in joining Rotary and other local civic organizations, building rapport with businessmen and community leaders in Bellingham and the surrounding area. He had a strong instinct for public relations and marketing and used those networking tools to build The Firs "brand" locally. He brought in several new staff members, including "Skip" Utech, Dan and Sally Moore, Mike Johnson, a Geneva local and old hand at Firwood who had just completed his Masters degree in biblical studies, Jim Schmotzer, another Firwood alum, and Jim Fosse, a Wheaton grad who had been a member of the Eleys' Berean Bible Church in Seattle. Mike Johnson ("Fonzi") took over the reins as director at Firwood, freeing Greg Kinloch, who had been Firwood director for over a decade, to become the overall program director for The Firs' three locations. Dan Moore became the conference business manager. Jim Fosse was initially employed at the conference center, but then took over as manager of the Chalet—a job he relished until the demands of an intense schedule and considerable isolation that precluded socializing and even church attendance most weekends caused him to rethink his options. For a single guy who hoped to marry and have a family,

1. Rom 8:28, NIV.

Mount Baker did not afford the greenest pastures.[2] Jim Schmotzer, who had previously worked at both Firwood and the day camp for several summers, took over leadership of the Fircreek program in the fall of 1979 and would add a new Firs Preschool program to his responsibilities in 1981. Dick had been his "summer supervisor" for several years and was an advocate and mentor when he and his wife Connie joined the full-time staff.

Most of those in this new crew, including Dick himself, were serious athletes, and the basketball court on the conference grounds was soon busy with spirited pick-up games before and after work and even during coffee breaks. Some of the staff and neighborhood kids got involved as well; Jon and Jason Kinloch, who honed their hoops skills at The Firs, were both impressive multi-sport high school athletes who would go on to collegiate careers in basketball.[3] The three Eley boys were likewise high school standouts in various sports and competitive gym and court rats.[4] Mike Johnson's son Ben was, like his dad, an avid basketball player. Even a relative old-timer, Hank Chamberlin, who was a Western Washington University hall-of-famer and had played in an adult professional league and officiated locally, joined the fray.[5] The energy and *esprit de corps* was palpable; The Firs was soon enjoying its own informal "fellowship of Christian athletes."

Dick saw himself as a bridge, he observed, from a family-founded and family-run organization to one poised for new ventures and a new identity that would give it equal status and prominence with other Christian camp and conference centers in the United States. The desire of his heart was, in his own words, that The Firs should become "the Forest Home, Hume Lake, or Mount Hermon" of the Pacific Northwest. With

2. Jim returned to Seattle, where he met his wife Marcie and enjoyed a storied thirty-three-year career at the Seattle Fire Department.

3. Jon, who achieved state and national recognition as a shooter even in his early teens, was Sehome High School's all-time scoring leader in multiple categories before heading to Gonzaga University for his college career. Jason was also a prolific high school talent and played college basketball at Trinity Western University and Seattle Pacific University.

4. Todd and Brent Eley were high school football standouts at Sehome High School.

5. The Chamberlins' grandson Roger, Jason Kinloch's teammate on the Sehome basketball team, went on to collegiate success at Multnomah, averaging nineteen points a game in his freshman season and named the team's Most Inspirational Player; their granddaughter Cari earned All State basketball honors at Sehome and enjoyed a stellar career on the court at Oral Roberts University in the late 1980s.

that mindset, he initiated management and personnel decisions that were intended to raise the profile of The Firs and move the ministry forward.

Grant Whipple was gracious and supportive through the transition, as some of these changes took hold; he also kept a generous distance, avoiding even the appearance of interference or intrusion on Dick's leadership and decision-making. The long-held commitment to "trust God to work in the other person" was habitual to him. "Aunt Ruth" Whipple, Otis's widow, perhaps remembering what it was like to come into this tight-knit community as a bit of an outsider, and to marry the patriarch, offered kindly encouragement to both Dick and Char. Dick's chief sounding board was Doug Anderson, who was by now the most senior and longest-serving member of the resident staff. He and Helen were in fact set to retire in 1980, after more than three decades of conference ministry. Doug built a home on Maple Lane, off Firs property but near enough to keep up modest involvement and to maintain relationships with Firs personnel and Geneva Community Church. His ongoing connections with the wider Bellingham community were evidenced in the frequency with which he continued to be called on to preside at weddings and funerals, as well as to share with local congregations the stories of his prolific overseas missionary labors.[6]

Helen and Chester Rutledge were also by this time retired and living off-site; they moved out of state in 1979 to live with their son Don and his wife Pat in Dallas.[7] Helen died there in 1980, at eighty-four years of age. Several years later, Chester returned to Bellingham for part of the summer to visit friends and to attend the dedication of a new Rutledge Education Center attached to Geneva Community Church, honoring his own and Helen's long service to The Firs. A distinctive and loving feature

6. In January 1987, Doug presented a slideshow of his travels in Indonesia to a local church. Just three months later, at age seventy-two, he went home to the Master he had served so whole-heartedly at The Firs and abroad. Helen lived in the home they had shared until moving into an assisted living facility; she died in 2013, at the age of ninety-five.

7. Don Rutledge, who grew up at The Firs and met his wife Pat on summer staff there, served for seventeen years in Guatemala with Central American Mission (C.A.M.) at Christian radio station TGNA. Several Firs acquaintances, notably Doug Anderson, made short-term trips to help with the work there. (Doug's daughter Jean settled in Guatemala permanently, with her missionary husband, Paul Swyulka; Barb met her future husband, Bruce Vander Meulen, on one such trip.) Don and Pat returned to Dallas in 1975, where Don was vice-president of Home Ministries at C.A.M. and where they were able to care for both Chester and Helen in their last years. In 1997, they had the pleasure of returning to Bellingham, where they would enjoy ten years of pastoral ministry at Northlake Community Church.

of the Rutledge building was a fireplace inlaid with hundreds of stones that Chester had personally collected, cut, and polished over three decades of itinerant missions in the Pacific Northwest and overseas.[8]

With the retirement of the Whipples, Andersons, and Rutledges, Dick's tenure represented an obvious changing of the guard. His vision and initiative as a change-agent was embraced enthusiastically by many, but for some of the longer-serving members of The Firs community, who still held to the old expectation of consensus, if not unanimity, in decision-making, the pace and direction of change were disorienting. That a person so new in leadership was moving with such alacrity caused some uneasiness, as did an apprehension that the distinctive character of The Firs, the very qualities that had brought them there, might be relinquished in the quest to make of it a "Forest Home or Hume Lake or Mount Hermon."

As in all organizational change, it is clear that personality played a major role; Dick's temperament was very different from that of his predecessor. Grant had been raised in the "school of waiting," with a disposition to seek clear biblical guidance and the mind of many counselors before making major decisions. He was never in a rush, and The Firs bore the imprint of that long patience as well as long obedience. The staff that served with him had grown accustomed to quiet composure, patient consultation, and a lack of drama. To some, the infusion of new energy and new young staff was obviously welcome, a breath of fresh air; to others, Dick could sometimes seem impolitic or hasty, intent on charting a new course at double-quick speed. He loved to laugh and enjoyed shenanigans of various kinds—whether skiing down the mountain highway from The Firs Chalet or parasailing at Firwood in his best pants and dress shirt. The same instinct for camaraderie and fun that drew young men to him seemed to others disarmingly casual, perhaps a little "unspiritual." A few members of staff began to feel and to express a degree of alienation that was, if not unprecedented, certainly rare in the annals of Firs history. Doug Anderson made an effort to mediate, with only modest success.

In the summer of 1980, tragedy struck the Fircreek day camp program, when a six-year-old camper drowned during an outing to Whatcom Falls Park. In his initial statement to the press, Dick (understandably protective of the reputation of The Firs) said that it was at that point unclear what had happened, but posited that the child might have wandered

8. Chester died in November 1988 at the age of ninety-six.

off from his campmates and counselors—a suggestion to which his parents took immediate and vehement exception, and which proved to be untrue. While the tragedy itself was devastating for all concerned, the inadvertent implication that the child may have borne some responsibility exacerbated pain and anger on the part of the grieving parents and prompted accusations of blame-shifting. The Firs ultimately acknowledged negligence on the part of camp staff, and agreed to an out of court settlement with the family.[9]

For all the heartbreak that this one incident caused, the ministry was in many obvious respects thriving. The Chalet and Firwood were busy; many kids and young people were coming to know the Lord. On the conference grounds, prominent speakers were featured at adult gatherings throughout Dick's tenure. One of the most unusual, perhaps, was Maria Hirschmann, better known as "Hansi," whose sensational account of escaping life as a devoted Hitler youth leader and coming to faith in Christ was published by Tyndale House in 1974 as *Hansi: The Girl Who Loved the Swaztika*. Hansi was at The Firs in 1978.[10] Luis Palau, an international evangelist and founder of Overseas Crusades, was by now a familiar and beloved speaker at the conference[11]; he and his wife Pat continued to visit frequently, as did Ray and Elaine Stedman from Peninsula Bible Church in Palo Alto, California. Other prominent guests included Alan Redpath of Capernwray Fellowship in England, Malcolm Cronk, David Jeremiah, Jack and Kay Arthur, Eugene Peterson, Elisabeth Elliot, and J. Vernon McGee, best known for his "Thru the Bible" program. (Dick later recalled the joy of hosting the McGees in his home while they were on site, and his special pleasure in watching Dr. McGee sitting on the floor, interacting with his young boys.) Additionally, in the time-honored missionary tradition of The Firs, there were regular conferences with a specific missions focus—notably Central American

9. This was the first of three accidental deaths to have occurred in a Firs-connected program in its hundred-year history. In 1994, a sixteen-year-old Firwood C.I.T., driving out of camp for his day off, slid off the access road and overturned the vehicle into a pond. His three passengers, all Firwood staff, escaped but were unable to rescue him. In 2017, a Chinese teenager visiting Firwood drowned while participating in a waterfront competition.

10. A lengthy interview conducted with Hansi at The Firs was published by the *Bellingham Herald*, July 28, 1978.

11. When Luis Palau conducted an evangelistic crusade in Bellingham in 1981, he told a reporter that he had by that point been to the area as a speaker at The Firs on eighteen different occasions.

Mission, with The Firs' own Don Rutledge, and Far East Broadcasting, with founder Bob Bowman.

In late 1983, as Dick began to come to terms with the fact that his dreams for The Firs were facing strong headwinds, he and the board agreed that he would step down as director. Shortly thereafter, Dick learned of a position opening at The Billy Graham Training Center (The Cove), nearly Asheville, North Carolina, for which he was an ideal fit. It was "God's creativity" at work, Dick reflected, and in early 1984 he formally commenced his new post, leaving Char and the boys behind so as not to interrupt his sons' school year. A few months later, he returned for Brent's high school graduation and packed up the family's belongings. Jeff, just having completed his freshman year at Sehome High, joined his parents in exchanging the Cascades for the Blue Ridge Mountains, but Todd (a rising junior at Western Washington State University) and Brent elected to stay on the west coast for university—the hardest part of the move, recalled Dick. If it were not for the clarity of the call they felt to The Cove, they might have looked for other opportunities in the Pacific Northwest.[12]

As he had anticipated when he took the role, Dick was indeed a bridge figure, one who sensed both the need and opportunity for significant revitalization at The Firs, that the ministry "must be ready to adapt resources to changing demands." He brought fresh ideas and fresh personnel to the conference. During his tenure, even in its apparently disruptive aspects, he was used of God not only to initiate some of that change himself but to prepare the way for subsequent leaders to address issues that had been long put on hold.

12. The Eleys, after leaving The Firs, enjoyed a whirlwind of ministry ventures. After four years at The Cove, Dick returned to pastoral ministry in an Asheville church, then pursued a doctorate in behavioral therapy and took up a series of roles in life coaching, pastoring, and leadership mentoring. He founded The Lamplighter Coaching. At the time of writing, "Doc" and Char are based in Florida, running a non-profit called The Center for Everyday Leadership, grateful that "in all of this, we have had the opportunity to be working for the Lord and seeing his kingdom enlarged."

# 15

# Conservation (1985–1995)

"Those who wait on the Lord shall renew their strength."[1]

WITH THE DEPARTURE OF THE ELEYS, The Firs Board reached out to Greg Kinloch—who was currently overseeing programming for all three properties—to take on the director's role on an interim basis. Having been on the resident staff with his wife Barb since 1970, he was a trusted colleague, familiar with all aspects of the ministry, who understood and valued both the aspirational and the more traditional perspectives within the constituency and was able to mediate effectively. It was not long before he was asked formally to consider the executive director position; after considerable prayer and conversation with Barb, he agreed.

In a mid-1980s edition of *The Firs Fellowship*, the ministry's quarterly newsletter, the featured side-by-side front page articles were "Memories of the Past," written by director emeritus Grant Whipple and "Perspective on the Future," penned by new executive director Greg Kinloch. Historic photos from the earliest years reinforced continuity with the founding character of The Firs, while Greg's essay called attention to priorities that would allow the ministry to remain relevant into and beyond the coming decade. Among the priorities Greg laid out were: (1) harmonious support of and cooperation with local churches; (2) designing programs, facilities, and recreation to meet the needs of families (many of which

1. Isa 40:31. The following lengthy chapter, tracing a very busy period in the history of The Firs, foregrounds six couples—Kinlochs, Johnsons, Wegeners, Walkers, Vander Meulens, and Smiths—though countless others had crucial roles in the ministry during those years.

were in crisis); (3) "having our house in order," so as to be prepared for financial uncertainties, government challenges, and bureaucratic intrusions within an increasingly secular milieu; (4) addressing the needs of an aging constituency—not only continuing to offer senior days, Elderhostel events, and seniors' conferences but also creating opportunities for retirees to participate directly in ministry by volunteering on site.[2] While "change is inevitable," Greg observed, "growth is not"; growth, in fact, would demand thoughtful, prayerful, and intentional calibration of the way "God's work, done in God's way" could and should meet the obstacles and opportunities represented by shifting cultural realities.

Greg leaned on a well-qualified and spiritually seasoned staff as well as strong board leadership as he began to assume his new responsibilities. Those who had been longest at The Firs were best prepared for the seasons of financial uncertainty that came and went periodically, typically as a result of factors well outside the ministry's control, such as fluctuations (sometimes drastic) in the Canadian exchange rate, which caused camper and conferee numbers to fall precipitously. The Firs had always had a sizeable Canadian constituency; Canadians sometimes filled nearly 50 percent of Firwood staff positions, and busloads and caravans of campers poured onto the grounds each summer from the Lower Mainland of British Columbia. As for adult programs, many women from north of the border were happy to combine conference attendance with shopping sprees in Bellingham stores, particularly as the Canadian dollar was at or above parity through the 1970s and early 1980s. But the "Loonie" fell to just over sixty-nine cents U.S. in 1986 and would continue to be volatile through subsequent decades, making planning difficult for a large part of The Firs' traditional base. Reflecting back on those years, Greg observed, "God was faithful, donors generous, and staff understanding. It was month-to-month, but each year God provided what we needed. Just like in the early days, we would often wonder at year end how he was going to provide, but he always did."

2. Two individuals who volunteered annually from April to October were retired members of the Los Angeles Police Department, Warren and Vicki Wilson. After moving to Salt Spring Island in the 1970s, they learned about The Firs from an acquaintance who needed a ride to a Luis Palau conference. They not only ended up driving her; they stayed for the two-week conference themselves, and fell in love with the ministry. Through their many years of giving their time and talents to the Chalet and conference center, Warren and Vicki became, like many such volunteers, cherished members of the extended Firs family.

Greg was charged with reestablishing financial stability through careful stewardship, increased use of all three ministry properties, and site and programming growth. He also, with board support, began to revisit some long-held patterns of housing and compensation for resident staff families. The original missionary concepts—(1) of couples or individuals being called to a lifetime of service and expected to devote all their working hours to The Firs, and (2) of compensation based on family size rather than experience or position—began to shift in favor of a hybrid model blending missionary principles with standard employment practices.[3] For the first time, family compensation would be configured as an essentially head-of-household pay model, with staff spouses eligible to work off-site if they wished, or to be compensated for work at The Firs, once a basic threshold of volunteer service had been met. A new policy was instituted that would permit some staff families to live off the conference grounds and even, in some cases, to purchase their own home.[4] Navigating these significant new distinctions with fairness required patient and prayerful diplomacy and good will all round.[5]

While resident staff were still the core of the ministry, additional full-time and part-time employees were also hired where needed—especially in peak seasons—in maintenance, food service, office, and housekeeping, and compensated at hourly levels consistent with those holding similar jobs in Bellingham. The latter change, made essential by the sheer volume of activity at the conference center, represented a significant outreach to the Geneva community, as neighbors, friends, and church members pitched in as occasional employees and local teenagers were drawn into the orbit of The Firs, often for their first work experience, serving alongside staff kids as waiters or dishwashers.

3. Once approved, these changes were implemented gradually, to minimize disruption and overall financial impact on the ministry.

4. The first staff members to take advantage of this policy would be Doug and Marie Walker, who purchased an off-site home in 2000 when they moved back to The Firs (having served earlier from 1988–1994) after a six-year hiatus in Spokane.

5. The obligations of residential community life, much like those of missionary or family life, had always been understood to be effectively 24/7. One was always available when needs arose; there was no "clocking in" and "clocking out." On the other hand, all meals could be taken in the dining room; housing, maintenance, and utilities, along with other benefits, were covered as part of staff compensation. Variations on these patterns took many forms following the initial changes under Greg's leadership; some families, even those living on site, preferred to prepare their own meals rather than eating communally in the dining room. Such flexibility was generally regarded as positive by the staff, and boosted morale.

Another unexpected community connection came when the Opportunity Council of Bellingham approached The Firs' food services director Brian Sondheim in 1987 about partnering in a Head Start government-funded meal program for low-income children. Head Start agreed to provide some new equipment for the venture and to lease The Firs' commercially licensed kitchen on a monthly basis to prepare breakfast, lunch, and snacks for local youngsters from October through May each year. The agreement was formalized in 1988; Head Start's collaboration with The Firs was to continue for over thirty years.

Meanwhile, under the energetic leadership of Mike ("Fonzi") Johnson and his wife Cheryl, Firwood was also in the mid-1980s reaching out beyond its traditional constituency through a scholarship program that provided camperships to foster kids, kids in juvenile detention, and others who would not otherwise be on the radar of The Firs, but for whom an opportunity to experience camp could be life-changing. Reflecting on those years, Mike credited a superbly talented and dedicated camp staff, including many Firwood alums, whom he recruited all over the Lower Mainland of British Columbia and the Pacific Northwest, for the way they welcomed, built trust with, and helped integrate these new campers into the Firwood community. Few such kids had ever gone to church or been exposed to the gospel; most were wary of adults; all had suffered various forms of neglect or abuse and taken on a protective "tough" persona in order to negotiate unfamiliar terrain. Firwood gave them something entirely new: a large, engaging, affectionate crew of young adult leaders, non-stop activity every day in a beautiful environment,[6] skits and games and pranks and outpost camping, and a daily evening gathering that featured contemporary Christian music and powerful talks about Jesus.

One story from those years stood out particularly for Mike. It began with a chance encounter at a local McDonald's restaurant, where Mike and his family were enjoying a meal together. Three teenage boys were making the rounds among the guests; Mike assumed, at first, that they might be panhandling, but it turned out that they had vouchers for free burgers, fries, and shakes but were unable to use them since none was over sixteen years of age. Happy to help them redeem their free food,

6. In additional to its already generous waterfront offerings, with multiple ski boats, canoes, and kayaks, Firwood by this time also boasted aqua-swings, parasailing, and paddle boarding, in addition to horseback riding, archery, riflery, a host of land-based team sports, and campcraft and survival skill options.

Mike extended the conversation, mentioning that he was a camp director. Would they be interested in attending camp for free that summer? The boys were somewhat taken aback and would later admit that they didn't know what to make of this garrulous stranger: was he just "a really great guy" or a crank of some kind? When Mike learned that the boys, unrelated to each other, lived together in foster care, he contacted and then visited the foster parent, secured permission, and made arrangements for a week at Firwood. When the trio arrived at camp, Mike asked them another unexpected question: were they smokers? They admitted as much. "I'll make you a deal," Mike offered, "I'll let you use one small designated area where you can smoke during your afternoon free time. Nowhere else in camp, and no other times of the day. If you break either of those rules, you'll be immediately sent home." It was a gesture that Mike thought important, though the board was understandably far from enthusiastic. No one remembers how much the three actually used their "smoking area"; they were quickly drawn into friendships and activities that filled up their days. But more importantly and memorably, on Friday evening, as camp wound down with a final time of reflection and interaction, two of the three boys stood up to give testimony to a changed life through newfound faith in Jesus. It was, in an already emotionally uplifting and spiritually charged gathering, a highlight for staff and especially for Mike himself. All three young men would return to camp on subsequent summers; the third, who never made a public profession of faith, was several years later tragically swept to his death off an Alaskan fishing boat; Mike has often fervently hoped that the gospel message, so clearly presented at camp, came back to him in those moments and that he cried out, like Peter, "Lord, save me!"[7]

In the fall of 1989, when longtime Firwood operations manager Frank Muench retired, Doug and Marie Walker (dubbed "Charmin" and "Snugli") moved to Firwood full time, taking up the Muenches' responsibilities and residence at camp.[8] They had come to The Firs in 1988 as young marrieds and initially served at the conference center, where Doug

7. Matt 14:30.

8. Their calling to The Firs, like so many, had its origin with "Uncle Doug" Anderson, who visited the Walkers' church in Vancouver, Washington when Doug was still in high school and invited him to come to Firwood and then to volunteer on various projects around the conference center. When Doug moved to Bellingham for university, he continued helping around The Firs, including construction of the Rutledge Building at Geneva Church, and was blessed to be part of a weekly breakfast meeting with Doug Anderson, who became an influential spiritual mentor.

joined the maintenance crew. But living at Firwood year-round proved a delight to them and their adopted daughter Kalynda—from the hectic, non-stop pace of the summer months through the peaceful solitude of the non-camping season, the unique kind of solitude that came of having neither landline nor cell phones (they used a pager) and only the most rudimentary of utilities. Marie served as camp registrar and oversaw the transition from paper to computer-based registration. Doug was involved in a host of facility improvements, including construction of new cabins, expansion of the Longhouse, and creation of a basketball court. The most momentous improvement of all was the introduction of professionally installed sewer and waterlines—which ended the practice of using filtered lake water for drinking, and permitted outhouses to be replaced with flush toilets and new shower houses to be constructed for boys' and girls' camps.[9] Additionally, power poles were replaced with underground lines buried in the road—which afforded both an aesthetic and practical improvement to power delivery. Mirroring his own life-changing experience of being mentored as a young man, Doug worked with the C.I.T. crew every summer, completing a long list of annual enhancements to camp, from resurfacing swim docks to clearing trees to provide pasture for horses.

As the physical property was continually being improved, program innovations were also happening under Mike Johnson's leadership, perhaps the most significant of which was the reimagining of the evening gathering that had long been called Fireside. For decades, these nightly events had featured traditional camp songs along with familiar hymns and choruses, typically accompanied by acoustic guitar or sung *a cappella*; a crackling bonfire centered the distinctive "fireside chat" ambience, at which a member of camp staff gave a devotional and/or evangelistic message. Then, as fire logs were reduced to embers and darkness settled, staff and campers joined in a melodic dismissal ("Good night, our God is watching o'er you; Good night, his mercy goes before you . . . ") before following flashlit paths to their cabins. Fireside was in the 1980s shifting in the direction of what would come to be called "Center Stage" (though a physical stage was yet to be built[10]). Many camp staff, some of whom were themselves musicians, were devotees of the new music

9. This major changeover and modernization of camp water and sewer services was made possible by a timely memorial gift to The Firs, which covered the entire cost.

10. Doug Walker, with help from his C.I.T.s, built the camp stage in 1991, allowing equipment and instruments to be up off the ground where the old firepit had been.

being promoted on Christian radio stations by pioneering songwriters like Rich Mullins, Michael W. Smith, Keith Green, and others. Electric lighting eventually replaced the campfire, electric guitars and drum-sets made their appearance, and contemporary music was adopted in place of old standards to which fewer and fewer campers had any attachment. With the new playlist came the new role of music and worship director, who trained the worship team and chose each evening's content, which varied according to the age of campers. Sometimes during high school camps, a local Christian band was invited to visit.[11] As the overall population of Firwood campers shifted from "mostly church kids" to mostly unchurched, this incorporation of contemporary music was seen as a means of translating the timeless character of the gospel message into a more accessible cultural idiom. Like the new biblical versions proliferating in the same period,[12] it demonstrated that the good news is not time-locked or archaic but "living and active," with continuing dynamic relevance for modern people, young and old. According to leadership records, more than 230 campers made a first-time commitment to Jesus each summer in the 1980s, while many others, including C.I.T.s, renewed their faith and reconsecrated their lives. It was a season of new wine, in new wineskins. A thoughtful balance was nonetheless required: in a *Firs Fellowship* editorial in 1993, Greg Kinloch cautioned against measuring program success "in decibels and amperage" or hype and glitz. Christian camping, if it moved in the direction of theme-park amenities, constantly upping the ante on program options, would invariably lose its essential countercultural quality: exposing kids to the awesome beauty (and even the silence) of God's creation.

One person who watched Mike's tenure at Firwood with special interest was his brother-in-law, Tom Beaumont, who likewise had long

11. A decade later, when Darell Smith was at the helm at Firwood, two "Firwood Center Stage" CDs, with original music tracks, were professionally produced by Rick Calhoun, a well-connected performer with Christian band Hokus Pick, at a Vancouver studio. They are now collectors' items.

12. The King James Bible was by this time no longer standard at camp. The New International Version (NIV) was often preferred by the leadership for its readability, though some staff used the New American Standard Version (NASV) or, more recently, the English Standard Version (ESV), sometimes supplementing also with paraphrases such as J.B. Phillips's *New Testament in Modern English* (1958) or Eugene Peterson's *The Message* (1993). Whereas in the 1960s and 1970s campers were expected to bring Bibles with them to camp, they were now provided with Gideon New Testaments (in a contemporary translation) to use during the week and then take home with them. For many, if not most, these were the first Bibles they had every owned.

experience in and a deep love for Christian camping. Tom had spent nine summers on staff at Trout Creek Bible Camp near Portland, Oregon and then served as camp director there from 1980 to 1984. Partly through that role and partly through contact with Mike, Tom began to become seriously interested in The Firs. When a job came open, he and his wife Mary accepted an invitation to join the resident staff, with Tom taking on responsibility as director of all conference center activities, including Fircreek, the summer day camp program that met across Cable Street from the main conference grounds.

Like Firwood, Fircreek was attracting record numbers of campers in the late 1980s and early 1990s. Ten five-day sessions were scheduled for junior campers, with distinct themes and activities each week; nearly a thousand children were registered annually for one or more of those sessions. In 1991 a new daytrip program, called Summer Jam'n, was added for junior high campers; the experiment was so popular that the program was extended from one week to six in subsequent years. Overall, it was becoming evident to many that the child and youth-focused ministries at The Firs and its secondary properties down the lake at Firwood and on Mount Baker—which had once been deemed satellite programs to the original focus on adult retreats and missionary conferences—were now areas of particular growth and opportunity.

In 1986, The Firs Chalet came under the direction of Phil Wegener, who had grown up on and around the grounds in a multi-generational Firs-connected family, was thoroughly acquainted with Firs personnel and programming, and knew every nook and cranny of Firs property. He had washed dishes in the conference dining room as a kid, spent a record number of summers on Firwood staff (camp name "Loco"), helped Doug Anderson and others on various building and maintenance projects, and assisted Tom Walton, Jim Fosse, and other staff at the Chalet over the years. The position of Chalet director had always been his dream job, but the timing was never right, it seemed, or the door open when he was available to walk through it. In 1981, having spent his entire life in the Pacific Northwest, he moved to Orange, California at the urging of former Firwood staffers Mike and Kathy Fisher,[13] who were pastoring a

13. Mike Fisher ("Rosebud") pastored the Evangelical Free Church of Orange, California for ten years and then became the senior pastor at Grace Bible Church in Dallas in 1986, following a line of notable predecessors including Dwight Pentecost and Chuck Swindoll. He and Kathy later traveled frequently to Myanmar (formerly Burma), training indigenous pastors and mentoring young believers. In these missionary endeavors, they were often accompanied by close friends Barb and Greg Kinloch. Barb recalled the

church there. Phil found work with a heating and air conditioning firm, put down roots in the church fellowship, and socialized with the college and career group, which included several acquaintances from Firwood summer staff. Through one of these, whose large extended family began including him in seasonal gatherings, he met his future wife Pam Wesley. They were married in 1983.

Several years later, while enjoying a family vacation in Bellingham, Phil learned that long-time Chalet director Tom Walton was stepping down.[14] The coveted opportunity having presented itself at last, Phil and Pam, with a clear sense of leading and with their eighteen-month-old daughter Heidi, made the move north to join the resident staff of The Firs in December 1986.

His new role had Phil "doing everything" at the Chalet: programming, planning, budgeting, maintenance, hosting. He hired all the speakers for Firs-sponsored retreats, the list of which typically included junior high, high school, college and career, and father-son weekends, as well as occasional women-only events or family mini-camps. Additionally, the Chalet still opened regularly to guest groups— having been the first Firs property to do so. Ever since the initial 1958 International Christmas Party hosted by Intervarsity Christian Fellowship at the Mount Baker lodge, church and parachurch groups, along with other non-profits, made frequent use of the facility.

A natural extrovert, Phil loved the interaction with campers and leaders, but he credited Pam, who came as often as possible to the Chalet with the children (Heidi was soon followed by twin girls Courtney and Kristen, then brother Jeffrey), with indispensable coaching on hospitality, creature comforts, and how to make guests feel at home. A longtime bachelor and longtime camp guy, for whom skits came more easily than some aspects of adulting, he welcomed the input. But it also became clear that the Lord had, during his California sojourn, prepared him in myriad practical ways for the role he had for so long hoped to fill. His sense of ministry had matured under the mentorship of Mike Fisher and, as a

thrill of encountering people in Myanmar with their own Firs connections, through those who remembered "Mama" Isobel Kuhn and her Rainy Season Bible School.

14. Tom stayed at the Chalet for much of the winter season of 1986/87, helping Phil acclimate to the myriad responsibilities he was taking on. He and his wife Patti then, after three decades of sacrificial service, elected to take early retirement from The Firs at the end of 1988, though they retained a home on the grounds and continued to help out on a volunteer basis. Patti had long been involved in women's ministries as well as various office and hospitality roles, and often sang at conference gatherings.

heating and cooling tech, he had learned skills that would prove indispensable at the Chalet when the whole building needed to be rewired and plumbed.[15]

Shortly after Phil came on staff, a decision to seek American Camping Association accreditation for The Firs Chalet set in motion a whole series of unanticipated and costly but necessary upgrades. A fire marshal who was sent to inspect the thirty-year-old A-frame declared it a fire trap that, in his view, ought to be closed and condemned; his report was passed on to the Forest Service, who agreed to allow continued use but with the proviso that a series of fire code upgrades and other safety improvements needed to commence immediately.[16] Architectural drawings and permits alone cost $20,000; actual construction costs would total upwards of $200,000—even with Firs personnel contributing most of the physical labor.[17] The Chalet generator and underground diesel tanks had to be moved into an external shed (built by Doug Walker and assistants in a frenetic, six-week weather window in 1991). Ten dormers, with specialized windows that opened both ways, were required for the upstairs sleeping rooms, to provide both light and fresh air. Bathrooms needed to be renovated and new furnace units installed on the upper floors. A four-story external stairwell/fire escape was mandated, as well as disability access. All these requirements and more came on top of the routine maintenance issues associated with an aging facility in a remote, often snowbound environment, not to mention normal wear and tear

15. Another indispensable specialist, who had for many years installed and serviced units at Firs properties, was local technician Ed Feller. With his wife Toni, Ed was active in all aspects of the ministry but had a special affection for the Mount Baker lodge; for twenty-five years, Ed and his family spent Labor Day weekend at the Chalet, during which time he would service all the equipment for the upcoming winter season. Ed's expertise sometimes took him overseas, to assist in missionary projects like Don Rutledge's in Guatemala or to service equipment in American embassies and consulates in more than fifty countries. But home was always where Toni was, and Toni loved The Firs. When diagnosed with terminal cancer in 2022, she began planning her own memorial service with characteristic aplomb, insisting that it take place at The Firs Chalet; three hundred came to pay respects at the first and only such service ever held there to date.

16. Phil maintained a good rapport with the Forest Service, hosting several Forest Service groups at the Chalet, which reinforced mutual cooperation and provided extra off-season income to The Firs.

17. Bruce Vander Meulen, Frank Muench, and Doug Walker headed up the work team, contributing endless arduous hours to Chalet improvements. They were assisted by many local volunteers, including Firwood director Darell Smith, local pastor Paul Petersen, building contractor Greg Swanson, and Firwood alum Phil Erickson, who spent some of their vacation time getting renovation projects at the Chalet completed.

and perennial weather-related crises (ice damming, leaks, etc.) The list of demands and the costs were overwhelming, and the short building season atop the mountain presented huge challenges. Nonetheless, the Lord provided: through generous donations and almost incalculable volunteer hours over most of a decade, The Firs Chalet was almost entirely renovated, to the satisfaction of appropriate authorities and enthusiastic reviews from campers and guest groups. In 1998, the Chalet would be open for more days than in any of its forty previous years of operation, with a single discipleship training program occupying the upgraded facility for twelve consecutive non-peak weeks.[18]

In the meantime, the conference center—though still a relative island of tranquility, with its majestic stands of mature fir trees and well-tended grounds—faced its own challenges, some of which mimicked those on Mount Baker (aging buildings, deferred maintenance issues) while others were entirely different. As some longtime staff members retired or passed away, resident staff houses became rental properties, though typically available only to Firs-connected individuals. The temporary nature of such arrangements added new burdens of care and upkeep, with remodeling, repainting, and upgrades becoming necessary as short-term tenants came and went. Moreover, the conference property, once secluded and rustic, was now surrounded on all sides by a busy suburban community; old seasonal cottages in the neighborhood were being replaced by upscale permanent homes, whose owners prized access to Lake Whatcom, and Cable Street was thick with commuter traffic every morning and evening.[19] As the remote and "set apart" character of the grounds experienced severe encroachment, a few members of council and board began to wonder about how to recover the sense of sanctuary that had defined the early decades of ministry at The Firs. For now, though, the tyranny of the urgent pushed such questions into the background: the year 1991 saw, among many other lesser projects, a total renovation of the original Whipple honeymoon cabin (the sentimental heart of the property), a remodel of the conference dining room, and a new roof for Geneva Chapel.

Involved in all these ventures, as well as upgrades to The Firs Chalet and improvements at Firwood, was a second-generation Firs

18. Sponsored and hosted by Youth with a Mission (Y.W.A.M.).

19. Census records show a 40 percent increase in the population of Whatcom Country from 1980 to 1995 (considerably outpacing both state and national growth), with a huge spurt in the early 1990s.

family—Doug and Helen Anderson's daughter Barb and her husband Bruce Vander Meulen, who came on staff in 1986, the same year as Phil and Pam Wegener.

Like all Firs-raised kids, Barb was conversant with everything and everyone in the ministry. Her dad, known as "Uncle Doug" to almost everyone, was Grant Whipple's right-hand man for many years, a visionary as well as a practitioner of all the many skills and arts of availability. An estimable jack-of-all-trades, he was as comfortable expertly toppling a seventy-foot fir tree or installing sewer lines as he was preaching at Geneva Community Church. His wife Helen had been a long-serving Firs registrar, whose welcoming and generous personality was the first introduction many had to the ministry.

As recorded in chapter 11 above, Barb's dad had visited Guatemala in 1964 in response to a letter from Don Rutledge (son of Firs staffers Chester and Helen Rutledge), who was serving with Central American Mission at the Christian radio station TGNA. The whole Anderson family, as well as numerous friends of The Firs from the Pacific Northwest, had subsequently spent time there on short-term missions. Barb's older sister Jean moved permanently to Guatemala City, married third-generation missionary to Guatemala, Rev. Paul Sywulka, and was employed with him at Central American Theological Seminary.

In 1976, after Guatemala suffered a devastating earthquake, Barb flew to Guatemala City with a small group of friends from The Firs to help with recovery and rebuilding projects. When they reached their destination, they found themselves sharing work, meals, Bible studies, and fellowship with a cohort of young men who had arrived previously from Grand Rapids, Michigan—members of a Berean Baptist Church that had its own ties to the Central American Mission. Among them, Bruce Vander Meulen struck up an immediate friendship with Barb, though no one saw a hint of romance until, after the Michigan crew flew home, Barb received a note from an apparently lovelorn Bruce, asking her if she would alter her flight home from Guatemala, detouring via Grand Rapids (which was admittedly not exactly on the way to Washington State). She was happy to comply, arriving in Michigan in January and there, as she recounted it, "became engaged before her first date." Lots of dates followed, and a wedding at The Firs, after which the couple spent the first eight years of their marriage in Grand Rapids, where Bruce worked in construction, janitorial work, and seasonal landscaping and snowplowing. Then, in 1986, the Lord opened doors at The Firs. Barb was more than ready to return to the west coast, and to be close to her recently retired parents; Bruce was looking for a change as well, and an opportunity to put his talents to work in a ministry context. As it turned out, nothing in his skill set or experience was wasted at The Firs; he was, like his father-in-law, not only multicompetent but also a quick study, ready to learn whatever he didn't already know how to do. With shared responsibility for housekeeping and groundskeeping, vehicle maintenance, updating of cabins, roof repair and replacement, upgrading of facilities at the conference center, Firwood, and the Chalet, creation of the façade for the Fircreek day camp, Bruce had a hands-on connection with virtually every part of The Firs property during his long tenure.[20]

Barb was happy to be raising their two sons, Doug Jr. (born 1979) and Andy (1982) in the same environment and among many of the people with whom she grew up. Having her own parents nearby in their late years was a special blessing. As the boys matured, she took on more and more responsibilities at The Firs in partnership with Bruce, especially involving maintenance and housekeeping. Her oversight of the housekeeping department would become legendary in later years, as she and a team of experienced employees and volunteers (many recruited from amongst her church friends) perfected the science of turnarounds between summer conference groups, with as many as 250 people vacating rooms and cabins in the late morning and similar numbers arriving to freshly prepared accommodations four hours later—an astonishing and demanding feat. Barb had an indefatigable work ethic, great organizational skills, a deep affection for beauty, and a Christlike heart for hospitality: "I love preparing places," she reflected, years later, with characteristic understatement.[21]

Hospitality had always been central to The Firs' character as a ministry. There were, in addition to the obvious public expressions of welcome

20. Bruce and Barb retired from The Firs in 2022, though at the time of writing they continue to live nearby; Barb retains an active ministry with women through her scrapbooking workshops (cropwiththefirs.org). Their son Andy, who was assistant Firwood director under Rob Lee, returned to The Firs fulltime in 2024 with responsibility for human resources, safety, and information technology. His wife Jen has served on The Firs Board.

21. There are many humorous stories from those years, some involving the efforts to which guests went to hide evidence of alcohol consumption; Jan Morell, who oversaw guest services for several decades and worked closely with Barb Vander Meulen, recalled Barb handing her a stubby of beer that she found stashed in the tank of a toilet in in one of the guest cabins. Jan kept it on a shelf in her office as an amusing conversation piece.

and kindness at every conference, retreat, or camp gathering, countless hidden (often sacrificial) gestures of generosity on the part of individual staff members. One such story involves a welcome extended to a Firwood alumnus who showed up unannounced on the Kinlochs' doorstep in the summer of 1984. Stacy Hebert (whose camp name, "Gumbo," owed to her Louisiana roots) had no idea that Barb and Greg had moved up the ladder from directing Firwood to overall direction of The Firs. She merely decided on a whim, while on a road trip with her sister from California to the Northwest, to check in on "Smudge" and "Smear." Hoping for a visit and possibly a meal, the two were taken in as houseguests for six weeks.

The whim may have been hers, but the plan was clearly God's. Stacy had just completed a degree in recreation at Biola, in large part inspired by her experience at Firwood in 1979, but she was carrying a lot of unresolved hurt and greatly in need of spiritual respite. The Kinlochs provided open hearts and listening ears, "just loving on us and caring for us," in Stacy's words. They also suggested, since camp was in session, a visit to Firwood. Amongst the staff, Stacy encountered several friends from her own previous summer, one of whom struck her as both familiar and entirely changed since they had last met. His name was Darell Smith, but she remembered him only as "Bubba," a somewhat remote "big man at camp." Now, there was something different, more approachable, about him that immediately attracted Stacy. When she was offered short-term employment at The Firs to help with housekeeping and college ministry, she jumped at the chance, not knowing that Darell was himself making the move from a longtime summer staffer at Firwood to a full-time staff position at the conference center. They ended up living next door to each other in staff houses. As they worked and shared life together in numerous roles on site, friendship deepened into romance. They were engaged six months later, and married in September 1986: it was a Firs love story that would have an extraordinary impact for decades to come.

Darell's initial role was at the conference center, but when Mike Johnson was called into a new ministry opportunity with Compassion International in 1991, Firwood directorship passed seamlessly into Darell's hands. Having spent many years on summer staff and worked closely with Mike, he was well prepared to ensure continuity, drawing on the successes and the style established in the 1980s.[22] Firwood was by

22. Darell was, when he took over, in the enviable position of having more applicants for summer staff than he had places to fill, as well as full rosters of campers for virtually every session.

now adding a somewhat more speaker-oriented ministry to its traditional counselor-centered approach. It was counselors who lived with campers, led Bible studies, and spent individual time helping kids sort through emotional and spiritual baggage, sharing Christ with them, while the nightly Center Stage programs carried much of the spiritual freight of evangelism. Darell recalled being "stunned by the growing number of kids attending camp who had never heard of Jesus Christ." It wasn't just that they didn't know who he was; they didn't even know his name, "yet every kid at camp was familiar with Satan." In addressing such a dearth of knowledge, Darell adopted a variant of a Young Life ministry model in introducing, on successive evenings, the reality and goodness of God, the problem of sin and evil, the person and work of Jesus, an invitation to become a Christ-follower, and the importance of ongoing discipleship and dependance on the work of the Holy Spirit once kids left Firwood. There was always an opportunity, on the last night of camp, for campers to stand and share their reflections, whether trivial, humorous, touching, or spiritually lifechanging. This was the occasion in which many, for the first time, testified to new faith in Jesus—or perhaps, a return to him after a season of wandering.

Darell and Stacy lived in camp accommodations during the summer months with their growing family, Jacob (born 1989), Abby (1991) and Baylor (1994), bunks having been built by Frank Muench and installed in an erstwhile storage closet to create a sleeping space for the kids. As a couple, they exuded extraordinary warmth; Stacy famously (and sometimes successfully) acted as a matchmaker for summer staff she regarded as well-suited, and she and Darell modeled a quality of empathy that allowed them to enter deeply into burdens as well as joys of those they served.[23] They maintained close ties with C.I.T.s and other leaders during the off-season, frequently hosting events in their home near The Firs. They laid the groundwork for an extension program for summer staff, dubbed Firwood Youth International, which would send a cohort of Firwood alums to Guatemala and El Salvador to assist with

23. Tragedy engulfed camp in 1994, when a sixteen-year-old C.I.T. lost control of the car he was driving out of Firwood on his day off, and slid into a pond. Members of his family and the pastoral staff of his Phoenix church stayed at The Firs while maintaining daily vigils at his bedside; he died in a Bellingham hospital weeks later. The experience was overwhelming for summer staff, as all wrestled with grief and "why?"-questions. Rivers of tears flowed, Darell remembered, and continued to flow all summer. But, in his words, "God showed up" in the midst of the heartache and walked through it with them.

programming and staffing local Christian camps.[24] They also initiated a program designed to connect new young believers who committed their lives to Christ at camp with youth pastors in their home area who could draw them into fellowship with other Christian kids and disciple them. The Youth Pastor Network wasn't a ringing success, Darell admitted candidly; it depended largely on active engagement of youth workers to follow up, and more than a few dropped the ball. But it was an effort that has continued through the years, and taken a variety of forms.[25]

Among new program offerings introduced at Firwood in the mid-1990s was a challenge course, incorporating trees and natural terrain in the old Ponderosa horse corral area along with cables, ropes, and harnesses. Combining both low and high course options (the latter of which permitted a spectacular view of the lake), the activities were almost all designed for team rather than individual challenges, and helped build relationships of trust, communication, and cooperation between campers. A climbing center, with a state-of-the-art thousand-square-foot climbing wall, would be added in 1998.[26] The horsemanship program got a boost with a new corral and barn and the addition of a full-time C.H.A.-certified wrangler, Kim Dugard ("Mickey") in 1993. She became a good-will ambassador in the local community of ranchers and horse owners, and ran a professional-quality and popular equestrian program for seven years.[27]

In these and other myriad changes and improvements to camp, though, the core of the Firwood experience was, and remained, to open the hearts and minds of young people to the Jesus they never knew, the only begotten Son of God—or, as the Smiths' four-year-old daughter

24. Though Darell and Stacy went on a fact-finding mission to Central America in late 1995, their dreams for a Firwood-connected missionary effort to commence in 1997 were sidelined by Darell's deteriorating health.

25. With the advent of cell phones and social media, it would eventually become possible for kids, once home from camp, to have "Firwood in their pocket," allowing staff to follow up directly with those interested in Christian musical, social, and devotional content, as well as personal discipleship.

26. Both the challenge course, which has been continually upgraded and modified over the years, and climbing center were available for use by guest groups in the off-season.

27. Kim married and moved to Camano Island in 2000. Several years later, after lengthy discussion about liability and procurement issues, the Firwood horsemanship program was phased out. In decades of operation, and despite some rambunctious "wild west" escapades (in the early years especially, under Pete "Hoss" Tjoelker), there was never a serious accident or injury associated with the program.

Abby memorably misnamed him, all too presciently, the "only *forgotten* Son."

# 16

## Heartwood (1996–2003)

"Be watchful, and strengthen the things which remain."[1]

As The Firs approached its diamond jubilee, there was within the community an obvious mood of thankful reflection on the faithfulness of God over seventy-five years of ministry. Signs of stability and continuity were evident, including a cadre of twenty-five mature and seasoned staff committed to the work for the long haul; there had been only modest turnover since the mid-1980s.[2] The fall council meeting held in late September, 1995 was well attended by friends and supporters from near and far, including seven members of the founding family. Doug Whipple, the first Whipple ever to serve as board chair, led the gathering, and at the outset invited his father to provide a personal retrospective of the ministry's history. Grant, now nearly twenty years retired from the position of executive director, recounted the decade-by-decade highlights of God's unfolding plans and purposes at The Firs, the choice individuals that he had called into the ministry, and his blessing of the work of their hands.

1. Rev 3:2. "Heartwood" refers to "the central, supporting pillar of a tree. Although dead, it will not decay or lose strength as long as the outer layers are intact. A composite of cellulose fibers and lignin, it is as strong as steel." U.S. Forest Service, "Anatomy of a Tree," https://www.fs.usda.gov/learn/trees/anatomy-of-tree.

2. When a friend of The Firs once observed to Greg Kinloch how remarkable it was that staff stayed so long, Greg jested about "high salaries, a short working season, and great recreational opportunities." Ignoring the quip, the other replied, with evident admiration: "Actually, I think the key to staff longevity is understanding and practicing true servanthood."

For all the emphasis on continuity, change was also clearly in the air and on the agenda. Grant recounted some of the policy amendments that had been made in the recent past and observed thoughtfully that even as the ministry grew and flourished, adapting where necessary and appropriate, those who loved The Firs ought never to "remove the ancient landmarks" (Prov 22:28), to forsake the distinctive character that had defined the ministry from the beginning. His brother Elden likewise later warned of the temptation to careless innovation with a verse from Jer 6:16: "Stand at the crossroads and look; ask for the ancient paths, ask where the good way is, and walk in it" (NIV).

As the jubilee was marked, then, there was something in the air, a tension—a creative tension perhaps, but a tension nonetheless. How to honor the past without making an idol of the status quo? How to adjust to new mission needs and opportunities without losing identity? How to move forward without forsaking the "ancient landmarks" or missing the "good path"? And how, in deciding all these questions, to retain unity in the bonds of peace?

Strategic planning had been undertaken in earnest several years earlier. An initial survey of staff and council members revealed, in Greg Kinloch's words, that "we have a lot of differences of opinion, a lot of ground to plow, no significant trend, but significant middle ground." Looking back, Greg's candor underscores some of the challenges involved in charting a course into a new millennium, especially given The Firs' historic commitment to "oneness" in major decision-making. Doug Whipple likewise, in a spring 1996 *Firs Fellowship*, noting that "the board faces many decisions that could dramatically change the nature of The Firs," acknowledged the difficulty of maintaining unity between the board, council, and members of the resident staff; his hope was that the strategic planning process would contribute to a renewed sense of spiritual concord within The Firs constituency.

At the heart of the discussion and of the "differences of opinion" was the conference center itself and its continuing viability as the centerpiece of the ministry. Firwood and the Chalet each had by now a unique and well-established identity, but the conference center had a history of being "all things to all people" over the years, adapting to meet a wide range of ministry priorities according the skills and talents of staff. The missionary conferences of the early years were becoming less frequent as local churches began to host such events themselves.[3] Couples' conferences had introduced video-based seminars, a radical departure from the typically more relaxed "fun and fellowship" format with well-known speakers; response was strongly mixed.[4] Family conferences still drew good summer crowds, though they increasingly featured lesser-known and often local speakers; the whole ecosphere of the Christian conference movement was shifting as the World Wide Web became publicly accessible and internet connections allowed "virtual" gatherings that brought well-known faces via screens into one's home or local church. As Greg Kinloch had projected when he was named executive director, one increasingly significant clientele for conference center programs was seniors, a large cohort of whom had grown up with the ministry and were now aging with it; perhaps for that reason they were unfazed by the somewhat dated accommodations and appreciated The Firs' unwavering adherence to its traditional biblical messaging. Carol Longston, a longtime staffer who had partnered with Grace Summers in women's ministry in the seventies and early eighties, embraced a new role as director of seniors' ministry in 1985, after a several-year hiatus with Bible Study Fellowship in San Antonio. Though, at forty-two, she was far from a senior herself, she was something of an "old soul" and had great rapport with her elders; she loved planning and speaking at luncheons, conferences, and Elderhostel events. Shortly after Carol addressed the aforementioned Firs council gathering in late 1995—recounting her long and varied association with the ministry since her first summers as a Firwood camper—she was diagnosed with an aggressive (glioblastoma multiforme) brain tumor. Through surgery, chemotherapy, and radiation treatments, she showed remarkable fortitude and grace, working in the office through much of the spring. In June 1996, at only fifty-three years of age, she preceded her many senior friends into the presence of the Lord.

Overall, the conference center calendar was increasingly dotted with single-day or weekend events rather than weeklong programs, leaving many open dates available for guest group bookings, which did not always materialize. Reduced usage did not equate with less maintenance, and the need to keep the grounds pristine and accommodations freshly

3. It is also clear that The Firs' historic ties to foreign missions—especially the China Inland Mission/Overseas Missionary Fellowship and Central American Mission—had weakened somewhat over the years, a fact that troubled some on staff.

4. Couples' conferences waned in popularity through the 1990s, and ceased altogether to appear on the annual retreat roster by the early 2000s.

repaired, painted, and updated was never-ending. Despite all these issues, and despite the fact that The Firs was surrounded on every side by a burgeoning suburban neighborhood, attachment to the property was still strong, especially among staff—not least because it housed, in physical terms, many of the historic markers of the ministry, though some were now hidden from any but the most discerning eye.[5]

Could the grounds be reconfigured or reimagined for new forms or dimensions of ministry, or its accommodations redesigned for the more demanding tastes of contemporary conferencegoers? One idea that had grown out of strategic planning was Anderson Lodge—an attractive and spacious two-story guest facility to be named for Doug and Helen Anderson. After extensive consultation with other camps and conference centers, a consensus was reached about location, size, layout, and style of accommodation and the project was turned over to architectural designers. A board committee examined various approaches to financing that would allow the project, a very significant capital expenditure, to be completed debt-free. For a donor base that was already deeply invested in the upkeep of existing properties, it was a big ask, but there was considerable excitement on the part of some that the lodge could revitalize the main. grounds. Before long, however, other factors began to intrude: the water district, in a legal battle with state and local authorities, put a moratorium on all new water and sewer permits. Regulations, permit obstacles, and mountains of red tape slowed the project to a virtual halt and reinforced the sensation of being "squeezed" by urbanization of the Geneva community and its various bureaucracies. What was the Lord saying in all of this?

Some were beginning to wonder if, despite its historic associations, the conference center might have run its course. Or, at the very least, if The Firs needed by some means to look for another property where one could recapture the original "set apart" feeling that defined ministry in the early years, but which was impossible to recreate as hundreds of cars whizzed by the Cable Street entrance daily. One might have thought that the Whipple family would have been the most reluctant for any such change, but the opposite was true. Grant was quietly pondering whether there was a way The Firs could be relocated down the lake to Firwood, and his son Doug, with other members of the board, began to consider whether the Lord might provide some completely new location outside

5. The original Whipple cabin, with its iconic fireplace, was entirely incorporated into a large meeting space known as the lounge (now the Alpine Room).

the hubbub of suburban Bellingham. Several exploratory trips were made to sites around the Pacific Northwest. In the midst of this provisional search effort, an unexpected call came from the Catholic Archdiocese of Vancouver, British Columbia, which was hoping to sell a camp property named Latona on Gambier Island in Howe Sound. Several Firwood families who had Latona contacts had suggested to diocesan officials that they should reach out to The Firs.

In response to this initiative, a committee was formed to consider the viability of Latona as a potential Firs property and Greg sent Rob Lee, one of the newest members of the resident staff, to spy out the land.

Rob, whose Canadian parents, Bob and Kay Lee, were longtime friends of The Firs and served on board and council, had a lengthy tenure on Firwood summer staff (camp name "Spray") and met his wife Val ("Fuji"), a Bellingham native, through Firwood connections. Rob and Val spent their first summer as newlyweds in lead counselor roles at Firwood, after which Rob found employment with Nordstrom, first in New Jersey and then in Seattle. In 1994, with two young children, he and Val elected to move to White Rock, British Columbia, where Rob joined his father's construction and contracting business. Having settled down at last near family and lifelong friends, Rob was surprised to receive a call from Darell Smith to ask whether he and Val might consider applying to come on Firs staff. The timing seemed all wrong and he quickly dismissed the idea, but Val felt a tug and began to pray. Within a few weeks, and despite his apparently perfect situation in living near his parents and working with his dad, Rob submitted an application. He and Val then went through an extensive interview and discernment process and ultimately accepted what they had both come to believe was a genuine, though unanticipated call.[6] They arrived in January 1995.

Rob's initial job description was focused on marketing and public relations, which involved his sharing The Firs "brand" and story with interested parties and making connections with other similar ministries throughout the Pacific Northwest. When Latona came into the picture as a possible new venue for The Firs, Rob reached out to Kirk Potter, executive director of Keats Camps on Keats Island, also on Howe Sound. Kirk

6. The Lees were the last staff couple hired under the original, missionary-derived "lifetime call" process at The Firs, which involved not only multiple interviews with executive director, executive committee, and all current staff, but a commitment to mutual prayer and an expectation of clear leading that this was of the Lord, usually through a specific text from Scripture. Rob and Val went on to serve on Firs staff in various strategic roles until 2017.

not only had a Firwood pedigree, having spent three summers on staff in the early seventies, but also knew Rob from annual Missions Fest gatherings in Vancouver, where both represented their respective ministries.

In the spring of 1999 Rob traveled to the Sunshine Coast to meet Kirk, along with Rob Bentall, a Vancouver businessman and founder of Barnabas Family Ministries, also on Keats Island. The three met at the Langdale ferry terminal and traveled by a Keats-owned boat to Latona, on the north end of Gambier Island, to evaluate the property and assess its potential as a Firs site. Rob Bentall and Kirk Potter, who knew Howe Sound well, were able to offer especially useful perspective on the benefits and challenges of operating a camp in this location. Many years later, Kirk recalled the pros and cons they discussed that day. On the plus side, Latona was a beautiful property in arguably the most stunningly beautiful part of Howe Sound, offering one of the finest boating, swimming, scuba diving, camping, hiking, and fishing environments in British Columbia. It encompassed 118 acres, adjacent to crown land, with 3,500 feet of waterfront. Having been used off and on as a camp facility, it had some rudimentary structures and fairly primitive cabins already in place (mostly old ATCO portables). If remoteness was desired, Latona certainly qualified: there were on Gambier Island no commercial enterprises, no shops or restaurants, no public facilities, no central road network—and no apparent appetite for development on the part of its few, passionately protective residents. It was pristine, rugged, and isolated. On the other side of the ledger, Latona was located within the shadow of mountains that kept it shaded and within the frost line through the winter months, limiting its usage to summer and shoulder seasons; its facilities were dated and quite rough, its septic treatment plant old and inadequate; it was inaccessible by public transportation (unlike Keats Island, which is serviced by B.C. ferries), meaning that campers, guests, and staff would need to come and go by charter boats, water taxi, or private vessels. Likewise for delivery of food, building materials, and equipment.

In short, the site was breathtaking, the logistics daunting. Both Kirk and Rob Bentall warned of the high costs associated with operating ministry on an island (with which they were well acquainted), but especially on a remote and inaccessible corner of an island like Gambier. (No particular concerns re operating a ministry across the border from The Firs' home base in Washington seem to have been raised.) Rob Lee carried their observations, along with his own reflections, back to The Firs.

Undeterred by the cautions and thrilled with the potential, Firs leadership arranged for a larger group, including staff, board members, and other interested parties, to visit the property and brainstorm. For those already disposed to see God's hand in this new adventure, the consensus seems to have been "we are well able to take it."[7] Latona represented for them a step of faith and timely expansion of The Firs ministry—reigniting some of the excitement that the acquisition of Firwood and the Chalet had generated in the 1950s and providing insurance of sorts against the possibility that Lake Whatcom activity might one day be curtailed by environmental or other concerns. The decision was made to proceed with purchase, and the board came up with a plan to fund the project through designated donations, through sale of several Firs-owned houses in the Geneva neighborhood, and through logging and sale of a considerable amount of timber on the Gambier Island property itself.[8]

That said, there was far from universal enthusiasm on the part of resident staff, many of whom already felt stretched between responsibilities for three locations and unconvinced of the need or appropriateness of this new undertaking so far away from the historic heart of The Firs. It was not obvious to them that this was the Lord's leading or that their hesitation represented a lack of faith. Some worried that as money and effort were prioritized for Latona, attention to maintenance and upkeep of the other Firs properties was bound to weaken. Might not the apparent abandonment of the conference center amount to something of a self-fulfilling prophecy, with those who questioned its continuing viability actually, by their actions, making it less viable? The Anderson Lodge project, centerpiece of the hoped-for revitalization of the main grounds—which had been temporarily stalled by local bureaucracy—was quietly shelved.

A planning committee was established to oversee necessary improvements and upgrades to get "Latona Beach," as it came to be called, ready for guest use; work commenced in the late summer of 1999 once the purchase was finalized. Doug Whipple, perhaps Latona's most ardent advocate, chaired the committee and was on site regularly, as were his wife Darlene and other members of the Whipple family, along with numerous board and council members and friends of The Firs.[9] Amongst

7. See Num 13:30. Caleb (in company with Joshua) encourages the people to possess the promised land, despite the challenges highlighted by other members of the surveillance party.

8. For more on Latona, see Rodgers, "Christ is All in All."

9. Doug and his wife Darlene ("Punkie"), who had lived in Seattle for three decades,

Firs staff members, Bruce Vander Meulen helped advise what needed to be done at the site to make it visitor-ready and arranged for purchase of necessary materials from Canadian suppliers. With other members of The Firs maintenance crew, including Frank Muench and Doug Walker, he traveled repeatedly to the site and, among other tasks, replaced the roof on both the existing main lodge and a caretaker's house. Typically, work parties would drive to Porteau Cove Provincial Park on the east side of Howe Sound (two and a half hours from Bellingham), where a boat would pick them up and take them to Latona.[10] Supply trips were more complicated; Bruce and his crew took a ferry from the Lower Mainland to Gibsons (formerly Gibson's Landing) on the west side of the Sound, from which they drove north to the Howe Sound Mill in Port Mellon and used the mill's dock to transport building supplies and equipment to the island. A local logger was hired to take down selective trees, both to sell and to use on site. Longtime friend of The Firs, Tim Aldrich (of Doris and Willard Aldrich's "mixing bowl" clan[11]), brought his portable sawmill to the property for several weeks, milling lumber, siding, shingles, etc. from available timber.

Norm and Michelle Bedard, who were living in nearby Gibsons, stepped into the role of caretakers, though they did not live on site. Firs staffer Jim Cooney acted as interim director for Latona Beach until in early 2001 Johnny Thiessen was hired to oversee operations. A Vancouver-area native and former youth pastor, Johnny's connection to The Firs stretched all the way back to attendance at a Firwood junior camp, when his counselor was Mike Johnson ("Fonzie"). He and his wife Tammy were tasked with directing camps through the summer months and building connections with churches and other organizations who might wish to use the facility.

An official dedication of "The Firs at Latona Beach" took place on July 26, 2000 during an Open House week at the site[12]; guest groups filled

moved to Sudden Valley in 1998 to engage more directly in day-to-day activity at The Firs. Darlene served as office manager and executive secretary. Doug, who was quietly and valiantly battling cancer for nearly a decade, died less than a year after the Latona purchase, on June 5, 2000, at the age of fifty-four.

10. On one such trip, Bruce Vander Meulen's maintenance truck was stolen from the park while he was on the island. It was eventually recovered by police, but with all tools and tool boxes missing.

11. See chapter 6, note 3 above. Tim and his wife Barb were frequent volunteers at Latona Beach in subsequent years.

12. Mike ("Rosebud") Fisher, a beloved former Firwood staff member and pastor of

out the rest of the summer schedule on the island that year and in 2001. In 2002, Latona's third summer in operation, twelve families participated in the first Firs-sponsored "Latona Family Adventure," a variant on the family summer conference held annually at the conference center; a team of volunteers from an Alberta youth group helped run a creative and well-received "Castaway"-themed program. Otherwise, the summer was filled with midweek school groups and weekend gatherings for British Columbia churches, all of which were new to The Firs and some of which were quick to adopt Latona Beach as "their" camp.

Jan Morell, who had just taken over responsibility for guest services at The Firs,[13] was an enthusiastic promoter of Latona's ocean-front location and pristine wilderness ambience; she helped spread word through brochures and other means to secure blocks of campers (mostly church youth groups from Bellingham, Seattle, and Vancouver, Washington) for this new Firs-connected venture. Among repeat users of the property was Northlake Church in Geneva, whose youth group under the leadership of Jon Hansen (Firwood's "Gonzo") attended "Latona Adventure Camps" on Gambier from 2002 to 2005.

Northlake was itself another icon of change in this season of The Firs story. Geneva Community Church—which was established in the early 1960s as a natural outgrowth of onsite Bible studies and fellowship gatherings with new converts meeting at The Firs[14]—was pastored by Grant Whipple for twenty years, with Doug Anderson as his long-term assistant. Though the church and The Firs were formally and legally distinct, Firs staff provided for many years major roles in leadership, and visiting speakers at the conference center were routinely invited to speak at Geneva services. By the late 1990s, the worship space was becoming inadequate for the needs of a growing suburban congregation, and the challenges of sharing the main sanctuary (built in 1962) and the Rutledge

Grace Bible Church in Dallas was guest speaker for the week.

13. Jan moved to the Geneva neighborhood in 1979, attended women's luncheons in the 1980s, and began helping the housekeeping crew at The Firs in the 1990s. She also worked in The Firs Bookstore with Julie Lingbloom (wife of retreat center maintenance coordinator Brian Lingbloom), selling books and merchandise and trying out her new skills as a barista, "little leaf designs" and all. (Bookstore managers Karl and Tammy Graham had introduced a popular espresso bar to the bookstore in 1996.) She was invited to take over guest services in 1999 and stayed in that role for 25 years. The Firs Bookstore, like many independent shops, was unable to compete with online booksellers and large retail outlets like Costco and closed its doors in 2003.

14. See chapter 10, above.

education building (built in 1983) with the retreat center were becoming more difficult. The last church service held in the historic venue took place on September 26, 1999, with Grant speaking and giving the congregation his blessing. In 2000, the congregation moved into a new, significantly larger worship center, several miles from The Firs, under the new name of Northlake Community Church. The old Geneva sanctuary ceased being used for regular worship, but after extensive (and expensive) repurposing of church spaces, served as a meeting place for numerous Firs programs and as a rented facility for local Christian non-profits. The first tenant, Evergreen Christian School, moved in during the summer of 2001 and occupied the building for six years.

The commencement of a new millennium, which turned out to be less disruptive than the Y2K soothsayers and doom-peddling media foretold,[15] ushered in a variety of milestones and personnel changes at The Firs. Darell Smith, who had been diagnosed with multiple sclerosis, found the 24-hour demands of living at and overseeing Camp Firwood to be increasingly untenable. He was able to pass the torch to Rob Lee, who took over as Firwood director in January 2000; Darell transferred to a role as overall children and youth programming director for Firwood, the Chalet, and the conference center. Phil Wegener, director of The Firs Chalet for a decade and a half, who had overseen a hugely taxing, multi-year remodel and safety upgrade of the facility in addition to running programs and triaging innumerable weather-related crises (e.g., roof leaks, broken windows, generator breakdowns, generator shed roof collapse, leaking waterlines under eight feet of snow), decided that his long-suffering wife Pam and four kids deserved to see more of him, especially in the winter months, and elected to step down and seek more traditional "nine to five" employment.[16] Doug and Marie Walker, who had taken a

15. Y2K involved a worldwide panic over whether computers, programmed with two-digit dating systems (e.g., "92" rather than "1992") would crash at the commencement of "00" on January 1, 2000, causing havoc for banking, utilities, hospitals, transportation systems, etc. Enterprising prognosticators produced Y2K-themed books, movies, and merchandise, including "survival guides" and kits—all of which turned out to be needless.

16. Phil and Pam moved with their children to a home in Sudden Valley. Pam worked part-time for The Firs, and Phil, after losing a software position when the dot-com bubble burst, eventually settled into a new career as a remodeling contractor. Tragically, Pam suffered a heart attack in October 2003, leaving him to raise their children on his own. Looking back, Phil reflected gratefully not only on those few years of enjoying a more normal family life but also on the Lord's timely financial provision for the family's needs.

hiatus for several years to be near their parents in Spokane, returned to full-time staff at The Firs, now with two children, having adopted son Jon while in Spokane.[17] The bookkeeping, maintenance, and food service departments also saw staff changes or additions in 2000, which was informally dubbed a "year of preparation" for the new millennium by Firs personnel.

In this same period, Greg Kinloch was beginning to transition out of his role as executive director, turning an increasing number of responsibilities over to Tom Beaumont as he and Barb prepared for an interim, pre-retirement stint as Firs ambassadors, and then full retirement several years later, with a move to Barb's home turf in the Yakima Valley. Tom, whose tenure at The Firs stretched back to the mid-1980s and who had served on the executive committee and worked alongside Greg as assistant executive director for several years, was well prepared to step into the traces. One of his immediate priorities would be to oversee a new board-approved capital campaign, "ploughing new ground for The Firs as we begin our ninth decade of ministry."[18]

In 2003, Grant Whipple, scion of the Whipple family whose radical faith and self-sacrificing love was the veritable heartwood of The Firs, passed into the Lord's presence at the age of ninety-two, a gracious, lifelong servant leader. He would be followed by his dear wife Bernice four years later; she was found by the family "asleep" in her home, having fallen silently between the kitchen and dining room, where she had bestowed hospitality on countless guests through decades of loving service to her Lord.[19]

17. Doug owned his own construction business during the family's Spokane years, which allowed him to extend and refine his construction skills, all of which would be put to good use when he and Marie returned to The Firs.

18. As the old faith policy continued to evolve, "The Firs board . . . endorsed a capital campaign to finance major projects that exist at all four sites . . . We will focus our attention on greater promotional efforts and look to see our base of revenue raise significantly" (*Firs Fellowship*, Spring 2000). For further discussion of the changes, see chapter 18, and Appendix B, below.

19. Grant's stepmother, "Aunt Ruth" Whipple, lived to celebrate her hundredth birthday before her own heavenly homegoing in 1996.

# 17

# Canopy (2004–2007)

"There will be a canopy . . . for shade . . . from the heat and . . . shelter from the storm and rain."[1]

ONE OF THE UNFORESEEN CHALLENGES that faced The Firs as Tom Beaumont was moving into his role as executive director was the post-9/11 political and cultural landscape. The terrorist attacks on the World Trade Center and Pentagon on a clear autumn morning in 2001 changed the country in incalculable ways, one of the most immediate and obvious being the tightening of security at the northern border. At 10:05 a.m. (ET) on September 11, 2001, the border between Canada and the United States was sealed shut without warning, causing massive traffic gridlock at the Peace Arch in Blaine, Washington. And although conditions eased over the following days and weeks, the relative effortlessness of pre-9/11 travel back and forth across the world's longest undefended border was never to return. Longer lines and more intrusive and time-consuming inspections became the norm, and a general apprehension about terrorism curbed the appetite for travel.

For a ministry like The Firs, which had always served a sizable Canadian constituency, the effects were drastic. Cancellations began coming in almost immediately, and the overall registration of Canadian conferees for the Chalet and retreat center, as well as staff and campers at Firwood, plummeted. Everyone had to scramble to plug the holes. For Jan Morell, the immediate need and priority was to introduce what The

1. Isa 4:5–6, ESV.

Firs had to offer to entirely new communities, churches, and families as potential guest groups: "We started to rebuild, we made a lot of phone calls, we touched base with a lot of people." Her winsome sales pitch and her tenacity proved indispensable in filling up the calendar with new groups and then encouraging retention. "Just come once," she would say, knowing that "once" would typically begin a long-term relationship. "They would worry about it being too suburban, too noisy, but once we got them here, under the canopy of these magnificent evergreens, they were amazed at how peaceful it was, how much of a sanctuary.[2] And they just kept rolling over. We called it our rollover policy," she observed with a smile. "I would say that out of hundreds of guest groups I booked over the years, there were only two I didn't rebook." One of Jan's favorites was always Royal Family Kids, an organization dedicated to loving and advocating for foster children and child victims of family abuse or trauma. For many years, Royal Family Kids brought several different groups for back-to-back camp weeks at The Firs. The transformation of wary and frightened children to happy and boisterous ones in the course of a week was always a thrill.

In Tom Beaumont's view, the move toward an increasing guest group presence at The Firs was providential; it took considerable strain off an already busy staff and cost the ministry much less to operate and manage. But it also ignited a new emphasis in ministry. "We began to realize that these groups were often doing, and doing well, things that we weren't especially focused on. We had historically hosted mostly Christians at the conference center. In partnering with local churches and parachurch groups, we were actually opening up to a more missional and evangelistic outreach; in some ways they were fulfilling one of our core missions better than we were."

As for The Firs' own programming, couples' conferences had been largely discontinued by this time, and seniors' and Elderhostel gatherings, women's weekends, and family camps were all to varying extents affected by the new situation at the border and the rising cost of travel insurance, which could in some cases exceed the conference fee.[3] Adult

2. Appreciative guest notes like the following were common: "I am so thankful for the vision of a group of Christians to build and hold onto these grounds for almost 100 years. There is a peacefulness when we come here that creates a safe haven for us to experience God's grace."

3. Special events, including "The Firs Noel" programs in December and community hymn sings, proved popular with locals, as did the later addition of "Scrapbooking Days" (initiated and led by Barb Vander Meulen) to the women's ministry schedule. The

camper days in Firs-run programs (which already represented less than half of the camper days filled by guest groups in 2003) decreased every year from 2003 to 2005, with projections for 2006 falling even further. The times were definitely changing.

One bright spot was an innovative new program initiated by Darell Smith in the early 2000s called Emmaus Road, which featured dynamic, high-profile Christian speakers for single-day Saturday conferences, where the emphasis was not on fellowship or recreation but (reflecting the Emmaus disciples, whose story is told in Luke 24) an intense, life-changing encounter with the risen Lord. Among notable Emmaus Road speakers were Brennan Manning (author of *The Ragamuffin Gospel*), Dan Allendar (Christian therapist and founder of the Seattle School of Theology and Psychology), Scot McKnight (author of *The Jesus Creed*), Gary Thomas (author of *Authentic Faith*), and Donald Miller (author of *Blue Like Jazz*). Emmaus Road proved an attractive offering to a whole new cohort of attendees, including younger working adults, for whom the combination of a shorter time commitment and a renowned speaker was especially appealing.[4] Most conferees came from Bellingham or the surrounding area, while others drove up from the Seattle or even Portland. Many had never been to The Firs before. The program proved an overwhelming success in terms of numbers (with as many as three hundred in attendance) and, according to evaluation forms, carried significant spiritual impact.

The Firs' Canadian outpost at Latona Beach, meanwhile, was focused primarily on Canadian rather than American guest groups; the tightening border simply reinforced that established pattern. The "Castaway" family camp in 2002 was a one-off, the only Firs-sponsored program to take place on Gambier, and even it drew mostly Canadians.[5] As noted previously, several church youth groups from Washington State enjoyed Latona Beach adventures in the early 2000s, but one of the original ideas for Latona—to provide a saltwater and wilderness extension to

latter afforded a niche opportunity for unchurched women to find a welcome at The Firs. The program was intimate, fun, and relaxed; relationships were built as beautiful keepsake books were created and simple meals and devotionals shared.

4. Optional housing for Friday and/or Saturday night was available for those travelling from a distance, and a midday meal was provided for all conferees on Saturday.

5. I am excluding here the Open House Week in 2000, and various work party weekends that American friends and supporters attended but that were not part of a formal program.

the Firwood experience for older youth and young adults (aged eighteen to thirty-five)—never really materialized.

In 2004, Johnny Thiessen stepped down from his pioneering role as director of Latona Beach to pursue a church planting ministry. The Lord provided an exceptional new director in John de Jong, a retired twenty-five-year veteran R.C.M.P. officer living in nearby Sechelt, who brought fresh energy, versatile skills, and a breadth of experience into the role. He and his wife Marian, a special education teacher, also had servants' hearts, as would become evident over the next several years as they and their four sons poured into the Latona Beach ministry. After a four-month initiation in the summer of 2004, they opened camp the following year in mid-March with a spring break retreat for Crossroads Community Church (the de Jongs' home church in Sechelt). They then hosted multiple camps through the summer, ending the season with an adventure camp for Collingwood School (in Vancouver) on October 3. Improvement projects were more or less continuous, with remodeled guest accommodation, a games/recreation hall, and a regulation-size beach volleyball court being completed that year. Given changes in caretaking and food services personnel during that camp season, it was not unusual during the late summer especially to find the de Jongs filling in with meal preparation, cleaning the dining facility and restrooms, driving a ski boat, or overseeing recreation activities.

In October 2005, John de Jong was invited to meet with The Firs Board and executive leadership at Manteo Resort in Kelowna, B.C. The purpose of the retreat was to prayerfully assess a whole range of issues facing The Firs, not least the ministry at Latona Beach. John's passion for the Latona project and his commitment to excellence in every aspect of the ministry were clear as he shared the transformative improvements in property and programming, relationships established, generous donations of materials and of endless volunteer help, and the overall impact of Latona Beach on those it served. The number of guest groups using the facility had grown steadily, and God had brought many to faith or to a deeper spiritual walk through their experience at camp. The challenges were nonetheless impossible to ignore. Though the location was spectacular, and Latona's niche as a youth camping guest facility had been more or less settled, facilities were still not where they needed to be and transportation costs and logistics presented a significant hindrance to many would-be camp groups. These same issues were a constant complication for camp operations themselves, especially food service. Cancellations proved not only inconvenient but extremely expensive. In its first five years of operation, despite dedicated, skilled, and self-sacrificing leadership, Latona had never broken even financially, and no one could realistically project that changing in the foreseeable future.[6]

In December, the board announced its decision that the 2006 season of The Firs at Latona Beach would be its last. Though obviously disappointed, John was exceptionally gracious in his response: "God's vision for Latona is much bigger than ours. My task now is to make Latona the very best experience ever for each and every person who sets foot on the property in 2006. Our partnership with [the Lord] can only bless us and those whom we strive to serve." He then asked that everyone in The Firs family "keep us in your prayers for a spirit of enthusiasm and perseverance."[7]

The decision to close down the Latona Beach program was, if anything, more contentious than the original decision to purchase the site had been in 1999, with some members of the community and council, for whom Latona represented a deeply personal investment of time and energy, feeling that the project wasn't given sufficient opportunity to come into its own and become financially viable. It was not easy to navigate such concerns, with which Tom Beaumont had considerable sympathy, or to manage the strong factional feelings within the constituency. In a 2003 newsletter, drawing on Paul's analogy of the body, he had previously warned of the "great challenge as a staff, board, and council, to see the big picture of The Firs" rather than to became partisans of one or another of its individual sites or programs. Greg Kinloch and Doug Whipple had each, in their own way, drawn attention to the same issue: the need for the community to pull together, intentionally and prayerfully, around a common, God-ordained identity and vision for The Firs as a whole.

In short, though Latona Beach was a flashpoint, it was only one part of a larger reassessment of the overall stewardship of The Firs legacy. And once again, the role of the conference center was foremost in everyone's minds. An outside consultant, Ron Mattocks, provided a rather stark assessment:

> The conference center . . . has not defined its primary market niche. The summer, in particular, magnifies the problem by

6. Losses continued in 2006, with fewer camper days, and revenue down 37 percent.

7. The property went up for sale in the spring of 2007 and was sold in June to Declan Lawlor, who had pre-Firs ties to Latona, for use as a non-denominational, multi-faith children's camp operated by the Camp Latona Society.

> relying on youth activity in an adult setting to be somewhat viable. Because of its low volume, the conference center is inefficient to operate, has very high overhead, and currently is the single greatest drain on Firs finances . . . The adult retreat market must be expanded, the calendar must be filled more, and double and even triple bookings must take place.

Kirk Potter, who came on the full-time Firs staff in February 2007, was named conference center director and immediately tasked with preparing a comprehensive evaluation of current use and a "short term action plan" for future ministry at the site. Kirk brought a wealth of relevant experience to the task. He had known The Firs since the early 1970s, when he served three summers on Firwood summer staff (camp name "Snap"), overseeing the sailing and outpost camping programs. He graduated from Biola (where he met his wife Debbie[8]) and Talbot Seminary with degrees in Christian Education focused specifically on camping. Subsequently, as a youth leader in West Vancouver and Tacoma churches, he maintained contact with Firs programs, accompanying junior high and high school kids to winter camps at the Chalet. And then, after a stint with Young Life of Canada, he was named executive director of Keats Camps, a position he held for sixteen years before coming to The Firs.[9] In a fall board meeting that year (2007), Kirk presented his report, which encouraged continued and enhanced use of the Geneva site and made numerous recommendations for upgrading the facilities and property for adult programming. The longstanding problem of deferred maintenance at the retreat center had, if anything, intensified during the Latona years, as money and effort flowed into the Gambier Island site. Now that the decision to sell Latona had been made, the crucial needs of the original Firs property could be addressed more readily. The board enthusiastically endorsed Kirk's recommendations and deferred maintenance projects at the retreat center were addressed with new urgency.

8. Debbie taught at Whatcom Discovery School (which met for several years in the former Geneva Community Church complex) with Val Lee, and was also involved in organizing women's retreats at The Firs.

9. Kirk also spent time with campers at Malibu Club, the Young Life camp on Princess Louisa Inlet on British Columbia's Sunshine Coast, and served several years on staff at Camp Homewood, a Quadra Island ministry founded by Alf Bayne and his wife Margaret in 1944 under the aegis of Pacific Coast Children's Mission. It is doubtful that anyone on The Firs staff before or since has had more extensive exposure to the panoply of Christian camps on the Pacific Northwest coast. I am deeply indebted to Kirk for answering my many questions and offering useful perspective during the writing of this book.

The Firs maintenance team, whose labors were generally invisible to visitors but absolutely vital to the ministry, already kept up a blistering pace with roof repair and replacement at all properties, construction and renovation of Firwood and Fircreek cabins, replacement of boat docks and other facilities at Firwood, and constant renovation and upgrades at the fifty-year-old Chalet. Renewed focus on the conference center would add a long list of new projects. It would also require new levels of giving, as part of a five-year stewardship campaign called Project Step-Up.

Kirk worked with Jan Morell in bringing fresh adult guest programming to the conference center (informally now called Cable Street North) and with Darell Smith, who moved over to a new role as Fircreek director, to enhance children and youth programming on the other side of the street (Cable Street South).

Darell's capacity to connect with children (even from a scooter or a power wheelchair) was as evident at Fircreek as it had been at Firwood. The gathering place in which all the children shared "Jesus and Me" time was code-named the "lap of God," a reminder of Jesus' welcome of little ones to his knee (Matt 19, Mark 10, and Luke 18). "Clearing a path to Jesus" was the explicit intent of all programming at Fircreek. In one among many memorable teaching moments, when Darell was leading kids in the Lord's Prayer, he paused over the petition for daily bread and made the distinction between prayers of genuine need and "gimme" petitions involving mere wants. He then asked if any campers wished to join him onstage in front of everyone and to ask God for something they needed. Lots of hands went up, and several children were chosen. They poured their hearts out with sincerity and candor. One young boy, in a foster home placement, prayed, "Dear God, please give me a family where I am loved, where I will be safe, and where I can stay for a long time. Amen." An eleven-year-old girl, whose parents were in the midst of an ugly divorce, prayed, "God, I pray that my parents would respect me and approve of my life." Another child said, "God, please help my grandfather. He had a heart attack, fell, and broke his neck. He needs to live." In a crowd of typically noisy children, there was an attentive, respectful silence as these youngsters addressed a loving Father with heartfelt concerns. Of such is the kingdom of heaven.

Fircreek had, since its inception in 1960, always been a summer-only program, a non-residential day camp that ran more or less simultaneously with Firwood—from the end of the school year to Labor Day weekend. In the early 2000s, the property and facilities that were home to Fircreek found a new purpose for school-year use with the opening of After School Adventure (A.S.A.).

Stacy Smith had been partnering with her husband Darell in ministry at The Firs since 1986, initially in an immersive role at Firwood, where Darell served as director for ten years. When Darell moved to a more administrative role at the retreat center in the late 1990s, Stacy opened a small daycare in her home, "just because I was lazy and didn't want to drive our kids all the way into town for preschool. They were all at my house anyway, and so I thought, Let's organize these kids and have a curriculum." A few years later, as her own children were aging out and into the school system, Tom Beaumont approached her about starting a community after-school program at The Firs. She would once again be working with Darell, but this time in a paid position. As Stacy recalled, she thought she would get the program up and running in 2001 and then look for a "big girl job." But she was soon captivated with the project, and within a few years she knew she had found her vocational niche, "creating spaces for kids who, a lot of times, were discarded or just in households that were too busy." She was ingenious in her programming and infectious in her enthusiasm, but the special magic in the "Adventure" she created was in her unabashed way of loving kids with the love of Jesus.

Five years after A.S.A. was inaugurated, there were more than seventy children on site daily at Cable Street South from 2:30 to 6:15 p.m., enjoying outdoor games and adventures in a beautiful woodland environment, as well as crafts, science projects, and homework help between the end of the school day and being picked up for home. A well-trained, energetic, and welcoming staff lavished attention and affection on the children, helping them grow in resilience and confidence as they played in a beautiful, safe environment. A state-licensed program, A.S.A. welcomed kids from six local public schools (Geneva Elementary, Carl Cozier Elementary, Wade King Elementary, Roosevelt Elementary, Silver Beach Elementary, and Northern Heights Elementary) as well as Evergreen Christian School, which was still meeting in the old Geneva Church facilities.[10] Stacy forged strong relationships with school counselors, administrators, and parents, which proved vital to the success of the program. Outreach to families went well beyond mere "hellos" when

10. Evergreen announced its intention to look for a larger space in 2007. Shortly thereafter, Whatcom Discovery School moved in for several years, after which The Firs' own After School Adventure and other childcare programs took over full-time use of the facilities.

kids were picked up. A.S.A. sponsored family game nights, moms' spa nights, dessert parties, and even end-of-the-year family overnights at The Firs Chalet. And as families faced particular challenges, the staff often found ways to extend extra care; when an A.S.A. parent had to undergo chemotherapy for cancer, camp personnel not only underwrote her son's increased program expenses, from three days to five, but also provided a special meal during her treatment regime.

The After School Adventure proved so popular with local working families (there was soon a waitlist) that it began sprouting whole new programs. A before-school program was added, providing early morning care (with occasional "Waffle Wednesday" or "Flapjack Friday" breakfast offerings) for over twenty children.[11] In September 2005, Stacy added "Kinder Adventure" to provide enrichment and outdoor play from noon to 2:30 p.m. for fifteen or more kindergartners, many of whom then stayed on for the After School Adventure program as well. And on school holidays and teacher workshop days, rather than taking a break, A.S.A. staff provided "All Day Adventures." Overall, while the conference center on the north side of Cable Street was occasionally too quiet, Cable Street South was becoming a year-round hive of raucous, happy activity.[12]

Down the lake at Firwood, things were also humming, with over two thousand campers spending a week or more in residence between mid-June and the end of August. Program offerings expanded every year as lakefront and land-based equipment was added to keep things fresh for return campers. Though the longtime horsemanship program was discontinued in the mid-2000s, the void was filled with paintball, skateboarding, a completely rebuilt and enhanced high ropes challenge course, and ever-expanding waterfront options (now including wake-boarding, water trampolines, inflatable slides, and a "blob"). But the heart of Firwood continued to be the forging of strong personal relationships between campers and staff, which in turn pointed campers to a personal relationship with Jesus. Rob Lee recounted how his ninety-member staff began each summer with a challenge "to see each camper with the eyes

11. An earlier, short-lived experiment with preschool programming had taken place in the 1980s.

12. A wish list for enhancement of Cable Street South, in a 2006 Strategic Plan, included an activity center, which could serve as a multi-purpose facility for Fircreek and a clubhouse for A.S.A. Ideally, it would include also a gymnasium for guest group use and an adjacent pool that would provide a safe onsite swimming area and reduce the flow of camper traffic to the lake. The activity center took a back seat to other priorities and never got past the idea stage.

of Christ—that is, to see past the behavior, the appearance, the fashion statements"—and recognize all of them as people beloved by God, for whom Christ died. Each summer, two hundred or more kids made a first profession of faith in Jesus; countless others renewed their pledge to follow him in a life of discipleship. Once the kids went home, dedicated counselors were finding ways, through popular websites like MySpace and Facebook, to keep in contact with them through the year, mentoring and encouraging them in their newfound or rekindled faith.

In August 2005, Firwood alumni celebrated the camp's fiftieth anniversary, an event which included all seven camp directors (Jerry Wilson, Dwight Whipple, Jon Aldrich, Greg Kinloch, Mike Johnson, Darrel Smith, and Rob Lee) and their spouses, as well as a large cohort of former summer staff. Master of Ceremonies was Paul ("Smacks") Petersen, 1975 Firwood counselor, local pastor, and member of The Firs Board. It was an evening of hearing testimonials, reliving memories through a five-decade compilation of photos and film, friendly competition in a Firwood trivia contest, singing old camp songs, renewing friendships, and receiving updates about current and future Firwood projects.

The primary item on the Firwood "to do" list, that had preoccupied leadership and the board since the late 1990s, was a new dining facility. Camp had simply outgrown the decades-old Longhouse. It was originally built to hold about eighty campers but had long since exceeded capacity, typically wedging in more than three hundred staff members and kids several times each day; this was not only impractical but unsafe, and the building could certainly not accommodate any increase in numbers. Its kitchen was also dated and inadequate to meet current health department requirements. A new dining space, with a large, modern, working kitchen would fill many needs; plans called for it to be used as a multipurpose facility, available not only through the summer camping season but also as a year-round site for Firs gatherings and guest group functions.[13] The iconic Longhouse, once it ceased to be a dining hall, would still be an asset for rainy day activities and a variety of program options.

By the middle 2000s, a projected plan for the dining room was complete and a site chosen. In 2007, Rob Lee reported that a "conditional use permit" had been granted by Whatcom County, and that a building permit was on the horizon. Fundraising had been ongoing for several

13. Expanding use of the beautiful and spacious Firwood property beyond the youth camping season was increasingly deemed not only advantageous to The Firs but a stewardship priority.

years, but The Firs' longstanding commitment to avoid indebtedness meant that the project would wait until sufficient funds were available. In early 2008, board chairman Dave Scheevel announced that the sale of Latona, which netted nearly double what The Firs had paid for it in 1999, was a provision unlike anything in The Firs' history, and would allow for the long-awaited dining room project, to be called Centerhouse, to proceed at last: "We are hopeful of making that leap of faith before the end of 2008."

Only eternity will reveal fully the many blessings associated with the seven-year ministry of The Firs at Latona Beach. But that God used it for good, to serve his manifold purposes, is indisputable—perhaps the one fact that everyone in the extended Firs family was able to agree on.

Seniors' retreat at The Firs conference center (1990s).

The Firs at Latona Beach, Gambier Island, British Columbia (1999–2006).

Fircreek campers at The Firs waterfront.

After School Adventure (A.S.A.) kids in the old Geneva Chapel building.

The Firs' forest preschool, Firs and Fiddleheads.

# 18

# Adaptation (2008–2016)

"Thou changest not, Thy compassions, they fail not.
As Thou hast been Thou forever will be."[1]

When reflecting back on his three-and-a-half decades at The Firs, much of it in the role of executive director, Tom Beaumont chose one word to sum it up: "Change!"

> I knew that change was happening when I arrived on the scene in 1985 and began working within Greg Kinloch's leadership structure. I got to be a part of the change in the eighteen years I worked with Greg and saw the inner workings of that change. Then when I became executive director, it became my responsibility to initiate and manage appropriate change. Change is inevitable and in many ways change is necessary. The families we serve, the churches we support, and the culture in which we minister all change, so change is needed for the growth and the impact we desire as an organization. The challenge is not so much to make sure that every individual change is the right one but that, in the midst of change, we don't lose sight of why we exist and the mission that needs to drive us.

The idea that Christian ministry adapts in different temporal and cultural settings is itself uncontroversial. All living things experience change, and organizational change is typically regarded as indicative that the

1. "Great is Thy Faithfulness," by Thomas Chisholm (1923), based on Lam 3:22–23: "Through the Lord's mercies we are not consumed, because His compassions fail not. They are new every morning; Great is your faithfulness."

organization is "alive" rather than moribund. But it is also obvious that not all change is good: "change" can imply innovation, improvement, renewal, reform; it can also suggest reversal, erosion, accommodation, compromise. Tom's emphasis on keeping the mission as primary focus was salutary.[2] All change needed to be made within a consistent effort to reinforce and strengthen the core identity of the ministry; otherwise, it could lead, unintentionally, to "mission drift."[3]

The mission statement formulated by Firs leadership had in fact adapted in several ways over the decades. In the mid-1990s, it commenced with the assertion that "The overall purpose of The Firs is to bring glory to God" and that the means to that end was "demonstrating in humble, practical ways the glory and power of God." It elaborated that in the "natural setting" featured in its camps and conferences, "the Bible-centered teachings of The Firs, together with time for personal and family reflection, helps people to accept Jesus Christ as their Lord and Savior, grow in their spiritual walk, strengthen their family life, and fulfill the Great Commission (Matt 28:19)."

A few years later, after the turn of the millennium, an updated and more concise mission statement was created, which read: "The Firs serves the local church and community by drawing groups and individuals to a camp and retreat setting where they will experience the biblical message of Jesus through instruction, creative activities, and significant relationships, resulting in changed lives."

The revised statement, especially when paired with an adjacent statement of biblically-defined "Core Values" (Impacting lives for Christ; Communicating the Bible as truth; Partnering with the local church; Serving well in a safe environment; Maintaining fiscal integrity; and Focusing on faith), shows no sign of theological drift (though some may regret the omission of formulating the ministry's ultimate purpose as bringing glory to God and in "demonstrating … the glory and power of God"[4]).

2. Board chairman Dave Scheevel rang the same themes in his 2006 annual report: "Just doing things because 'we've always done it that way' is not working in today's world. We need to be responsive to current requirements . . . if we are to compete with other camping and conference organizations. In addition, being sensitive to ministry needs and opportunities that change from time to time is also critical. [Equally important] is the need for clear vision and mission about the future ministry of The Firs."

3. The term was coined in the early 2000s and gained widespread attention with the important and influential book by Greer and Horst, *Mission Drift: The Unspoken Crisis*.

4. This initial statement echoes the Westmister Shorter Catechism, the first question of which, "What is the chief end [i.e., purpose] of man?" is succinctly answered,

Nonetheless, emphasis shifted in several subtle but noticeable ways. The old missionary identity, though silent in the 1995 statement, is explicitly redefined in the newer version: the focus is local; the central mission is serving church and community that are geographically proximate to The Firs.[5] Indeed, "serving the community" is itself a new emphasis—one borne out in the creation of A.S.A. and related state-supported programs outlined in the previous chapter. Moreover, the language of "experience" and "significant relationships" and "changed lives" seems intentionally crafted to be more culturally accessible than the traditionally worded 1995 statement.

Among the obvious programming changes effected under Tom's early watch were the ending of ministry at Latona Beach and sale of the Gambier Island property, and the decision to discontinue family camps at the conference center, the market for which had diminished significantly. The concomitant decision to "zero in on youth and children's ministries" and "to pursue greater involvement in student ministries" was another major decision affirmed by board leadership.[6]

And, perhaps for the first time, the vision laid out by Tom and his leadership team made explicit a new aspiration regarding The Firs' financial health: "The Firs will be a sound, thriving, and prosperous institution. It will achieve operational solvency; it will practice aggressive development, and it will focus all of its resources on meeting the needs of others."[7] While the terminology is a far cry from Otis Whipple's early twentieth-century statements about waiting on God's provision, however modest, it reflected a clear biblical concern for faithfulness in matters of financial management in a large, multifaceted, twenty-first-century ministry. Avoidance of debt was still clearly stipulated. But "solvency" and

---

"Man's chief end is to glorify God and enjoy Him forever." The latter phrase quietly reflects the "faith" focus ("helping people believe").

5. The view of many within The Firs constituency was that churches had taken on support for cross-cultural and overseas missions and were doing it well. For others, the loss of The Firs' historic connection to and active involvement with the global church was regrettable.

6. The idea of hosting a resident student ministries program at the conference center that percolated for many years under various names ("Firs Leadership Apprenticeship Program," "Village Discipleship Training Community," "Lectio," "Collegium") would finally take hold in 2023 as "Radicle and Rooted" (see chapter 20 below). College student Bible studies and university retreats had a strong early presence at The Firs, as indicated in the early chapters of this book; a residential option would allow for more intensive discipleship in the context of accountable Christian community.

7. From "Strategic Planning: The Firs 2006." See also Appendix B.

even becoming a "thriving and prosperous" institution were now definite and articulate goals—not as ends in themselves but as a means of serving others in Jesus' name.

In this light, "Stewardship" was the theme that retired physician Bruce Whipple[8] chose as a focus for community prayer and community involvement when he was named board chair in 2007; the following year he chose "Faith," reasserting that "The goal and mission of The Firs have remained unchanged, although the method and programs seem to be in constant change." In 2010, Bruce recounted that in 2007 the board had set a mandate "to achieve in three years a net budgeted operational surplus of 5 percent—a huge step of faith." Having budgeted for, and achieved, a net income in excess of $100,000 after years and years of "flirting with breaking-even" was an extraordinary testimony of God's ongoing provision, to which the only appropriate response was "praise for the past and trust for the future." In 2011, in his last public reflection as board chair, Bruce drew attention to "the amazing unity" that pertained "in a very diverse group working through difficult decisions and processes"—which he attributed to the prayers of God's people: "I am convinced that this is fundamentally the most important resource of The Firs, since God is the one who supplies according to his riches. All other contributions that we make are of secondary importance." As Dick Eley had trenchantly summed it up three decades earlier, it was essential that "we not just dwell in a philosophy but actually live on our knees."

With new realism about challenges and clarity about objectives, some changes were more readily agreed upon, including personnel changes. The Chalet, having been managed by Tom Walton for thirty years, followed by Phil Wegener for fifteen years, proved increasingly difficult to staff because of its remoteness, its exceptional demands on family life, and its constant need for repair and upkeep. Bobby and Carol Anderson, both of whom had been involved in food service at The Firs, were popular Chalet hosts for several years, followed by Jeff Milsten, alumnus of a Young Life camp in Oregon, who brought building skills, outdoor leadership qualifications, and an entrepreneurial spirit to the role, but after four and a half years found the intense schedule incompatible with raising a young family; he left to take a firefighter position on Bainbridge Island. In 2014, Rob Lee added the role of Chalet manager to his position as Firwood director—balancing programs in opposite seasons and

8. Bruce Whipple, Grant and Bernice's eldest son, returned with his wife Lillian from Alaska to the Geneva neighborhood in 2004.

finding dedicated staff and volunteers to host and manage the Chalet on weekends. For a time, Firwood cook James McClure acted as Chalet cook during the winter season. Doug Walker, who had loved the Chalet since spending weekends there with Tom Walton in the early 1980s, assumed year-round operational responsibilities, aspiring there, as at Firwood, to make the environment safer, better kept, and more attractive for campers.

At Firwood, meanwhile, one of the longest-awaited and most heralded changes came in 2010 with the completion and dedication of the new dining hall, Centerhouse, made possible by the generosity of countless donors and by an infusion of significant funds from a favorable sale of the Latona property. With an 8,000 square foot main floor, a 4,000 square foot basement, and a 2,000 square foot deck, it featured a vastly enlarged and improved kitchen, space for comfortable family-style dining for as many as four hundred guests, and ample room for indoor recreation, including a stage with light and sound systems. Centerhouse was hugely popular among campers and also provided a beautiful space for off-season gatherings for guest groups and Firs staff and council events.

Apart from obvious physical improvements at Firwood,[9] other forms of adaptation were shaping the camp experience in significant ways. By the late 2000s, a noticeable "migration indoors" had taken hold among American children and teenagers, effected largely by increasing attachment to technological devices and screens. What had once been the most natural and sought-after environment for kids, especially in the summer months, was too frequently exchanged for inside spaces behind closed doors. "Kids no longer knew how to play outside in God's creation," observed Rob Lee. The flip phones they had first brought to camp in the early 2000s gave way to internet-connected smartphones, which in turn prompted all too many parents to expect 24/7 access to their kids.[10]

9. Doug Walker, having returned with his family to The Firs in 2000, was again the prime mover of physical enhancement at Firwood. Apart from his involvement with Centerhouse, some of his more noteworthy projects were construction of a new shower house and infirmary, director's apartment, camp office, and a gazebo which served as a memorial to Anne Hutcheson (Grant and Bernice Whipple's daughter). In addition, swim docks, sail dock, and food dock were all replaced, the horse barn and corral converted to a paintball venue, skateboard ramps built, etc., etc. Old cabins were constantly being repaired; in one memorable instance, Doug and his crew had to rebuild a cabin that was destroyed by fire during the camp season (August 2001) in a matter of days, since it was needed to house a new batch of incoming campers.

10. Though there was a requirement to turn in any devices that kids brought to camp, it was not uncommon for campers (and parents) to try to get around the policy by bringing or sending two phones—one which was meekly turned in and a second

Getting everyone to "detach" for a week or two was not easy, but it was essential to the camp experience: "As we taught campers to unplug the cell phones, iPods, and personal video gaming systems, they began to pull apart from the things of the world and enjoy one another in a beautiful setting, in a safe community, where God's word was open and fragrant."

Staff culture at Firwood was also itself in flux, for some of the same reasons, but also for others that Rob reflected on years later:

> The landscape of summer staff changed dramatically in the 1990s and 2000s. When I was on summer staff, many of us came from evangelical homes, were connected to a local church, and knew the Bible very well. From the middle of Darell's ministry through mine, we noticed a huge shift. For many of those who served at camp, Firwood summer staff was their only faith community and I was the only pastoral figure that they had in their lives.[11] They did not come from a home where there was any faith journey: they met the Lord through Young Life or a college ministry. (Or, in some cases, through summers at Firwood.)

But it was also Rob's observation that even among those who had gone to church their whole lives, "many came to us completely biblically illiterate. They were great kids for the most part, they loved to worship, they loved to be in community, but they just didn't know the Bible at all."[12]

In such circumstances, vetting summer staff for a capacity to lead campers to an understanding of the claims of the gospel was challenging. The old pipelines from schools like Biola, Multnomah, Trinity Western University, and Regent College had largely dried up. Many applicants for summer staff were camper alumni, who loved everything about Firwood but whose knowledge of the Christian faith lacked depth and maturity. The demands on camp leadership to mentor inadequately prepared staff

(usually a burner phone) kept hidden in luggage.

11. This issue was evident in many areas of Firs youth ministry. Darell Smith recounted being approached by a father of two Fircreek campers in 2014, asking if he was a pastor. "No," Darell replied, "but I guess I'm the pastor at Fircreek." To which the dad responded, "Fircreek is the only church we know." The imperative in an increasingly post-Christian environment not only to "serve the church" but to "be the church"—in an informal sense, at least—brought both unprecedented opportunities to welcome and love people for Christ's sake ("helping people believe") and a special obligation, where possible, to point people to a faithful community of worship and fellowship.

12. Biblical illiteracy in the pews has been much commented on in recent years, as exegetical preaching has diminished and, even in many self-styled Bible churches, congregants are no longer "people of the Book." See, e.g., Berding, "The Crisis of Biblical Illiteracy," and his book-length study, *Bible Revival.*

were taxing. Different kinds of curricula were experimented with, including video-based series prepared by other Christian ministries, but retention was often minimal—a trend that got worse every year, Rob observed. And regardless of format, "it was very difficult to train counselors how to teach a forty-minute Bible study, even following a carefully designed lesson plan; many just did not have the ability."

Disciplinary issues among staff members were cropping up more frequently as well. Though staff were, during the training week at the outset of every camping season, led by camp leaders through the staff manual—including its statement of faith and conduct code—debate and pushback over what some regarded as "outdated" (or "Pharisaical") views were sometimes heated during these years, according to a former staff member. In the digital environment habituated by young people and the cultural landscape of the Pacific Northwest, it was typical to view certain biblical moral norms as incongruous, if not repressive. Almost every year in the 2010s, one or more staff members were sent home for "breaking contract" (i.e., engaging in prohibited behavior) during the camp season. In 2012, a completely different issue emerged when Firwood had to serve a record number of campers with an inadequate staff cohort, the smallest in recent memory. Dramatically fewer applicants for the C.I.T. program materialized, and several male counselors reneged on their contracts just prior to staff training week, leaving leadership to scramble to cover bases with short-term volunteers. Far from having a wealth of suitable applicants for summer staff to choose from (a regular issue in earlier decades), Rob and his team sometimes found themselves praying to fill staff bunks.

There was increasing recognition that Firwood, like Fircreek, needed to embrace a new, purposeful discipleship mindset as it welcomed teenage staff, especially, to its camp programs. In Tom Beaumont's words:

> It once seemed easy to get kids who said the right things, came from the right families, and attended the right church to join us on staff. Once there, we expected them to have appropriate behavior and to serve in the variety of capacities that we had to fill. Truth be told, we didn't know where they were in their spiritual lives for the most part, and we didn't intentionally see them as an object of our ministry. Fast forward to today, and the picture is much different . . . We are much more aware of the needs of the kids we call on to serve. We realize, as well, that they come with far more questions about their faith; they come trying to figure out who they are in their faith; they come with a greater level of biblical illiteracy; they live in a context and a

> culture that is moving rapidly away from Christianity. I dare say that the ministry we have with our summer staff is greater than even with our campers, and has the greatest potential for long-term impact for the sake of the gospel.

Tom's words are borne out in the remarkable testimony of Payton Saunders who, at sixteen, applied on a whim for a C.I.T. position at Camp Firwood, a place she remembered fondly from several summers as a junior camper, years earlier.[13] Though she didn't grow up as a church kid and had never really understood any of the "religious stuff" that camp leaders talked about ("I was the sort of camper who would fall asleep in her bunk during Bible study"), she was thrilled when her application was accepted. Neither her friends nor her family understood why, and even she was a bit perplexed. Her only explanation, years later, was that "the Holy Spirit grabbed ahold of me":

> Our first week was staff training week, led primarily by the director, Rob Lee. I felt extremely in over my head. I found myself constantly thinking, "I have no business being here. What am I doing?" I almost quit. But I stayed one more week, which turned into another, which turned into an entire summer. A lot of that first summer [2014] was defined by learning who Christ was and learning about what the body of Christ was. By the end of the summer, I wasn't fully convinced, but I was hungry for more. I returned in 2015, and God spent a second summer drawing me to him.

In 2016 Payton moved to Seattle and entered her freshman year at the University of Washington, attending classes and enjoying sorority life. By her own admission she "tucked Jesus away." And when the prompting came to reapply to Firwood, she decided to ignore it. Other plans were afoot; she had a job lined up and a place to live in Seattle for the summer. As the nudging continued unabated, she argued with God, still unpersuaded about the whole Jesus story, and dared him with a prayerful challenge: "Convince me!"

Within less than two weeks, all of her summer plans fell through. Relenting at last to a God who seemed unwilling to take "no" for an answer, she called the women's lead at Firwood, who surprised Payton with

13. Payton (camp name "Chaturonga") actually had a multi-generational connection to The Firs, though her family was not particularly grounded in faith; both her paternal grandmother and her mother had attended camps at Firwood and the Chalet in years past.

the news that she had been praying specifically that she would come to camp as a counselor that summer.

> I packed my car and drove straight to camp. It was as if a light had been turned on within me. I was convinced! That week, I accepted Jesus as my savior. Two weeks later I was baptized.[14] Seeing Christ work through me to teach the gospel to my campers had a transforming impact on me: that summer was defined by the saying "God doesn't call the qualified, he qualifies the called."

As ever, God's unfailing faithfulness is the story behind Payton's story; in the complex weave of her life, he called her by name and demonstrated his persistent love and mercy for her, as well as "the plans he had for her, plans to prosper . . . to give her hope and a future" (Jer 29:11, NIV). She spent two more summers in leadership at Firwood, one on the media team and one as C.I.T. lead, before pursuing a calling in the legal profession, a career she had long aspired to, but initially thought might be incompatible with her faith ("I had never met a Christian attorney!").[15] Through an internship with Vision House, a Christian non-profit in Renton, Washington that provides transitional housing to homeless families and children, she was put in contact with a Christian lawyer in Seattle, whose firm represented churches, religious educational institutions, and parachurch organizations. With her sense of calling confirmed, Payton pursued a law degree at Texas Tech University in Lubbock, Texas, where she met her husband, Kellin. The Lord then opened the door to return to Seattle, where Payton focuses on civil litigation and advocacy on behalf of Christian non-profits. Two siblings followed her into serving on Firwood staff; "God has used The Firs to draw not only me to himself, but my entire family."[16] To which an old hymn's lyrics provide the perfect com-

14. Baptism of Firwood summer staff in Lake Whatcom was a new phenomenon, reflecting a desire of young converts (especially those without an established church home) to make public profession of their new life in Christ. In 2016, Rob Lee recounted, nineteen such baptisms took place at camp.

15. As she was wrestling with this issue, Payton was introduced to Bob Goff's bestseller, *Love Does*, by another Firwood counselor. Goff, himself a Christian attorney, encourages Christians to take on the adventure of engaging with the world in its need, for Jesus' sake. In discerning how, he argues, pursue something that "already lights you up. Something you already think is beautiful or lasting and meaningful . . . Pick something you feel you were made to do" (216–17). This was exactly the counsel Payton was looking for.

16. I am deeply grateful to Payton Saunders (now Payton Tompkins) for sharing her story of conversion and vocation with me, and for extending permission to includes it here, in précis.

mentary: "Leave to your God to order and provide; / In ev'ry change He faithful will remain."[17]

There was less obvious change at the conference center than either Firwood or the Chalet during these years. Maintenance staff were kept busy with an endless list of repairs and upgrades to facilities on the grounds, aided by occasional work parties, the largest of which in 2015 brought well over a hundred local volunteers to help with everything from painting to landscaping. Guest groups continued to dominate the schedule, providing 90 percent or more of total camper days. In 2015, the one Firs-sponsored retreat that drew a large and enthusiastic crowd was an adult conference featuring former Firwood directors, Greg Kinloch and Jon Aldrich, as well as Don Anderson.

One especially gratifying exception to the "change" ethos was in the food services department, in which, for many years, the demands were such as to make it a place of constantly revolving doors. In January 2007, Jim Donath arrived from Lake Elmo, Minnesota with his wife Julie, sons Jacob and Nick, and daughter D'Andra. Jim brought a wealth of experience from the St. Paul School District and Covenant Park Bible Camp on Park Lake, thirty miles southwest of Duluth. He not only had the skills and temperament necessary to manage the complex requirements of menu planning and food preparation for large conference events, but also proved an excellent (and demanding) mentor to local youngsters who worked part time as dishwashers, hosts, kitchen assistants, and servers. The family settled in well, trusting that the lovely, large home they left behind in Minnesota would sell quickly. No one knew at that point that a market collapse and the Great Recession were just around the corner. As months went by without a buyer, and mortgage payments stacked up, Jim began to wonder if he had made a mistake in bringing his family across the continent. The staff joined the family in praying fervently for an answer. And then, just as Jim was on the brink of resigning his position, the Lord provided a sale. Some of the old-timers around the ministry had seen this kind of thing plenty of times before. For the Donaths, it was both test and confirmation of God's call to The Firs. They dug in and stayed the course; Jim became one of the longest-serving and best-loved food service directors in the history of the ministry.[18]

17. "Be Still, My Soul," by Catharina von Schlegel (1752), translated by Jane Borthwick in 1855.

18. During the pandemic, Jim worked for the Opportunity Council in Bellingham, a position that had an "essential service" designation. He returned to his old role as food

# 19

# Shaking (2017–2021)

"And the fir trees shall be terribly shaken."[1]

ONE OF THE MOST OBSCURE and difficult verses in the brief Old Testament prophecy of Nahum describes, in the King James Version, "the fir trees" being "terribly shaken." Most modern translations, recognizing the original Hebrew as both idiomatic and metaphoric, render it more prosaically.[2] But it is a verse that, in its older wording, comes to mind as one reflects on a four-year period when, indeed, much of the ground under The Firs seemed to be quaking.

By all accounts, the summer of 2017 began as a banner season at Firwood. Full cabins, good weather, non-stop activity during the day, and energetic music and worship each evening at Center Stage. The summer's first high school camp was in full swing during the fourth week of July. As in several previous years, it included a cohort of teenagers from mainland China. They were sponsored by an organization called EduKeys USA, based in Seattle, that partnered with Beijing in providing cultural exchange opportunities for Chinese students. The participants typically had limited English, but beginning their tour of the United States with an action-packed week of fun with American peers in a beautiful setting was seen as a welcome introit. They were housed together in a single cabin,

services director at The Firs in 2023.

1. Nahum 2:3, KJV.

2. Referring to the fall of Nineveh at the hands of the Babylonians, it uses language that has vexed translators and prompted wildly variant readings.

and participated in all aspects of the camp experience, including shared meals, activity classes, free time games, Bible studies, and Center Stage.

One of the perennial highlights of high school camp was a popular all-camp competition with prescribed contests taking place throughout the entire property, woods to waterfront, over the course of several hours; it was a raucous, chaotic, and fast-paced "Amazing Race"-styled relay—with detailed rules and staff observers at every stage of the event. On this particular Tuesday, the competition was in full swing when someone noticed that one of the Chinese campers was not participating in some of the activities. His cabin mates initially seemed unconcerned, assuming he had simply lost interest in the event and retreated to his cabin; no one regarded him as "missing" until later in the afternoon, when he could not be found in his cabin or elsewhere in the main camp area. Search teams were organized and scoured the entire property. Police were alerted and arrived with their own searchers; media vans showed up at the camp entrance, boats with news crews arrived off shore, drones flew overhead. The search was eventually discontinued at nightfall without success, but resumed the next morning. A camper had found some of the young man's clothing; police tracking dogs alerted their handlers to a specific waterfront location—not the swimming beach but the boat dock area where one of the relay activities had involved swimming to a nearby sailboat, tipping and righting it, and then returning to shore. Divers using underwater cameras located the missing camper in about thirty feet of water, just past a drop-off, and retrieved his body on Wednesday afternoon.

Rob Lee wept when he shared the news. It was the first and only camper death in Firwood's six decades of operation.

The young man's Chinese cabin mates, who themselves had only minimal English, indicated that he hadn't participated in the waterfront drill, as he was not an experienced swimmer. A counselor had specifically told him to sit out that part of the competition. No one saw him enter the water, including the on-duty lifeguard, or heard any call for help. Did he merely wade partway out from shore, unaware of the drop-off, and then slip from view? He was not wearing a life-jacket.

The young man's parents were contacted through EduKeys and eventually made their way from China to Bellingham, where they held a private, grief-filled ceremony remembering and honoring their son on the shore of Lake Whatcom.

Sorrow and soul-searching engulfed everyone on staff, not only at Firwood but throughout the organization. How could this have happened? Were language barriers an issue? Almost certainly. Was culture relevant, especially if there was a perceived element of shame in not participating in a camp activity? Possibly. Could better safeguards have been in place? Yes. Though camps went ahead as scheduled for the rest of the summer, the emotional weight of the drowning was unrelenting: how to make sense of such a tragedy, and how to ensure that something like this never happened again? An external safety review was conducted, which produced guidance and protocols to enhance and reinforce camp safety for all participants. Tom Beaumont, reflecting on the loss, said that "the harsh impact on the whole of our organization runs deep. Yet our resolve is even firmer, looking forward. And as we respond to the unknowns, the unexpected, the unwanted . . . we do so with an unshakable faith in a trustworthy God."

2018 brought a variety of personnel changes, including the arrival of Jon Epps, who was appointed overall director of camp and retreat ministries. Jon grew up in southern California, but made Bellingham his home while studying at Western Washington University, where he became deeply connected to a campus ministry known as The Inn, affiliated with First Presbyterian Church. Jon served in numerous roles there, first as a student leader, then a staff member, and eventually as director. He and his wife Shannon stepped down from leadership at The Inn in the spring of 2018 to take up a new role at The Firs. Rob Lee transitioned away from The Firs, where he and Val had been on staff for over twenty years, to become executive officer of the Building Industry Association of Whatcom County; Rob's Firwood assistant director, Steve Jagich, took over as director both at Firwood and the Chalet.

Guest groups continued to dominate the schedule at the conference center. In 2018, Firs-sponsored programs—including a weeklong adult retreat, various scrapbooking events, and The Firs Noel—brought in 319 attendees, while nearly 7,000 visitors attended guest group retreats. Sometimes a single church group filled the entire facility and its more than two hundred beds; at other times as many as three different groups were hosted simultaneously, each with its own meeting rooms and accommodations. And as Jan Morell had predicted, many groups that had "come just once" in the early 2000s were now Firs regulars and had become good friends of the ministry.

Children's programming across Cable Street was thriving—both the After School Adventure program, with its various spinoffs, during the school year and Fircreek day camp in the summer months. In 2018, the largest registration in Fircreek history was recorded, with nearly half of all campers attending for more than one week. Darell Smith offered a lovely retrospect:

> In the midst of nine weeks of crazy themes, hard work, miles of colored butcher paper, gallons of tempura paint, hilarious skits, original all-camp games, an assortment of wild and fun activities, cool art projects, catchy camp melodies, and insightful discussions about God's love, little children as well as some adults became familiar with the voice of God as he whispered in their ear, "Jesus." They had experienced his presence, but many just didn't know his name. Now they do.

During one of those nine weeks, Stacy Smith was the "J.A.M." ("Jesus and Me") speaker. With her typical story-telling wizardry, she presented Paul's words to the church in Rome (8:28)—"All things work together for good, for those who love God and are called according to His purpose" —against the backdrop of the 1972 children's classic, *Alexander and the Terrible, Horrible, No Good, Very Bad Day.*[3] She had the kids memorize the Pauline text, repeating it aloud with actions, and then added another layer of instruction later in the week with a skit related to cake-baking: campers were invited to come on stage to sample individual ingredients in a cake recipe, most of which tasted unpleasant on their own but, when mixed together, would create something wonderful. On Friday afternoon, to reinforce the lesson, each cabin group was given a plate with cake slices to be shared among the campers. When asked, "Why are we eating cake at Bible study today?" the answer came back, "Because God works (mixes) all things (nice and not-so-nice things) together for good (cake) for those who love God (hold his hand) and are called according to his purpose."[4] It was a beautifully conceived, child-friendly presentation, and one likely to bind Romans 8:28 to many young hearts and minds.

The Apostle Paul's confidence in the sovereignty of God at work in even the hardest and messiest seasons of life, bringing good out of the most challenging and "not good" of situations, was perhaps an apt preparation for the summer of 2019, which proved the most difficult in the history of The Firs.

Darell and Stacy Smith had for decades built a loving, welcoming environment at Cable Street South for children and families, especially

3. Written by Judith Viorst, published by Atheneum Books.

4. The question-and-answer format mirrors the practice of Jewish and Christian catechesis, as an ideal way of passing on biblical truth to the next generation.

those dealing with various forms of dysfunction and trauma. Parents or guardians who dropped off children each day knew that they would be safe, surrounded with loving attention, provided with hours of well-supervised outdoor and indoor recreation, and introduced to the person and teachings of Jesus. There were, in Stacy's mind, important ministry objectives not only for the child campers, but for teenage and young adult leaders as well, many of whom were themselves unchurched.[5] As Darell observed, "The A.S.A. staff is a ministry in itself. A lot of the staff come with not really any type of tangible experience of spiritual things, but as a result of being on staff, they leave with one." Even among the many for whom these child-centered programs were the closest or only approximation of "church" in their lives, The Firs had a sterling reputation.

All that changed in spring 2019, seemingly in the blink of an eye. A young man well-known and well-loved by the Smiths and by the entire Firs staff applied to serve as a Fircreek counselor. He had been part of the program himself as a youngster and had enjoyed part-time positions in the kitchen and dining room at The Firs conference center over the years. Shortly after his application was accepted, a social media post surfaced, indicating that he was publicly expressing commitments that did not align with expectations for leadership at The Firs.

When Darell became aware of this, well before the program actually began, he reached out and asked him to come in for a conversation. Darell explained The Firs' long-standing commitment to a biblical framework for personal conduct and leadership, and shared that, given the candidate's publicly stated commitments, this particular role would not be the best fit for him. It was not an easy conversation, but it was a gentle and respectful one, and the young man left disappointed but understanding, agreeing that his application would be withdrawn.

Some community members responded on social media, expressing concern and questioning the decision. Their posts were shared widely and soon gained significant attention. As the press became involved, the story expanded across radio, television, and print media. Tom Beaumont provided a statement explaining The Firs' position, but it did little to calm the waters.

5. Unlike Firs-sponsored programs (including Fircreek), A.S.A., which was state-funded, was obligated to specific hiring protocols that precluded choosing staff for religious affiliation or "alignment with ministry." Stacy had an uncanny ability to select individuals who, wherever they were on their faith journey, were capable of loving kids deeply and providing a joyful, life-giving experience for them. Many were themselves touched and changed by the gospel message as they served A.S.A. families.

A few picketers showed up with signs during the early weeks of June; a larger protest, organized online, was planned for the opening day of Fircreek, June 24, at which more than a hundred individuals participated for several hours as local reporters recorded interviews.

Throughout the summer, sporadic protests continued. Houses up and down Cable Street and throughout the immediate neighborhood displayed symbols of solidarity with the protesters. Firs personnel received strongly worded phone calls, and the ministry was criticized across both social and traditional media. Down the road at the entrance to Firwood, the camp sign was repeatedly vandalized and eventually removed; news vans and watercraft appeared once again, as they had in 2017. Several guest groups canceled events at the retreat center and many local parents withdrew their kids from camp: both Fircreek and Firwood experienced a nearly 20 percent drop in registrations. Summer staff were uneasy wearing Firwood apparel around Bellingham. And the Opportunity Council announced publicly that it was closing its Head Start kitchen that had been operating at The Firs since 1987, ending a long and cordial relationship.

Darell was heartbroken, especially given his deep affection for the young man in question, whom he had known for his whole life. Years later he was still troubled about whether and how he might have handled things differently.

As conversations in the broader culture shifted on questions of identity and personal conduct, The Firs continued to hold to its long-established understanding of Scripture. The organization had for years welcomed any and all people, knowing that some attendees at retreats, camps, and other programs likely had different views and experiences. In Tom Beaumont's words, "We operate from a position of 'inclusiveness' in terms of any children or youth or adults who register for one of our programs. We don't screen people . . . and we don't turn anyone down on pretty much any basis."[6] The hope of The Firs is that all who attend its programs will encounter Jesus and experience the love of God.

Part-time employees who washed dishes, bussed tables in the dining room, or filled lifeguard positions were not asked to sign a doctrinal

6. "When Faith Meets Up With Culture," an unpublished address to the Christian Camp and Conference Association (2020). In his statement to media in the midst of the 2019 crisis, Tom said, "We are a faith-based organization whose mission is not only to love kids but to introduce them to a God who loves them as well. A God who we feel reveals himself primarily in the Bible. We seek to accomplish this mission through our programs and within the context of approved Statements of Faith."

statement or questioned about faith commitment or personal lifestyle. They were simply expected, in recognition of the mission of The Firs, to refrain from behaving in any way contrary to its values. For young leaders and counselors in Firs-sponsored programs, however, there was an expectation of active alignment with the mission and agreement with the faith statement.

The Firs' commitment to upholding its long-held understanding of marriage and Christian life—formally codified in its doctrinal statement in 2004—had always been assumed as part of its biblical identity. But, as Tom Beaumont put it, the ministry learned that it needed to find ways to "give feet to our doctrine":

> We weren't prepared for how "what we believed" would need to navigate through the community we sought to engage. We didn't think enough about how to communicate truth that appeared to conflict with other equal truths. And we didn't ask enough "what does it mean?" questions as we looked beyond the statements into relationships . . . Giving feet to doctrine doesn't mean backing off the truth of what we believe or weakening our resolve, but it does mean applying grace to that truth. It means paying as much attention to practice as doctrine. We don't lead with doctrine on a normal basis, so we shouldn't start now. We lead with relationship. It is possible to show radical love and still hold on to solid, evangelical, traditional understandings of sexuality and marriage.[7]

These are issues that continue to resonate, and to challenge everyone associated with the ministry. Leading with love while upholding truth, especially countercultural truth, has never been an easy calling. The only one who has ever done it perfectly is Jesus.

Eventually the furor died down, and as summer edged into autumn, many local families, having made their point during the weeks of protest, were prepared to reenlist their children in programs at The Firs. Stacy and Darell had enormous credibility in "leading with relationship," and even some parents who had joined the protests later said that, though they had other childcare options, their children "did better with Jesus."

Stacy's passion "to love kids and serve families" was as expansive and innovative as it was deep-rooted, and she added yet another program to The Firs repertoire in September 2019— a forest preschool called Firs & Fiddleheads. It welcomed children from ages three to five to an

7. Beaumont, "When Faith Meets Up With Culture."

outdoor classroom in a beautiful four-acre wooded area of Cable Street South where, under the towering firs and among the ferns and flora, they enjoyed endless opportunities to explore the wonders of God's created world. Rubber boots and rain slickers were part of the uniform for much of the year; the program was play-based and child-led; its facilities included an outdoor mud-kitchen, obstacle course, science and art classrooms, and a reading nook, where Stacy was often featured sharing favorite stories in her uniquely engaging way. Because Firs & Fiddleheads was a "school without walls," it established a very low ratio of one staff member to every six children, and drew on a team of teachers, led by Danielle Strasser ("Javelina"), who were passionate about the importance of outdoor education, especially in the formative years, before "school" would mean sitting at desks.

Firs & Fiddleheads quickly established itself as a new favorite offering for local families. It provided multiple schedule options to accommodate different family needs, including all-day or morning-only sessions, and over the years it would add a homeschool enrichment program for older kids (ages six to eleven), a Forest Friends option for parents who wished to join the activities along with their toddlers, and a summertime Forest PreKamp that partnered with Fircreek.

In the short run, though, there would be an interruption, that no one anticipated, for all Firs programs.

In the third week of January 2020, the first reported case in the United States of a mysterious new respiratory disease occurred in Snohomish County, Washington—between Bellingham and Seattle. The individual in question had just returned from visiting family in Wuhan, China, where a "novel coronavirus" with pneumonia-like symptoms that did not respond well to conventional treatment had been reported several weeks earlier. By the end of January, person-to-person spread of the virus was confirmed, and cases were beginning to balloon internationally; sickness, sometimes fatal, connected to "Covid-19"—especially within vulnerable populations with preexisting health conditions—was causing widespread alarm. The first known outbreak in an American long-term care facility occurred at the end of February in Kirkland, Washington, where three dozen residents would ultimately succumb to the disease.

With Washington State being the apparent epicenter of Covid-19 in the United States, the state governor declared an official state of emergency in February 2020 and instituted a stay-at-home order in March, initially intended to last for two weeks. As cases continued to explode, mandates intended to mitigate the spread and protect the public were extended and expanded: masking, social distancing, compulsory testing and quarantine, restrictions on the size of gatherings (both inside and outside), and limitations on in-person work, recreation, shopping, dining, and worship. All K-12 schools were ordered closed for six weeks, effective March 17, and then, following that six-week period, shuttered for the remainder of the academic year. Many businesses were forced to shut down; others were able to modify from in-person to remote (i.e., computer-based) employment. Individuals in designated "essential" categories (law enforcement, healthcare, farming, construction, transportation, childcare, etc.) were permitted to continue working, with restrictions, including in some cases mandatory vaccination.

In the early stages of the pandemic, The Firs conference center was open, but guest groups quickly dwindled and then ceased altogether by the late spring of 2020. The Chalet was likewise forced to close its doors. And, for the first time since it opened in the 1950s, Firwood was completely shut down; there would be no camp programs for either the 2020 or 2021 seasons, as all residential camps and conferences were labeled high-risk. On the other hand, childcare was deemed "essential" under state guidelines, so both the Firs & Fiddleheads preschool and A.S.A. were licensed to stay open, and offered daily programs. A.S.A. provided before-school care, "zoom school" through the Bellingham school district, after-school care, and even summer care ("Awesome Summer Adventure") from 7:30 a.m. to 5:30 p.m. for state-subsidized children. These programs, along with Fircreek day camp (following strict C.D.C. guidelines), continued unabated through the pandemic, providing an immensely valuable service to parents and offering stability, connection, safety, and fun for children in an otherwise confusing and frightening time.

Though its revenue was slashed by program closures, The Firs chose not to lay off staff. It reduced salaries somewhat and tweaked job descriptions in order to keep people busy in new ways, taking advantage of the unprecedented quiet on all three properties. Maintenance, repair and upgrade of buildings (even empty buildings), landscaping, etc., were all still necessary, and did not take seasons off. At Firwood, Center Stage was completely rebuilt, with expanded seating, new lighting, and a larger stage area. At the Chalet, where for four summers a Christian couple previously unknown to The Firs had poured extraordinary financial resources and countless volunteer hours into both functional and aesthetic improvements (bathroom remodels, kitchen upgrades, replacement of heating/cooling units, a new generator, etc.), the summer of

2020 allowed, through their financial gifts, for dormer windows, exterior painting, and a much-needed new roof to be completed.[8] The Chalet was once again completely revitalized, for whenever it would be permitted to welcome back guests.

The Lord's people proved exceptionally generous through the pandemic season as they recognized the unprecedented need. Donations exceeded expectations and, as Tom Beaumont recalled, despite the disruption in normal operations, "God graciously sustained our programs." Additionally, The Firs took advantage of relief programs made available through various levels of government to businesses and organizations (including Christian non-profits), which proved a significant factor in avoiding layoffs.[9]

Tom had been planning his own retirement from the executive director role for some time, ideally to take place in January 2021. Indeed, he had worked out a detailed schedule with the board as early as 2018, providing thoughtful notes and guidance as to how he thought the transition should proceed. Nothing went quite as planned, however. A headhunting firm was hired to provide to The Firs a list of potential candidates; the process was extensive and costly, but resulted in a failed search. Then, with the advent of Covid-19, everything changed at an existential level both on the grounds of The Firs itself and across the national landscape of camp and conference ministries. Noone was making major decisions about moving or changing affiliation when so much was uncertain. Tom and the board agreed that he would retire on schedule, having effectively navigated the early stages of the pandemic, and that Jon Epps would step in as interim director while the board initiated yet another search.

It was a strange and challenging time for everyone, with none of the kinds of festivities that would typically attend the departure of a consequential, long-term executive director. Once it became clear that Covid restrictions would be extended through 2021, several other staff announced their departure as well, including Kirk Potter, who had overseen a decade and a half of conference center seasons, from the heyday of non-stop guest group activity to the now eerie silence of a property essentially under lockdown. Firwood director Steve Jagich departed for

8. God's amazing provision, through the generosity of this couple, who wished not to be named or given public recognition, is one of the notable miracles in The Firs' recent history. See also Appendix B.

9. There was a brief flurry of local reporting concerning whether The Firs' receipt of such funds was appropriate, given the public controversy regarding its hiring practices in 2019, but the moneys were not held up (*Bellingham Herald*, May 2, 2022, A5; August 31, 2020, A1, A3).

Oregon; his assistant Angie Brionez left The Firs to work for her old Firwood boss, Rob Lee, in Bellingham. Marc Watson, who with his wife Karen, had been on staff for over thirty years, announced his intention to retire in January, but was persuaded to stay on until October.[10] Several others departed as well; 2021 saw the number of full-time employees at The Firs fall to fifteen. Overall, though children were happily occupied across Cable Street at A.S.A., the forest preschool, and Fircreek, it was a time of unsettling isolation for many; the loss of fellowship, community, and service meant there was a huge hole at the heart of The Firs.

Kim Hendrickson, who had been on site since 2013 as registrar for children's programs, was tasked with trying to revive guest services at the retreat center once pandemic-related impediments were removed. Along with Jon Epps, she reached out to prospective individuals and groups with information about "Phase 3" options in the late spring of 2021 at all three sites. As Jon reflected in a June newsletter, "For every sign of optimism, there are setbacks, frustrations, losses, and uncertainty." Some of the earliest gatherings were scrapbooking events led by Barb Vander Meulen and held at Firwood's Centerhouse in May and June. The boathouse at Firwood was also made available for friends of The Firs who were suffering pandemic fatigue and wanted to get away for a "family summit" or personal prayer retreat. By late June, guest groups were beginning to regather, though in modest numbers and with masking and screening protocols, at both the main grounds and Firwood. The centennial celebration of ministry at The Firs that everyone had long anticipated was put on hold, but the "shaking" of the last half-decade seemed at last to be quieting.[11]

In July 2021, The Firs Board formally reopened its search for a new executive director.

10. Marc had come to The Firs in 1989 as food service director but shifted over to bookkeeping in 1992 and then ultimately to a long-term role as a very effective and well-regarded business manager. Karen wore many hats at The Firs, serving at various times in housekeeping, as dining room hostess, receptionist, Firwood registrar, and Chalet guest services director. The Watsons had a huge heart for the ministry; even after his official retirement, Marc continued to help out in the business office and—given post-pandemic staffing issues—sometimes agreed to cook at Firwood and the conference center.

11. Heb 12:28 offered perhaps the most poignant encouragement after hard years: "Let us be grateful for receiving a kingdom that *cannot be shaken*, and thus let us offer to God acceptable worship, with reverence and awe" (ESV). There were, as it turned out, still tremors on the horizon, as the next chapter documents, but through which a new confidence and clarity of direction emerged.

# 20

# Stand (2022–2025)

"Stand fast in one spirit, with one mind striving together for the faith of the gospel."[1]

Tom Beaumont, in a 2018 "Three Year Focus" document for The Firs Board and Council, astutely observed that when he stepped down as executive director in 2021, that role would almost certainly, for the first time in The Firs' hundred-year history, be taken up by an "outside" person. Every previous executive director had considerable staff experience and was familiar not only with current personnel but also with the distinct character and unique demands of the ministry.[2]

In the late fall of 2021, the board announced a candidate had been hired, though he was not introduced to the community by name until January 2022.[3] Lemuel ("Lem") Usita was a gifted and accomplished educator, with advanced degrees from Biola, and a pastor with extensive experience in youth ministry and leadership training. At the time of hiring he was serving as Academic Dean at an innovative leadership college connected to Daybreak Church in Carlsbad, California. But he had local connections as well, having previously served on the pastoral staff of Christ the King Community Church in Bellingham, during which time he visited Firwood as a speaker at Center Stage. Lem was engaged

1. Phil 1:27.

2. Dick Eley shadowed Grant Whipple for several years before stepping into the executive director role. All other directors had a lengthy affiliation with the ministry.

3. Jon Epps, who served as interim director after Tom retired and navigated much of the pandemic season, left The Firs in early 2022.

to Christa Katona, whom he met on the pastoral team at Daybreak; their wedding was scheduled for April, shortly after Lem's term as executive director commenced.

For the board, Lem seemed well positioned to lead the organization forward, especially given The Firs' increasing focus on children's ministry and youth evangelism, discipleship, and mentoring. Though Lem himself candidly acknowledged in a blog post that "I have never done anything like this before," his contacts were extensive both in Bellingham itself and within church circles up and down the west coast. According to the board's announcement, "he has already taken great initiative in assembling potential strategic hires" for a depleted Firs staff.

Perhaps the greatest strategic need was a Firwood director, since camp had not been open since the summer of 2019 and would require both an enormous physical effort to rejuvenate the grounds and cabins and a thorough rebuilding of staff and camper relationships before it could reopen in the summer of 2022. While Lem was in conversation with the board about assuming leadership at The Firs, he reached out to a former student and friend from San Diego with the query, "Would you ever work at a camp again?" Kyle Kerchner, whose Christian life began at camp twenty years earlier and who had spent ten summers working at Hume Lake, was intrigued by the idea. After weeks of self-reflection and consultation with friends and family, he accepted Lem's invitation and loaded up his truck with his two dogs and a few worldly possessions and drove to Bellingham to take up his new role as director of Camp Firwood.

The responsibility of reopening camp under such circumstances would have taxed anyone. Only five weeks of camp were scheduled for Firwood's first post-pandemic season, but camper registrations were down and many staff positions unfilled as the July opening neared: "We could use seven more guy counselors, six guy C.I.T.s, six lifeguards, and an R.N. for three of the weeks. There are a lot of roles to fill." A piecemeal staff was pulled together, augmented with part-time help, and camps went ahead as scheduled, though it was a far from normal summer.

Meanwhile, Fircreek, along with other programs at Cable Street South (A.S.A., Firs & Fiddleheads), which had the advantage of continuous operation through the Covid years, were full and busy. Fircreek operated a full ten weeks of day camp in the summer of 2022, with some weeks having to establish a waitlist as early as May.

One of Lem's early initiatives, that he hoped would make a difference for Firwood recruitment the following year, grew out of his interest in and experience with "gap year" programs for students who had graduated from high school but were not yet sure of their next steps. Mirroring some of what he had done in California at Daybreak Leadership College, he introduced what he called Collegium, a year-long residential "discipleship community" at The Firs. The young adults who were accepted to Collegium would be mentored in life skills, intern with local Christian ministries (including The Firs' own programs, such as the forest preschool and A.S.A.), act as hosts and kitchen staff in The Firs dining room, and also commit to serving at Firwood the following summer.[4]

The first cohort of Collegium students included a young woman named Autumn Ellis, who had, though only twenty, a fairly lengthy history with The Firs; she spent five summers on the Fircreek staff under Darell Smith's leadership and then worked at Firwood in the abbreviated 2022 season with Kyle Kerchner. But her Firs connections stretched back much further even than that. Her parents, Robb and Kelly Ellis, had served on Firwood staff in the 1990s (camp names "Snewt" and "Shnookums" respectively); they met and fell in love as Firwood counselors in 1996. A few years later, as young marrieds, they returned to The Firs in two successive summers to assist Darell with family camp, leading the kids and teen program.

As Autumn settled in to the Collegium program at the retreat center, she learned about various employment openings at The Firs and contacted her parents—remembering the many times that she and her siblings, Joey and Riley, had heard stories about Robb and Kelly's years at Firwood and their oft-repeated hope that the Lord might someday call them to The Firs. Such an assignment, they often said, would be their "dream job."

Kelly was at this time area director for Young Life in Lincoln City and Newport, Oregon, a role she had filled since 2018. She had previously been Head of School for Neskowin Valley School, an innovative indoor/outdoor kindergarten to eighth-grade private school on the central Oregon coast (2014 to 2019). Robb was a school counselor and wrestling coach at Taft High School in Lincoln City. Between the two of them, they had for years been involved in raising, advising, coaching, loving, and mentoring not only their own kids but their kids' friends, and serving

4. As previously noted, there had been earlier experiments in youth mentorship/internship programs at The Firs over the years, including the Firs Leadership Apprenticeship Program (FLAP) in the early 2000s, The Village Discipleship Training Community in 2005, and Lectio in 2007.

children and teenagers in various school and ministry settings. They knew youth culture intimately, and they were experienced in engaging teens in Jesus' name and for his sake.

With their own children "launched" and with unexpected news of openings at The Firs, the timing seemed right to consider their dream job.[5] After taking the matter to the Lord, they submitted applications, and both were hired in October 2022: Robb was named The Firs' operations director, and Kelly became Lem's executive assistant. Kelly's soon proved to be an especially auspicious appointment, drawing on yet another set of skills and experience beyond her educational and ministry background. She had strong entrepreneurial and business acumen, having owned and operated a retail store in Lynden, Washington from 2007 to 2012.[6] As such, she had managed inventory, staffing, payroll, accounting, customer relations, marketing and sales, and strategic planning—employing a whole range of executive abilities that complemented her proficiency in ministry. In her first spring council meeting, she led the business portion of the gathering, providing a concise overview of overall budget details, donations, capital projects, and projections for the following year.

While the Ellises' appointments filled crucial holes, the depth chart was still thin, with many staff positions unfilled or in flux. Fortunately, senior leadership of children's programs across Cable Street (Fircreek, A.S.A., Firs & Fiddleheads, etc.) was seasoned and steady, with Stacy Smith, Ellie Fowler, and an experienced team in place. Ellie, who had served on Fircreek staff for several years, stepped into the director role when Evan Bryant left for a full-time position at Northlake Church; her husband Will was named to the crucial role as Chalet manager in late 2022. Jenny Greenleaf, long-term receptionist and office manager, stepped down after twenty-eight years of service. Sarah Morell took over her role at the front desk and also assisted Kim Galoia (née Hendrickson)

5. Joseph Ellis (22), was at the time serving with his wife Kenzie as a youth pastor in Salem, Oregon. Joseph ("Sharpay") had an established Firwood pedigree, having worked at Firwood in 2018 and 2019; he would be named assistant director in 2024. Kenzie ("Blundstone") was to join him on staff in 2024 and 2025, and then serve as lead teacher in the Firs & Fiddleheads preschool program. Riley Ellis (19) was studying theology at Corban University in Salem, Oregon when his parents moved to Bellingham. He too was on Firwood staff ("Von Schweetz") in 2023 and 2024, his wife Jordyn ("Carmex") serving with him in 2024 and again in 2025. Autumn ("Pashaw"), with many summers on Firs camp staff under her belt, met her husband Tyler Grehan ("Totoro") at Firwood in 2023; they would go on to serve again in 2024.

6. Sole Obsession Footwear.

with guest groups (a responsibility her mother-in-law Jan had managed for many years). But housekeeping and maintenance faced a critical need for new oversight and staffing, as Bruce and Barb Vander Meulen were scheduled to retire in December after thirty-six years of herculean service to The Firs.[7] In the providence of God, Doug Walker, who had worked with Bruce for many years, stepped into a new role as supervisor of the maintenance department, a position for which he was ideally prepared. Lem moved Jen Ryan (who had been with guest services since 2007, specifically at Firwood and The Firs Chalet) into a newly created role as human resources manager, to serve as a liaison between staff and the executive director, with responsibility for job postings, health benefits, retirement, etc.

Overall, it was clear that recovery from major staff turnover and the long shutdown during Covid represented significant hurdles. It was an immense task to reopen a large and complex operation, with several properties and numerous programs, after a virtual standstill, and to reengage a community that had grown accustomed to detachment from church attendance and from "gathering" generally. Lem worked to connect with local pastors, hoping by that means to rekindle the potential for adult ministry at the conference center, which he referred to aspirationally in the spring 2023 council meeting as "the [spiritual] garden for Whatcom County"—where "the Word could make its way into the hearts" of visitors. His hope was, in fact, to revitalize virtually all of the historic retreats and ministries that he had read about in *Work of Faith, Labor of Love.*

On May 13, 2023, the long-delayed centennial gathering, marking The Firs' founding in 1921, drew 215 guests to Firwood to celebrate ten decades of ministry. The event was beautifully choreographed, including testimony, a slideshow of historic photos, a Firs history trivia game, skit, video, and a lovely buffet meal. After others reflected on the past, Lem shared his vision for the future. The formalities concluded with prayer, and a moving rendition of "The Benediction," led by the song's composer, Seattle-based musician Timothy James Meaney. His signature track had been sung at the conclusion of every Center Stage since the 1990s, often with Meaney himself onstage to lead it.

7. Their last month on staff was spent renovating the lower floor of El Nathan, one of the oldest and most iconic Firs residences. Barb has continued her popular scrapbooking ministry (which she started in 2012) post-retirement.

Master of ceremonies for the evening was Jon Hansen (Firwood's "Gonzo"), an apt choice, given his lifelong familiarity with the ministry; he grew up revering his parents' generation of Firs people—not only eminences like Grant Whipple, but also folks whose lives were transformed at The Firs.[8] He was a Geneva kid and attended Northlake Church, which was filled with Firs staff and friends and which gave him a secure grounding in Scripture even as a child. And then, in fourth grade he attended and fell in love with Firwood for the first time; camp became the spiritual capstone of every year for him—as a camper, and in subsequent years on staff. As a youth pastor at Northlake, before he established a real estate business, and as a regular speaker at Center Stage, he continued to be a bridge between new generations of young people and the historic ministries of The Firs.

As May 2023 came to a close, staffing for a slightly longer (seven-week) Firwood camping season was once again running behind schedule and somewhat inchoate. Some members of the staff who had been hired intended to work for only part of the summer and a few seemed inadequately vetted for Firwood leadership. Lem, acknowledging gratefully Kyle's hard work against long odds in the daunting post-Covid environment, especially as a relative newcomer to The Firs' ministry culture, decided a change needed to be made.[9] Kelly Ellis, who had already transitioned from being Lem's executive assistant to a new role as assistant executive director in April, stepped in as interim Firwood director for the summer, and began to assemble a team of trusted staff and seasoned alums.[10] Kelly's first call, though, was to Jon Hansen. And for Jon, it was God calling—almost literally.

Ever since he had been asked to emcee the centennial festivities, Jon hadn't been able to get Firwood off his mind. The camp that he had loved since he was ten years old, that had sat idle for two pandemic summers,

8 Jon's parents were David and Kay Hansen. David pastored Silver Beach Community Church from 1966 to 1977 and then taught an adult class at Geneva Community Church for decades. Jim Thurston, David's best friend, committed his life to full-time service while attending a Firs retreat in the 1960s, pledging to live by faith and "to go wherever you send me." Jim served the Lord as a missionary in Chile for six decades. In March 2024 he returned to The Firs to speak at the annual meeting, where he gave a powerful "faith-raising" challenge to those present to reinvest in the ministry in a sacrificial way.

9. Previous directors had typically come from the ranks of summer staff and/or established connections with The Firs' overall ministry; as such, they were familiar with the distinctive culture of Firwood.

10. These included several members of her own extended family. See note 5, above.

was not functioning well. Since someone else was in charge, his only role was to pray, but he could not escape the burden of concern he was feeling. Shortly after the centennial gathering, while sitting with his dad on the lawn of his home across the lake from camp, he confided his unrelenting but confusing anxiety about Firwood. The two of them prayed together that if the Lord had some plan for Jon to reconnect with Firwood in a significant way, he would make that clear without any hint of input from Jon himself—indeed, that someone from The Firs would actually reach out to him. Three weeks later, the phone rang: "We need you at Firwood this summer." It felt like a miracle—the "fleece" he had set out, with only his father as witness. And he was ready. Jon agreed to lead spiritual life and programming for the whole camp season and, arranging time off from his real estate business, poured every waking hour into preparation for camp. His vision for ministry at Firwood included intense mentorship of counselors, who would then make deep connections with campers through a host of crazy, trust-building games and activities, one-on-one conversations, and daily Bible study.

Adjustments were made and a cohort of suitable staff members gathered, trained, and mentored through the summer months; new hires were paired with alumni. A Bible study curriculum based on Paul's epistle to the Ephesians was adopted. Staff attended services together as a group at several Bellingham churches on Sundays throughout the summer. And hundreds of kids came to the Lord: during one Center Stage, over fifty campers shared how their lives had been spiritually upended that week, including several who admitted they had not come to camp for "the Bible stuff" but were now intent on following Jesus. According to one longtime friend and board member, 2023 proved a "miracle turnaround" summer—not with respect to budget, but missionally—and reestablished a firm foundation for future years.

Meanwhile, Lem himself was beginning to wrestle with his own long-term future at The Firs. Christa, who was expecting their first child in July, had not really put down roots in the ministry or the community, and was homesick for California. Lem informed the board that he would be taking a three-month paternity leave following the birth of their baby. Kelly, as assistant executive director, would fill in in his absence.

By this time, Kelly had been manifesting a striking range of executive competencies as well as flexibility and resourcefulness in filling numerous unexpected and often divergent roles. At the board's direction, she met with staff, led them in a time of worship and devotion, and then invited candid conversation and feedback, in a circle rather than at tables, to reestablish a sense of fellowship and trust that had become somewhat frayed. It was a restorative meeting.

When it became clear that Lem needed, and apparently wanted, to step down, The Firs Board named Kelly interim executive director. Lem and Christa, with their baby boy, Zeal, left for California in the early autumn of 2023, with prayerful good wishes from those who had hoped for a much longer and more successful tenure.[11]

In many respects, this period can be thought of as extending the "shaking" of the previous decade. But, in the words of Bruce Whipple, "the Lord's fingerprints were all over the situation," and he was, in his everlastingly amazing way, untangling what seemed to many an unimaginable predicament, working all things for his glory. It was Lem's hiring that led to the establishment of Collegium, that in turn led Autumn Ellis to inform her parents about openings at The Firs. And it was in the midst of intractable staff issues, the repercussions of Covid, concerns about discontinuity and spiritual drift, and a general loss of confidence in The Firs' historic mission that Kelly's strengths were revealed. Though she would never have thought to apply for the role of executive director at The Firs, God managed to get her in position to take on that mantle in his time, in his inimitable way. In February 2024, after a renewed search—in which her candidacy was expressly invited[12]—the board "unanimously and enthusiastically" named Kelly Ellis the executive director of The Firs. In accepting the position, she reflected:

> The past several months have been a journey of introspection and prayer as I've sought God's guidance for both the organization and my role within it. Through this time, God has continually provided his reassurance and affirmation in his steadfast plan for The Firs, and I believe he has many blessings in store. As I embrace this position, I am fully committed to championing The Firs' mission alongside our dedicated staff and stakeholders.

11. Once the family resettled in San Diego, Lem went on to found a company called Identity Specialist LLC, providing identity coaching, consulting services, and leadership mentoring for the next generation. He is also, at the time of writing, an instructor at California State University San Marcos.

12. Kelly was at first reluctant to be considered. She had been given an extended closeup of how demanding the role was and, in her words, "the weight of it all felt overwhelming." But she was ultimately, through a season of prayer with Robb and others, convinced that if God was calling her, he would provide for her: the words of Heb 11:7 and a divine "fear not" quieted her anxiety about the enormity of the task and prompted her to step out in faith.

> While there is much work to be done, we have an incredible opportunity to grow our impact in sharing and teaching the hope of Jesus Christ. Together, we will carry on the legacy of disciple-making that has defined this organization for over a century.

The interim months between Lem's departure and Kelly's official appointment as executive director were anything but easy. Several planned retreats at the conference center had to be canceled. Kelly's husband Robb, who had moved from general operations to serving as conference center director, left The Firs staff to return to education.[13] The Collegium program was disbanded, without plans to continue the following year. Each day brought new challenges and newly moving parts.

But in other respects, a fresh wind was soon felt to be blowing. For the first time in several years a sense of unity of purpose and confidence about the future was being restored. There was evident clarity about identity and mission—in the Apostle Paul's words, a clear trumpet.[14] A conscious and forthright reaffirmation of The Firs' biblical heritage (as expressed in its doctrinal statement) was paired with a new forward-looking emphasis on youth evangelism, with mature adult believers in a supportive role.[15] The mission statement (i.e., the "why" of ministry) that had been adapted several times during Tom's tenure ("The Firs serves the local church and community by drawing groups and individuals to . . . experience the biblical message of Jesus" to a more streamlined "The Firs exists for people to encounter Jesus and experience the love of God") was replaced in 2024 with a distinctly youth-focused "Equipping young people to share the love of Jesus and radically transform the world."[16]

Kelly tasked her sister, Nicole Roberts, a professional graphic designer, with providing fresh logos for The Firs and its various ministries—sleek and modern, but aptly capturing the ethos of the organization. The website received a facelift. Communication with the constituency

13. Robb accepted a position as school counselor on Lopez Island, part of the San Juan archipelago, about two hours from Bellingham by car and ferry. He and Kelly maintain a home on the island as well as in Bellingham.

14. 1 Cor 14:8: "For if the trumpet makes an uncertain sound, who will prepare for battle?"

15. The historic emphasis on foreign missions, which has greatly diminished in recent years, was re-envisioned in terms of the "mission on the doorstep," especially among American youth.

16. As for the "how," a vision statement added "We partner with families and churches to ensure the next generation is well-equipped to live their life on mission for Christ."

became frequent and focused, typically including photos and short-form online content. And the board, which had been in what seemed like perpetual crisis mode for several years, was able to engage in collaborative and prayerful partnership with Kelly, confident in her ability to balance appropriate process with decisiveness.[17]

Jon Hansen joined the full-time staff at The Firs in the fall of 2023, turning over his thriving real estate business to a manager in order to focus exclusively on ministry. He was given the title of director of spiritual growth and named director of Camp Firwood—an unexpected fulfillment of a childhood dream.[18] He was also given responsibility for helping redesign a residential discipleship ministry for young adults at The Firs, called Radicle and Rooted.[19] With some of the features of Collegium, it was anchored in a focused and accredited biblical curriculum.[20] Accreditation was only possible because of Jon's seminary training, pursued many years earlier at the encouragement of Grant Whipple. When, as a young man who had fallen in love with youth ministry at Firwood and Northlake Church, Jon sought advice about whether he needed a theological education, Grant was emphatic, "Go get your training." And though he had never needed it previously in any formal sense, it was, in Jon's own words, "a thread of the Lord's sovereignty" that he followed Grant's counsel twenty-five years earlier. "God just keeps providing for

17. This was one of the "key spiritual personal characteristics" outlined in the board's executive director search document. In 2024 Marcus Brotherton joined The Firs Board and in 2025 he agreed to serve as board chair. A nationally-known author, Marcus has an invaluable, three-generation connection to The Firs; his paternal grandparents were friends of Otis and Julia Whipple during their Vancouver days and, like them, strong supporters of the China Inland Mission. His father grew up attending youth conferences on the main grounds, and he himself attended Firwood as a camper in the early 1980s and then spent five summers on camp staff. He and his wife Mary Margaret have ensured that their three children also enjoy strong Firs connections.

18. As a ten-year-old, just home from his first year at camp, Jon told his bemused father that he thought he "was born to run Camp Firwood." Under Jon's leadership, Firwood has continued to improve, expand, and diversify the camp experience, with mountain biking and laser tag, among other activities, added to the range of options in 2025.

19. The noun "radicle" is botanical, referring to the embryo of a seed that will shoot down into the soil and become its primary root, but contains also obvious wordplay with the adjective "radical." As the program was initially conceived, the "radicle" year would be followed by an optional "rooted" year—extending the lessons of intensive Bible study and discipleship into practical vocational options.

20. Accreditation was provided through Anchor Christian University's partnership program.

what he wants to do to make his name known. And in the end, he gets the glory."

God provided another key player to The Firs executive leadership team in 2024, completing a "three-stranded cord" to ensure strength and stability.[21] Tony Neal grew up in Southern California, where he came to faith as a teenager and began to pursue a life of serious and intentional discipleship. He attended Moody Bible Institute, after which he and his wife Robin moved to the Pacific Northwest to pastor Calvary Creekside Church in Everson, Washington. Among their congregants in the early years of their twenty-year tenure at Creekside were Robb and Kelly Ellis, who lived at the time in nearby Lynden.

Even after the Ellises moved to Oregon in 2012, the two families kept in touch periodically. But it wasn't until 2023, when Tony felt the time was right to step down from pastoral leadership at Creekside, that he and Robin became interested in serving the Lord at The Firs. Seeing a job opening for the position of director of advancement, Tony reached out to Kelly to discuss a prospective role for which his varied gifts and experience might be a good match. In addition to his two decades in church leadership, he had business experience and had served as a chaplain, directed a children's home, coordinated mission trips, and partnered with several relief organizations. Kelly's vision for a Christ-centered, gospel-focused ministry across all aspects of The Firs' programming was compelling to him, as was her clear commitment to ensure that the Word of God was the foundation and the glory of God the animating and motivating objective. Tony could see that, even in a time of rebuilding, The Firs' capacity to connect with over three thousand young people in the course of a year, introducing them to Jesus and promoting hearts of discipleship, represented one of the greatest ministry opportunities in Whatcom County. He and Robin were welcomed onto the full-time staff in the summer of 2024. Like most Firs personnel Tony took on multiple roles, from donor relations and fundraising to special construction projects and major capital investments—in his words, "whatever needs to happen to make a positive contribution to the ministry."

Along with Jon Hansen, Tony also stepped immediately into a teaching role with the first cohort of Radicle and Rooted students, grounding them in the Word of God and teaching them how to put it into practice. "Not just a gap year. A God year" provided the motto and described the

21. Eccl 4:12.

ethos. Each day began with a brief time of worship around a passage of Scripture, then individual quiet time, with subsequent shared and guided discussion. More formal class time followed, with inductive scriptural study and/or theological discussion based on a book such as Alistair Begg's *Christian Manifesto*, a study of Jesus' Sermon on the Plain (Luke 6). The afternoon typically involved work practicums, either at the conference center or Firwood. Retreats and service projects were part of the package as well; in early 2025 the students traveled to Los Angeles, both to visit Biola and to partner with Samaritan's Purse in the aftermath of the devastating Palisades Fire. One of the students sent an onsite update back to The Firs:

> We have sifted through six houses now and have [found] unbroken china, pottery, mementos, gold, silver, coins, jewelry, rings, etc. Each day is unique and I can totally see God working. I believe that five people have come to the Lord through us showing up with servants' hearts and our leader Gene, who has the great gift of evangelism, sharing the good news.

The nine-month program, for the first Radicle and Rooted students, was life-changing, providing both growth in personal discipleship and practical tools for evangelism, all in the context of accountable Christian community. The 2025/2026 cohort has continued this experience, with in-depth studies of several Pauline letters and an Introduction to Theology course, along with a track discussing biblical manhood and womanhood. Tony's wife Robin, who led women's and youth ministry at Creekside for many years, was added as an instructor and mentor for young women.

Tony sees tremendous potential in the Radicle and Rooted project (which he believes the Lord could potentially grow into a larger Bible school) and The Firs' overall youth-focused ministry. Like many, he senses "rumblings of God breaking through" in revival among the young. "Last year there were over a hundred young people committed to serving the Lord at Camp Firwood, representing an absolutely incredible open door for discipleship in one of the most starved demographics in the country. Many of them showed tremendous growth and tremendous love for Christ and tremendous sacrifice as they served." Jon Hansen shares the same passion for The Firs' strategic mission to young people: "I think revival is going to come through the youth," he observed, reflecting on the hundred-year ministry of The Firs and its place in the wider sphere of God's activity. "In the past, we were largely focused on adults, and then the Lord surprised us by adding on the youth piece. Now, I think it's going to be the youth first—kids that have never held a Bible or gone to church coming to faith in Jesus. And guess what? These young people can't grow in their faith without adult mentors. For a long time, the inner circle was adults and it spilled out to the youth, but now it feels like that's flipped."

In the summer of 2025, every single week at Firwood saw thirty to fifty campers commit their lives to Christ for the first time—not always "on cue" at the end of a full week of exposure to the gospel. In the Tuesday evening Center Stage of the first high school camp of the season, Firs board member Norm Funk, a Vancouver pastor, opened his Bible and shared a simple, unornamented message about Jesus. No funny stories, no emotional hype. After which, he felt compelled to give an invitation. A few long moments passed in silence, no one moving, until one camper stood to his feet. And then another, and another, and more and more, as "the room rippled with the power and presence of the Holy Spirit."[22]

"This is what we pray for, every week," recounted Jon Hansen. "And then, when these new believers go home, we continue to hold them up and to provide resources that will help them grow as disciples." In the last several years, Firwood kids have begun to start Bible clubs and prayer groups in their secular high schools, testifying to their faith with confidence and courage.

At the same time as youth ministry at all three Firs locations was becoming an explicit priority, "serving the local community" in state-affiliated childcare programs like the After School Adventure and its various spinoffs, was becoming less tenable, as state regulations impinged to a greater and greater degree on employment practices. When it became clear that signing the Washington State Licensing Agreement jeopardized The Firs' overall commitment to faith-based hiring,[23] the decision

22. This story was recounted by Marcus Brotherton, board chair, at the fall council meeting in November 2025. He was present at Center Stage that evening and deeply affected by witnessing the response of teens to the simple gospel: "nothing . . . except Jesus Christ and him crucified" (1 Cor 2:2, NIV).

23. The Board formalized a resolution concerning "Faith-Based Hiring for Ministerial Roles," on January 13, 2025, stating that "The Firs Directors and Officers will only sign contracts that do not limit The Firs' ability to hire based on faith as defined and clarified by its faith and doctrinal statements." Under Kelly's leadership, The Firs has leaned into its commitment to faith-based hiring, designating all employment roles as "ministerial" and adopting job descriptions that clarify ministerial expectations. Everyone hired by The Firs, even part-time or short-term, must affirm its Christian identity and doctrinal convictions and demonstrate a capacity to share his or her faith

was made to close A.S.A. after twenty-five years of joyous, generous, self-sacrificing service to children and families by Stacy Smith and her team. For Stacy, who had blessed hundreds of staff members and campers with the love of Jesus for two and a half decades, living out the motto that "play is the serious work of heaven," the shutdown was emotional:

> After years of laughter, learning, and a lot of love, A.S.A. is coming to a close. From little feet running through the big fir woods to lifelong friendships formed right under our roof, A.S.A. has been more than a program. It's been a home. A place that has touched the hearts of children and grownups alike. We are beyond grateful and blessed for every moment, every family, and every memory. The adventures we had will stay with us forever.

A Family Fun Night and Reunion, featuring "BBQ, dodgeball, and a whole lot of love"—as well as more than a few tears—took place on Sunday, June 8, 2025, followed several weeks later with a massive liquidation sale of games, props, toys, art supplies, décor items, furniture, and sports equipment. The Geneva Chapel-turned-classroom-and-activity-center was cleared and cleaned, restored to the kind of stillness it had not experienced in years. As hard as the relinquishment of these precious programs was at first, the Lord provided his peace and—when Stacy confronted an unexpected health crisis later in the summer—assurance that the closure was providentially timed. Stacy took on a new, strategic, and more manageable role as director of alumni and family engagement, maintaining and restoring connections with those who, after a period of uncertainty, were beginning to rebuild trust with The Firs. She and Darell would continue to be indispensable ambassadors for the ministry, and for the Lord they serve.

A yet more momentous decision—perhaps the most momentous in The Firs' hundred-year history—was announced at the annual meeting on March 29, 2025. The board had, after months of prayerful deliberation and following upon many years of discussion, unanimously voted to put the conference center properties of The Firs on both sides of Cable Street up for sale. As has been documented in these chapters, the halcyon days of year-round conferences at The Firs were long gone, as the whole concept of adult retreats in historic buildings and a fairly rustic environment has lost its appeal for many—for two opposite reasons. On the one hand, those desiring to hear the kind of high-profile Christian speakers who

---

with ministry guests.

had once come routinely to The Firs now encountered such speakers (in person or through video-conferencing) at church-hosted events, often in upscale hotel environments; on the other, those who had long cherished the "set apart" quiet of The Firs, with its relaxed recreational options, now found the busy, suburban neighborhood of Geneva a drawback. It was also true that the number of guest groups booking events at the retreat center had markedly declined, especially since Covid. While the Radicle and Rooted program made use of dorm and dining facilities, many accommodations and meeting spaces on the Geneva campus stood empty for much of the year.

Along with the decision to put the original Firs property on the market came the determination to "reposition resources for maximum impact," which would eventually include expanded, year-round ministry at both Firwood and the Chalet. But board and leadership were also emphatic that the initiative to market the property was taken with complete openness to God's leading in whatever form that would show itself—either by providing a suitable buyer who would (ideally) continue Christian ministry on the site, or even, by some unforeseen means, allowing The Firs itself to continue to steward its legacy in a new way in its original location. It was another "fleece" of sorts, or perhaps a willing sacrifice, in the spirit of Abraham on Mount Moriah, with a singular desire for the Lord's provision and direction.[24] "We're in a season of discernment," observed Kelly, "trusting that God's plan will unfold in his perfect timing." She challenged the community to "move forward in courageous unity, grounded in trust," keeping intense, prayerful focus "not on what is seen, but on what is unseen, since what is seen is temporary, but what is unseen is eternal."[25]

Until such time as the answer is clear, Firwood is expected to become a busier hub of activity not only during the traditional camp season but throughout the year. In September 2025, The Firs hosted its second annual alumni day, which dovetailed with a scheduled family camp at Firwood. The property was bursting at the seams and filled with exuberant energy as old friends and new connected over meals, waterfront and land-based activities, and Center Stage worship. Plans are being explored

24. Gen 22:1–19. Abraham was prepared to offer his son Isaac at God's command, an act of unimaginable faith, but the Lord intervened miraculously with provision of a substitute. The "acceptable sacrifice" was in this instance obedience itself, a radical willingness to trust God.

25. 2 Cor 4:18 (NIV).

for moving both the Fircreek summer program and the Firs & Fiddleheads preschool to Firwood, with transportation of campers back and forth each day, in the short term at least, from the Geneva campus.

One surprising recent development has brought "new things" and new personnel back into direct, tangible contact with The Firs' history. Tony Neal and his wife Robin, who had been hosting a home fellowship for several years, were praying about moving into a more permanent location since the group had outgrown their house. In conversation with Kelly about Grant's pastoral ministry at The Firs—beginning with home Bible studies, which morphed into regular worship and fellowship in The Firs lounge (now called the Alpine Room), and the eventual establishment of Geneva Community Church in the early 1960s[26]—an idea emerged. The Geneva Chapel building was no longer occupied, since A.S.A. had moved out. Within a few weeks, chairs were provided, hymnals located in a storage cupboard, and a new, small congregation under the name Whatcom Fellowship began to meet where Grant Whipple, Doug Anderson, Don Rutledge, and countless conference speakers and missionaries had once preached. Tony, thrilled to add a regular pastoral role back into his already busy life, welcomed this as a divine opportunity: "I believe that God has opened a great door of outreach and support for The Firs as we are studying the Scriptures and worshipping the Lord in Geneva Chapel once again. The prayers of the saints that have gone before are still being heard in this place and I believe that the Lord has great things ahead."

As this book closes, then, a vibrant history is still being written by the Lord at The Firs. Though many aspects of the future are unclear, its mission has never been more focused.

Through more than ten decades, in seasons of growth and pruning, clarity and uncertainty, stability and upheaval, the bracing words of Hudson Taylor that "God's work done in God's way will never lack God's supply" continue to sound a perpetual challenge and promise to those who love The Firs. In this beautiful corner of Whatcom County, a ministry founded in faith as a labor of love, has (sometimes against hard odds) endured in hope—that the gospel, faithfully taught and lived, will continue to bear fruit for today, for generations to come, and for eternity.

26. For details, see chapter 10, above.

Camp Firwood and Reveille Island.

Firwood's new dining facility, Centerhouse (completed and dedicated in 2010).

Mountain bikers ready for the trails.

A Firwood baptism.

Center Stage.

The Firs' first cohort of Radicle and Rooted students.

# Appendix A

## *The Firs Doctrinal Statement*

The wording of the doctrinal statement adopted by The Firs has changed in several ways since the ministry's founding; these changes do not reflect any fundamental change in doctrinal positions, but (1) clarification of credal beliefs that would once have been assumed and/or (2) responses to points of doctrinal controversy in the wider Christian world. The description of the Bible as "inerrant," for example, was not included in the original doctrinal statement (though it was almost certainly assumed), but added in 1977, at the height of the inerrancy debate in America; the current version leaves out the term "inerrant" and returns to more accessible categories ("divinely inspired, infallible, entirely trustworthy, the supreme authority"). Likewise, insistence on a premillennial return of Christ was not formally written into the statement of belief until the 1970s; it too has been left out of recent versions, with no dispensational timetable for Christ's "personal, visible return to earth in righteousness and glory." There is now no explicit reference to the eternal punishment of the lost; that expectation is subsumed under a reference to the ultimate consummation of Christ's "salvation and judgment." An emphasis on the expectation of personal sanctification is included, and in that context, an explicit affirmation of the biblical and evangelical position on marriage and sexuality. Scripture references accompany and validate each of the beliefs laid out in the current statement.

Alongside this brief, public-facing statement, The Firs also now provides on its website a more expansive "What We Believe" overview, which goes beyond the essentials of credal affirmation to an explanation of the biblical "love story" of God for humanity and his redemptive purposes revealed in the person of Jesus Christ.

For comparison, the statement that pertained when *Work of Faith, Labor of Love* was published follows immediately here, after which is included the current statement (as of 2025).

1977

-Belief in the Bible to be the inspired, inerrant, only infallible, authoritative Word of God.

-Belief that there is one God, eternally existent in three persons: Father, Son, and Holy Spirit.

-Belief in the deity of Christ, in His virgin birth, in His sinless life, in His miracles, in His vicarious and atoning death, in His bodily resurrection and His ascension to the right hand of the Father, and His personal, bodily, and premillennial return.

-Belief that, because of the fall of man and his consequent moral depravity, there is absolute necessity of regeneration by the Holy Spirit for salvation.

-Belief in the resurrection of both the saved and lost; the saved unto eternal life and the lost unto eternal punishment.

-Belief in the spiritual unity of believers in Christ.

2025

We believe that the Bible is the Word of God, divinely inspired, infallible, entirely trustworthy, and the supreme authority in all matters of faith and conduct. (2 Timothy 3:16–17; 2 Peter 1:20–21; 1 Corinthians 2:13)

We believe that there is one God, eternally existent in three persons: Father, Son, and Holy Spirit. (Matthew 28:19; 2 Corinthians 13:14)

We believe in the deity of Christ, in His virgin birth, in His sinless life, in His miracles, in His vicarious and atoning death, in His bodily resurrection and His ascension to the right hand of the Father. We believe in His personal, visible return to earth in righteousness and glory to consummate His salvation and His judgment. (John 1:1–2; Romans 3:21–26; 1 Thessalonians 4:13–18)

We believe that, because of the fall of humanity with the resulting sinful state and subsequent separation from God, there is the necessity of new birth, in salvation by faith in Jesus Christ alone. (Romans 3:23; 6:23; Ephesians 2:8–10; John 1:12)

We believe that God has called Christians to a life of sanctification through the Holy Spirit and to a life fully committed to the will of God in Christ. (1 Peter 1:14–16; Titus 2:11–14)

We believe in the Christian church as the one universal body of Christ. Christ is the head of His church and calls God's redeemed people to be set apart for His purposes in the world. (Ephesians 1:22–23; 5:25–30; 1 Peter 1:9–10)

We believe in the institution of marriage defined in Scripture as the covenantal union between one man and one woman. We believe that the Christian standard is faithfulness within the marriage covenant and abstinence outside of it. (Genesis 2:24; Matthew 19:5–6; Ephesians 5:31–33)

We believe that every person is created in the image of God, that human sexuality reflects that image in terms of intimate love, communication, and fellowship. We believe that God created humankind as two distinct sexes, male and female. (Genesis 1:27; Matthew 19:4–6; Mark 10:6–8)

# Appendix B

## *Faith Ministry at The Firs (1921–2025)*

"But who am I, and what is my people,
that we should be able thus to offer willingly?
For all things come from you, and of your own have we given you."[1]

An essay in a Firs newsletter, "The Cable Street Chronicle," dated December 2004, posed the provocative question: "What Ever Happened to Faith at The Firs?" It addressed head-on a concern that was current within The Firs community at the turn of the millennium about the gradual shift in what "faith ministry" had come to mean in the eight decades since The Firs was founded.

As recounted in the early chapters of this book, The Firs was established within a very specific tradition of faith ministry that took its inspiration from the examples of George Muller, founder of the Ashley Downs orphanage in Bristol, England, and Hudson Taylor, the British-born founder of the China Inland Mission. Otis and Julia Whipple, after reading the biographies of these two remarkable men, believed they were likewise called to a life of wholehearted dependence on God to provide for their material needs. When they opened their humble honeymoon cottage to friends in the 1920s, and then when they established the Lake Whatcom Bible and Missionary Conference in 1929, they did so with an explicit emphasis on "living by faith" and thereby "helping people believe." Theirs was a quietly radical missionary spirit: they expected their

1. 1 Chron 29:14, ESV.

faith to be tested (which it was) and they expected God to "show up" miraculously in his way and time, to provide for their needs and the needs of The Firs (which he did).

Those who felt God's call to The Firs resident staff in its early decades embraced that missionary spirit wholeheartedly and were, themselves, schooled in a life of countercultural faith, which was costly in material terms but richly rewarding spiritually. They lived on site, they shared meals communally, and they were all paid from a common purse and with a common stipend, the only distinction being on the basis of family size.

As the decades went by, as the ministry grew from one site to three, and as family culture and the cost of living changed so that most households required two working parents to get by, the missionary model became ever more challenging. Stacy Smith recalled that when she and Darell applied as newlyweds to join the fulltime staff in 1985, "We were young and didn't fully understand the implications of 'living by faith'. I may have thought, 'How hard could it be?' I soon found out, real hard at times, especially when raising children in a relatively affluent area." As other aspects of the communal living model codified in The Firs' early years were slowly beginning to change in the 1990s (allowing staff to own their own homes and spouses to work off site, and providing a graded compensation package), The Firs was moving inexorably, though not necessarily intentionally, in the direction of a "Christian non-profit" rather than a "missionary" identity. Even the prerequisite for all potential fulltime resident staff to demonstrate a specific biblical confirmation of their call to The Firs was eventually dropped.

The original emphasis on "no financial appeals" was also moderating, but somewhat more tentatively, in the same period.[2] As recounted in early chapters of this book, even in times of dire need, Otis and Julia Whipple took their petitions to God and waited on him to supply by his means, in his time. Most of the early members of The Firs staff experienced periods of severe financial testing when they joined the ministry. But even in those early years, the calling on the wider circle of friends and council members, and of others who loved The Firs, was recognizably different. Some of those drawn into the orbit of The Firs by God were themselves business leaders and people of considerable wealth.

2. The issue of debt was adapted only insofar as to allow, in certain circumstances, short-term indebtedness with assurance of repayment, effectively "debt to ourselves." All of The Firs properties and assets are debt-free.

Their challenge was to prayerfully discern how to invest in the Lord's work, to partner with him in providing for the needs of those on the front lines of ministry. The relationship was always regarded as a spiritually precarious one: Otis Whipple, and Grant after him, felt as strongly as had George Muller that they should neither talk about financial needs nor take up public offerings. Within the context of a closed gathering of The Firs Board and Council, needs could be mentioned, but the only way to distinguish between "consecrated" and "unconsecrated" money[3] was to allow God to guide potential givers just as surely as he guided the recipients, through prayerful obedience.[4] And it was imperative to give thanks as readily and sincerely for a "widow's mite" or castoff building supplies as for a large gift from a wealthy donor.

Once Firwood and the Chalet were added to the ministry, several things began to change. Having moved beyond missionary-style gatherings and into a youth camping and recreation ministry, The Firs became more obviously public-facing; its outreach expanded dramatically into the community, as did its evident need for equipment, materials, and supplies; it was subject to more external regulation, licensing, and permitting. Guests were charged modest fees for retreats and camps but the "general fund" that kept everything going was supplied by unsolicited donations from the Lord's people. By the 1980s, even some of The Firs' most faithful and generous donors began to suggest the need for greater financial transparency and accountability—arguing, on biblical grounds, that (1) silence would contribute to a mistaken public perception that the operation was fully underwritten and had no material needs, and that (2) potential donors were being denied the joy of contributing to the Lord's work at The Firs. The line between "letting needs be known" and "solicitation of funds" was a fine but important one and constantly emphasized through the 1990s; outside consultants provided guidelines as to how to maintain both integrity and transparency through print materials and newsletters, correspondence with individual donors, and explanation of The Firs' policies to guests and conferees.[5]

3. See Prologue, quoting Taylor: "We can have a little as the Lord chooses to give, but we cannot afford to have unconsecrated money" (*Growth of a Work of God*, 42).

4. Donors, including those who gave most lavishly, typically insisted on anonymity. Consistent with the ministry's own character, and the words of Jesus in Matt 6:4, their generosity was unassuming, often hidden—"known to God" rather than advertised to the community.

5. The Firs became an accredited member of the ECFA (Evangelical Council of Financial Accountability) in 1990.

These were not easy matters to wrestle with, especially for those who grew up in the missionary generation and cherished the "ancient landmarks" that Grant Whipple alluded to in a council meeting in 1995.[6] Tom Walton, grandson of Otis and Julia, son of Grant's sister Lois and her husband Nate Walton, was a missionary kid in China until, after internment in a Japanese prison camp, the family came home to Bellingham and took up residence in a modest cottage at The Firs in 1943.[7] These were lean times. And when, fifteen years later, Tom and his young wife Patty (née Rasmussen) were called to serve on The Firs resident staff, there were lean times still. "I can remember six months when we never got paid; that was the longest period. But I can honestly say we were never concerned. The Lord provided every single time just in a miraculous kind of way: a farmer who had a cow would give us a quarter of beef or a family would bring us a gunny sack of potatoes or corn and Bernice [Whipple] would find a way to divvy it all up. Honestly, it was genuinely exciting to see how the Lord was going to meet our needs."

As much as he cherished those experiences of "waiting and seeing" what God would do, Tom acknowledged that he found a way to adapt when the policy was eventually somewhat loosened. As the first and longest-serving manager of the Firs Chalet, he began carrying around a list of current and future needs in case someone asked, "How can I help?" When a well-known donor did just that, Tom told him that he needed a stove for the Chalet kitchen. The response was, "I'll give when I know the exact amount." Tom was ready: the stove in question, delivered up the mountain, would cost $1,263.23. The necessary funds, so designated, were immediately provided.

Tom also had a hand in being the Lord's intermediary in the purchase of the Baker property, now called South Cove. The property was bought and sold several times after The Firs acquired Firwood, but although it clearly represented a crucial asset, no consensus to purchase had been reached by the board and no funds set aside. When Tom bumped into the current owner in town, he initiated a conversation about the property and learned that a developer was interested in building condos on it. Tom commented that The Firs would be very interested in the land because it was adjacent to Firwood and controlled the right of way but acknowledged that "we don't have a nickel to put toward it at the moment." The

6. See chapter 16, above.

7. For more detail, see chapter 7, above.

gentleman invited Tom to visit his nearby cabin at Wildwood and talk further, and a friendship evolved in the course of regular Saturday get-togethers. Whenever the subject of the Baker property came up, Tom reiterated both how strategic it was for Firwood and how The Firs had no funds in hand to purchase it. Though there was a developer in the wings, the Lord continued to forestall the sale. Sometime during this same season, when Tom and his wife were making a routine family visit to an uncle in Tacoma, Tom was asked, unprompted, "The Lord has been very good to us. Are there any significant needs I could help with in the ministry?" Tom explained the situation; the land in question was actually familiar to him, since he had bow-hunted with Tom at Firwood in the off-season. After further discussion, he said, "I'll take care of it. You go talk to the owner and do what you can with the details."[8]

Having shared nothing at all to this point with Grant Whipple, Tom brought him the surprising revelation that not only was the owner willing to sell, but that a friend of The Firs was willing to buy. No board committees or deliberations had been involved in this instance; it was the Lord's doing and the Lord's timing, mediated through an unlikely friendship and an unexpected inquiry.

Since 1999, modifications of the financial policy have allowed greater transparency about the overall fiscal situation at The Firs and the cost of maintaining and improving specific programs; board-approved capital campaigns are permitted, as are appeals within The Firs constituency regarding specific and immediate needs. Local fundraisers such as golf and cornhole tournaments to raise campership funds for underprivileged kids to attend Firwood or Fircreek, or to support Firs-adjacent ministries like Royal Family Kids Camps, have also become regular events. For people whose lives have been blessed by the Lord through The Firs, these "asks" are understated and generally welcome. The Firs has never employed third-party fundraisers; it scrupulously avoids aggressive appeal letters, phone calls, or the manipulative tactics used by many Christian organizations. In keeping with its spiritual legacy, the first and most crucial ask is always for prayer. Given the spirit of such requests, most appreciate being informed of ministry needs and having a part in meeting them.

And God still does the completely unexpected, as when a Christian couple with no connection to The Firs, on a weekend alpine drive near

8. Details were worked out graciously and generously on all sides; the downpayment was deposited, a modest mortgage rate agreed upon, and monthly installments sent until everything was paid off.

the Mount Baker summit, happened to notice the Chalet. Curious, they got out and walked around the property, smitten by its obvious beauty but struck, too, by its weather-worn condition. God stirred their hearts and when they returned home, they searched the internet to learn about The Firs, and specifically about its Mount Baker property and program. Prompted by a clear sense of divine calling, they volunteered time, energy, and generous assets over several years that virtually transformed the Chalet. Wishing no recognition for themselves, "May God be glorified" was their heartfelt benediction on this remarkable offering.

Just as this book was going to press, The Firs' executive director Kelly Ellis was spending a quiet Saturday confiding in the Lord about a specific financial need for The Firs that seemed overwhelming in human terms; the amount had been set prayerfully but not announced publicly, and the deadline for its arrival was imminent. Though feeling anxious, she reflected on the decades of God's faithful and timely provision outlined in these pages, and left the matter in God's lap. The next day, someone approached her at church and pressed an envelope into her hand; it contained a check with the precise amount that she had mentioned before the Lord and no one else. Not long afterward, another friend of The Firs provided the same amount again, unprompted. The loving answer of a generous and attentive heavenly father was overwhelming: "good measure, pressed down, shaken together, and running over" and poured into *her* lap (Luke 6:38, NIV).

Living by faith in the twenty-first century is as countercultural as ever, though it may not be circumscribed by a particular policy, as the 2004 article in "The Cable Street Chronicle" observed. Faith in the Old Testament context could mean standing still and waiting for God's provision; it could also mean marching, fighting, building, making, or even asking others to "bring an offering" (Exod 25:2). But as everyone who has been involved in leadership at The Firs would unhesitatingly say, faith means first and foremost dependence on God and the certainty that "we can do nothing without his provision." Whether by capital campaigns and short-term appeals, purposeful silence and waiting, or even prayer and fasting, it is God who supplies every need: all things come of him. As The Firs seeks God's kingdom above all else, laying its needs before the Lord expectantly and receiving his blessings thankfully, it continues to live by faith. There is a latent temptation, as Tom Walton observed thoughtfully, to become a business rather than a ministry, "giving lip-service to our faith tradition while behaving as though God doesn't exist or that he is unaware of our needs or unprepared to act on our behalf." Such a temptation must be forthrightly resisted. Whatever the future holds for The Firs, its ministry will surely thrive in the shadow of the ancient landmarks, with the conscious recognition of God's unfailing faithfulness, and in the experience of "joy and peace in believing."

# Bibliography


Aldrich, Doris Coffin, and Ruth Walter Whipple. *The Firs of the Lord*. 2nd edition. Chicago: Moody, 1961.

Austin, Alvyn. *China's Millions: The China Inland Mission and Late Qing Society, 1832–1905*. Grand Rapids: Eerdmans, 2007.

Basham, Megan. *Shepherds For Sale: How Evangelical Leaders Traded the Truth for a Leftist Agenda*. New York: Harper Collins, 2024.

Bayne, Alfred V. *A Candle on the Coast, 1944–1994: A Fiftieth Anniversary History of the Pacific Coast Children's Mission and Camp Homewood, by the Founder*. Campbell River, BC: Pacific Coast Children's Mission, 1995.

Beaumont, Tom. "When Faith Meets Up With Culture." Address to the Christian Camping and Conference Association Super Sectional Meeting, Coeur d'Alene, ID. February 2020.

Bentall, Rob, and Kathy Bentall. *Barnabas: When God Plants a Vision*. Vancouver, BC: Independently published, 2025.

Berding, Kenneth. *Bible Revival: Recommitting Ourselves to One Book*. Bellingham, WA: Lexham, 2018.

———. "The Crisis of Biblical Illiteracy." *Biola Magazine* (May 29, 2014), https://www.biola.edu/blogs/biola-magazine/2014/the-crisis-of-biblical-illiteracy.

Biery, Galen, and Dorothy Koert. *Looking Back: The Collectors' Edition: Memories of Whatcom County / Bellingham*. Bellingham, WA: Grandpa's Attic, 2003.

Black, Lorna Whipple. *Heritage of Faith: A Chronicle of the Otis and Julia Whipple Family*. Enumclaw, WA: Pleasant Word, 2006. Extended excerpts online at https://www.weihsien-paintings.org/DwightWhipple/WhippleWWII(web).pdf.

Brauer, J.C. *Protestantism in America*. Revised edition. London: S.C.M., 1966.

Broomhall, A.J. *Hudson Taylor and China's Open Century*. 7 vols. Sevenoaks, UK: Hodder & Stoughton, 1981–1989.

———. *The Shaping of Modern China: Hudson Taylor's Life and Legacy*. 2 vols. Manchester, UK: Piquant, 2005.

Brown, Katherine. *Work of Faith, Labor of Love: A Spiritual History of The Firs*. Portland: Multnomah, 1980.

Burkinshaw, Robert. *Pilgrims in Lotus Land: Conservative Protestantism in British Columbia 1917–1981*. Montreal: McGill-Queen's University Press, 1995.

Cailliet, Emile. *Young Life*. New York: Harper and Row, 1963.

Canfield, Carolyn. *One Vision Only* [Isobel Kuhn]. Chicago: Moody, 1959.

Carmichael, Amy. *Though the Mountains Shake*. New York: Loizeaux Brothers, 1946.

Cole, Stewart. *History of Fundamentalism.* Westport, CT: Greenwood, 1971.

Dawson, Alene. "The Value and Virtues of Summer Camp." *The John Templeton Foundation Newsletter*, February 10, 2025.

Engels, JoAnn. "Calloused Hands and Tender Hearts [Doug Anderson]." *Power for Living Magazine* (October 1969) 3–10.

———. "Let Joe do it!" *Impact.* (December 1971) 7–12.

Foster, Robert D. *The Navigator: Dawson Trotman.* Colorado Springs: NavPress, 1983.

Gasper, Louis. *The Fundamentalist Movement.* The Hague: Mouton, 1963.

Gish, Edna Whipple. "My Missionary Life." Undated memoir, ca. 1987. https://charleswhipple.org/pdf/My%20Missionary%20Life.pdf

Goff, Bob. *Love Does.* Nashville: Nelson, 2012.

Green, Maude Whipple. "Family History of the Whipples." Unpublished manuscript, 1971.

Greer, Peter, and Chris Horst. *Mission Drift: The Unspoken Crisis Facing Leaders, Charities, and Churches.* Bloomington, MN: Bethany House, 2014.

Grubb, Norman. *C.T. Studd: Cricketer and Pioneer.* London: Lutterworth [1933], 2014.

Guinness, Howard. *Journey Among Students.* London: Anglican Information Office, 1978.

———. *Sacrifice.* 6th edition. London: Intervarsity, 1975.

Handy, R.A. *History of the Churches in the United States and Canada.* Oxford: Clarendon, 1976.

Hannah, John D. *An Uncommon Union: Dallas Theological Seminary and American Evangelicalism.* Grand Rapids: Zondervan, 2009.

Hitz, Charles W. *Through the Rapids: The History of Princess Louisa Inlet.* Kirkland, WA: Sitka 2, 2003.

Hunt, Keith, and Gladys Hunt. *For Christ and the University: The Story of InterVarsity Christian Fellowship of the U.S.A. 1940–1990.* Downers Grove: InterVarsity, 1991.

Johnson, A. Wetherell. *Created for Commitment: The Remarkable Story of the Founder of Bible Study Fellowship.* Carol Stream: Tyndale, 1982.

Kuhn, Isobel. *By Searching.* Chicago: Moody, 1957.

———. "My Spiritual Mother: A Memoir of Mrs. Otis Whipple." Unpublished essay (ca. 1940). Appendix B in Katherine Brown, *Work of Faith, Labor of Love: A Spiritual History of The Firs.* Portland: Multnomah, 1980. 205–220.

Lyall, Leslie T. *A Passion for the Impossible: The China Inland Mission, 1865–1965.* Chicago: Moody, 1965.

MacLeod, A. Donald. *C. Stacey Woods and the Evangelical Rediscovery of the University.* Downers Grove: IVP Academic, 2007.

McIver, Bruce. *Riding the Wind of God: A Personal History of the Youth Revival Movement.* Macon, GA: Smith and Helwys, 2002.

Miller, Felix James. "Summer Camp: An Ailing American Institution." *Public Discourse*, August 14, 2023; June 23, 2024. https://www.thepublicdiscourse.com/2024/06/90569/.

Murphy, Belva Atkinson. *Mommy of the Mixing Bowl* [Doris Coffin Aldrich]. Chicago: Moody, 1959.

Orr, J.E. *The Second Evangelical Awakening in America.* London: Marshall, Morgan, and Scott, 1952.

Phillips, David. "The History of the Inter-varsity Christian Fellowship in Western Canada." Masters thesis, Regent College, Vancouver, BC, 1976.

Pierson, Arthur T. *George Muller of Bristol.* 5th edition. London: Nisbet, 1901.

———. "The Proof of the Living God as Found in the Prayer Life of George Muller of Bristol." In *The Fundamentals: A Testimony to the Truth,* edited by R.A. Torrey and A.C. Dixon (1910) 1:70–86. Reprint edition, Grand Rapids: Baker, 1972.

Pousett, Gordon H. *The Keats Island Story: Celebrating 75 Years of Christian Camping (1926–2001).* Vancouver, BC: Forms Galore, 2001.

Rayburn, Jim. *The Diaries of Jim Rayburn (Founder of Young Life).* Edited by Kit Sublett. Houston, TX: Whitecaps Media, 2008.

Rayburn, Jim III. *Dance, Children, Dance: The Story of Jim Rayburn, Founder of Young Life.* Carol Stream: Tyndale House, 1984.

Reason, Joyce. *Searcher for God: The Story of Isobel Kuhn.* Cambridge: Lutterworth, 1963.

Repp, Gloria. *Nothing Daunted: The Story of Isobel Kuhn.* Greenville, SC: JourneyForth, 1995.

Rodgers, Jane. "The Firs: Christ is All in All. Profile of The Firs Bible and Missionary Conference and Executive Director Greg Kinloch." *The Grapevine* (Winter 2000) 4–8, 18–20.

Ruskin, John. *The Works of John Ruskin.* Edited by E.T. Cook and Alexander Wedderburn. 39 vols. London: George Allen, 1903–1912.

Sandeen, E.R. *The Roots of Fundamentalism.* Chicago: University of Chicago Press, 1970.

Skinner, Betty Lee. *Daws: The Story of Dawson Trotman, Founder of The Navigators.* Grand Rapids: Zondervan, 1977.

Smith, Christian. *Soul Searching: The Religious and Spiritual Lives of American Teenagers.* Oxford: Oxford University Press, 2005.

Sorenson, Jacob. *Sacred Playgrounds: Christian Summer Camp in Theological Perspective.* Eugene, OR: Cascade, 2021.

Sweet, W.W. *Revivalism in America: Its Origins, Growth, and Decline.* New York: Scribner's, 1945.

Taylor, Howard, and Geraldine Taylor. *Hudson Taylor's Spiritual Secret.* Chicago: Moody, 1932.

———. *The Growth of a Soul.* London: Religious Tract Society, 1911.

———. *The Growth of a Work of God.* London: Religious Tract Society, 1918.

Taylor, Hudson. *To China With Love* ("A Retrospect"). Reprint edition. Minneapolis: Dimension, 1976.

Vidler, Alec. *The Church in an Age of Revolution.* London: Penguin, 1974.

Wickett, Adele, ed. *Cool Waters Beckon Me: Celebrating Fifty Years of Camping at Pioneer Pacific.* Toronto: InterVarsity Christian Fellowship, 2004.

Woods, C. Stacey. *The Growth of a Work of God: The Story of the Early Days of the Inter-Varsity Christian Fellowship of the United States of America.* Downers Grove: InterVarsity, 1978.

www.ingramcontent.com/pod-product-compliance
Lightning Source LLC
LaVergne TN
LVHW050619100826
845148LV00011B/1647

* 9 7 9 8 3 8 5 2 7 5 8 3 0 *